PETER O

Peter O'Reilly

THE RISE OF A RELUCTANT IMMIGRANT

Lynne Stonier-Newman

Christmas, 2010

Dear Sandy & Jersey,

Warm wishes from Brian &

Lynne

Stonier-Newman

TouchWood
Editions

TouchWood Editions
www.touchwoodeditions.com

Library and Archives Canada Cataloguing in Publication
Stonier-Newman, Lynne, 1941–
Peter O'Reilly : the rise of a reluctant immigrant / Lynne Stonier-Newman.

Includes bibliographical references and index.
ISBN 978-1-926741-04-8

1. O'Reilly, Peter, 1827-1905. 2. Judges—British Columbia—Biography. 3. Civil service—British Columbia—Biography. 4. Indian reservations—British Columbia—History. 5. Gold mines and mining—British Columbia—History. 6. Immigrants—British Columbia—Biography. 7. Irish Canadians—British Columbia—Biography. 8. British Columbia—Biography. I. Title.

FC3824.1.O74S86 2010   971.1'03092   C2010-900255-5

Editor: Marlyn Horsdal
Proofreader: Elizabeth McLachlan
Design: Pete Kohut
Cover images: C-03910 (top) and D-02847 (bottom) courtesy of Royal BC Museum, BC Archives
Author photo: Helen Knight

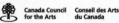

BRITISH COLUMBIA ARTS COUNCIL

Canada Council for the Arts   Conseil des Arts du Canada

We gratefully acknowledge the financial support for our publishing activities from the Government of Canada through the Canada Book Fund, Canada Council for the Arts, and the province of British Columbia through the British Columbia Arts Council and the Book Publishing Tax Credit.

Mixed Sources
Cert no. SW-COC-001271
© 1996 FSC
FSC

The interior pages of this book have been printed on 100% post-consumer recycled paper, processed chlorine free, and printed with vegetable-based inks.

The information in this book is true and complete to the best of the author's knowledge. All recommendations are made without guarantee on the part of the author. The author disclaims any liability in connection with the use of this information.

1 2 3 4 5 13 12 11 10

This book is for
Garth and Kimberley
Mandy, Shavon, Sue and Ron
and, as always, Brian.

CONTENTS

Peter O'Reilly had just turned thirty-two when he arrived from Ireland in 1859.

CHAPTER ONE

O'Reilly's First Months as a Colonial

Peter O'Reilly grasped a spindly pine tree, bent forward nervously and gazed down the steep slope. Two hundred feet below, whirlpools tossed massive trees around in the Fraser River's boiling waters. When he looked across to the rock-sided canyon on the east bank, he was dumbfounded by the sheer cliffs. Each granite monolith stretching up toward the grey clouds was covered by a tapestry of vine-like structures. More like a spider web than a trail, the ropes, poles and connecting, flimsy bridges wove intricately across the perpendicular slopes, high above the turbulent river.

Now he understood why they said a white man needed an Indian guide to traverse that treacherous pathway and why many judged it impassable. Experienced at mountain climbing himself, he pondered the challenge as he watched two men spread-eagled along the mountain face, moving slowly north. As a probationary gold commissioner and stipendiary magistrate, he expected he would soon be crossing it himself. When O'Reilly had arrived from Ireland two months earlier, Governor James Douglas had temporarily appointed him to the prestigious administrative position for the new colony of British Columbia; it was Chief

Gold Commissioner Chartres Brew who would actually decide whether he was suitable.

"See those Indians, Mr. O'Reilly? The trail is less than two feet wide at that point. Ever been on a route like that?" Brew asked.

"No, sir, but I would like to make that trip someday."

"Really? I crossed it once. Felt it important that the Indians and gold miners be aware that I could—and would."

O'Reilly stepped carefully backwards onto the narrow path where their horses were tied. "Quite a demonstration. Those precipices certainly are steeper than the ones I've climbed in Ireland," he admitted to Brew, a fellow Irishman.

∽ ∽ ∽

O'Reilly had seen little of the colony. During his first seven weeks, Brew had kept him at Fort Langley as its stipendiary magistrate and to supervise three administrative clerks. Those overworked men were still frantically sorting the paperwork for 1858, even as the 1859 gold licences and claim information began to arrive. In mid-June, when Brew ordered O'Reilly to accompany him on an inspection trip up to the Fraser goldfields, he had been relieved.

They had been paddled up the Fraser to Hope in a long, heavily loaded Indian canoe whose freight included a ripe-smelling side of beef. Then they had switched to horses to wind along the trail that cut through the dense rain forest to Yale. O'Reilly had been stunned at how many prospectors they had encountered, even more so when he heard their numbers from Yale's gold commissioner, Ed Sanders. He reported to Brew that he estimated ten thousand gold miners were already between Hope and Spuzzum along the Fraser's banks.

Brew asked, "Returning men or new ones? Are they causing any problems so far?" While the prospectors waited for the torrent of spring flooding to recede, so panning for nuggets could begin, they had little to do. Each new man searched for an available piece of riverfront to stake a claim, while those who already had one protected it against interlopers and Indians, often ruthlessly. The previous year, some conflicts had grown into actual warfare when prospectors had invaded the local Indians' traditional fishing grounds.

"It's been relatively peaceful, sir, so far," Sanders reported.

As O'Reilly listened to Brew and Sanders, he was amazed by what being a gold commissioner seemed to involve. Apparently the river levels would not be ideal until August, two months from now. He wondered what the miners would do while they waited. Brew was predicting that thousands more miners would arrive in 1859, as gold rushes usually expanded in their second season. Last year, an estimated thirty thousand miners had been stretched out along the Fraser.

"Now, Mr. O'Reilly, are you beginning to understand the chaos of 1858 and why Governor Douglas stepped in to try and stop the fighting between miners and Indians? And what complex duties you have as a gold commissioner?"

"Yes, Mr. Brew." O'Reilly hoped his nervousness did not show; he knew he looked more mature with the full beard he'd grown since turning thirty-one last March.

British Columbia had not officially become a colony of the British Empire until November 1858. Previously, the approximately two hundred and fifty thousand square miles called New Caledonia had been a protectorate, occupied by fewer than five hundred white traders and over seventy thousand Indians, directed by Vancouver Island's governor, James Douglas, who was also the chief factor for the Hudson's Bay Company's Pacific forts. As the thousands of prospectors had flooded into the Fraser area in the spring, an unknown number of Sto:lo and Nlaka'pamux Indians and would-be miners had died in the conflicts over access to the Fraser's rich shore.

When the warfare grew, Douglas and Royal Navy marines from the ships at Fort Victoria went up the Fraser. Douglas designated fishing areas for the Indians where miners could not pan and appointed magistrates to enforce those reserves. Then he wrote Sir Edward Bulwer-Lytton, head of the Colonial Office, warning of future bloodshed and recommending the area be formally organized as a British colony. The various tribes of Indians affected had had a large gathering, and a powerful chief, Spitilum, had urged peace with the whites rather than war, but only if their territory was protected. To maintain claim to these lands, Britain had to take control over the mainly American miners.

O'Reilly, coming from the troubles over land in Ireland, understood the urgency, and he had also heard the rumours in Fort Langley. Some Americans had evidently not agreed with their country's treaty with Britain, which made the forty-ninth parallel the border between the US territories and the British colonies and protectorates in North America; they threatened to ignore it and claim ownership of BC land and water.

As they left Yale's small government building, Brew asked O'Reilly how much he knew about BC's recent history. "For instance, do you know why the vigilante incidents occurred last year?"

"All I know is that you and Colonel Richard Moody and some Royal Engineers wintered in Yale to maintain control of the area."

"Yes, and Begbie. It took us from December until March to sort out that silliness." Brew explained that a power struggle between Ned McGowan, leading the miners' vigilante committee from Hill's Bar, and Dr. Max Fifer, spokesman for the miners of Yale, had degenerated into a potentially dangerous situation.

"Governor Douglas has since judged that such a stay was probably unnecessary as well as outrageously and inefficiently expensive. Begbie, Moody and I disagree with his assessment, but he is the governor and has to be zealous about controlling colonial costs. Do you understand what I am telling you?"

"Yes, sir. Government employees have to be frugal," O'Reilly said gravely as he nudged his horse behind Brew's.

The chief gold commissioner thought that O'Reilly probably did understand; he had been in the Irish Revenue Police after the potato famines when most administrative costs, even shoeing a government horse, had been disallowed. In fact, the reason that Brew had accepted his own contract in BC was because his pay as an inspector in the Royal Irish Constabulary had been reduced. He had arrived nine months earlier, in time for the ceremonies on November 19, 1858, when British Columbia was declared a British colony. He had been sworn in as chief inspector of the future BC Constabulary by the new colony's first judge, Matthew Begbie, as had all officials. Then, a month later, despite Brew's protests about the terms of the contract he had signed with the Colonial Office, Governor Douglas had insisted he also become the colony's chief gold commissioner.

Trying to combine policing with taxing was convoluted and O'Reilly found his new position confusing. During the trip up the Fraser, he'd asked, "Is it true that gold commissioners have to supervise the constables? And how many of those are there, sir?"

"Currently, a total of nine. A constable is assigned to a specific gold commissioner and they are responsible for all law and order, and licensing miners, in their area." Brew had explained that a gold commissioner could also hire temporary constables in emergencies, if suitable manpower was available.

"Nine?" O'Reilly had blurted. In Dublin, he had been told that Brew had resigned from the Royal Irish Constabulary to create the usual model of civil policing system for the new colony. And he had considered applying as an officer as he'd heard that its initial projected manpower was to be one hundred and fifty constables.

"Sir," O'Reilly had asked, "am I really to be an area's chief of police, mining supervisor *and* tax collector?"

"Yes."

Since that conversation, the more O'Reilly thought about one man having the power to tax, enforce law and also make some judicial decisions, the more he worried about how that could all fit together. When he was a lieutenant in the Irish Revenue Police, they were not involved in constabulary work except during general upheavals. Now, as a gold commissioner, he would collect licences and ensure the proper staking of claims, keep the peace, lay charges and then, as a stipendiary magistrate, judge those same misdemeanours. There could be potential conflicts, he knew, amazed that Brew had been willing to continue under Douglas's new directives. Then O'Reilly realized that the chief was probably in a situation similar to his own: Brew had also cut his ties in Ireland when he chose to come and work in this new colony.

As Brew took O'Reilly into various miners' camps along the Fraser, he continued to emphasize how each gold commissioner had to control his assigned area. "I need to be able to trust that each of my commissioners and constables will use common sense as well as authority." Then he announced that he was delaying the decision about O'Reilly's permanent appointment and extending his probationary period.

O'Reilly knew why his suitability was in question. He had shown poor judgment by incorrectly taxing the respected Captain William Moore's barrel of pork and then offending the man further by being overly authoritarian. The incident had been enthusiastically reported in the colonies' newspapers, how O'Reilly had seized the pork from Moore's steamboat and then fined the captain an additional forty dollars when Moore had complained. The much-censured probationer would always be able to recall, word for word, Moore's letter to the editor in the *British Colonist*'s May 1859 edition:

> Fined . . . by a magistrate, who holds the law in the palm of his hand. I am, therefore, led to believe that this is a new style, instituted by the said O'Reilly, for raising the wind.[1]

After the incident, Brew had been furious with him, and had pointed out that even though their mothers were friends, O'Reilly had to demonstrate he had the abilities to be a gold commissioner. "Do you understand that you have to establish authority by making astute decisions, Mr. O'Reilly? Often in completely isolated areas, you have to be able to control and calm large groups of men, impose governance and enforce the colony's laws and taxes."

"Yes, sir." O'Reilly had braced himself for the expected dismissal.

"Most of all, a gold commissioner and magistrate needs to gain respect." Brew had pointed out that no other gold commissioner had generated angry letters to editors, nor a letter of complaint from Governor Douglas. "Can you explain why—before you exercised your high-handed lack of wisdom, Mr. O'Reilly, thoroughly embarrassing and lessening the credibility of all the colony's administrators—you did not ask someone for an opinion when Captain Moore objected?"

O'Reilly apologized again and said, "Sir, if I had considered better, I would have asked appropriate questions. I did not think about the consequences of my actions and I deeply regret that."

"One more unsuitable action and you will be dismissed."

O'Reilly suspected he had been allowed to continue as a probationary gold commissioner mainly because of his ability to find suitable horses. The colony desperately needed more mounts for its officials.

Only four weeks after the pork incident, the chief appointed O'Reilly to be Hope's gold commissioner, but warned him he was still on probation. Brew also told him that he was authorized to find, purchase and supervise a herd of government horses at Hope.

"Yes, sir." Although O'Reilly was unsure about how to be a suitable gold commissioner, managing horses was his favourite occupation; he preferred it to working with people. And though the American Civil War was causing a severe horse shortage in BC, he knew he could find horses that even Brew would judge to be good buys. He had brought his four-year-old stallion, Tom, with him to the colony, and Tom's desirable bloodlines attracted horse breeders who wanted his stud services. Those men would willingly help O'Reilly.

Brew emphasized that he would be continually reviewing O'Reilly's performance and, if it was unsatisfactory in any way, his contract would be ended. "Listen to people. Learn the vocabulary miners use. Go panning for a day, Mr. O'Reilly. Find out how hard it is to stand in cold water, shovelling gravel from dawn to dusk, searching for colour."

O'Reilly beamed, his dark blue eyes losing their usually guarded expression. "Yes, sir. Thank you, sir. My mismanagement around Captain Moore's pork has taught me many lessons."

"Good. Even when you're a grey-haired and successful man, someone will still recall your first mistake. Do not make any more."

O'Reilly laughed. As he and Brew continued their inspection tour of the mining camps, the general excitement appealed to him and so did the way the miners welcomed them and shared their news. Each man either dug out the licence he had purchased earlier or paid up willingly. Some even showed the gold flakes and nuggets they had panned from the more manageable creeks flowing into the swollen Fraser. Tents ranged from primitive to luxurious, as varied as the occupants, who came from many countries. Some were not able to speak English, yet all seemed to feel a general camaraderie. He also quickly realized how respected Chief Brew was and, hence, himself.

When he and Brew returned to Yale, it was a Saturday night, and miners and Indians swarmed into the makeshift town, crowding the main street as tightly as bees in a hive. Businesses were operating out of flimsy shacks and tents, some selling pickaxes, shovels and food while others offered whiskey, card games and women. When O'Reilly commented that any white woman there had to be a floozie, since proper women would never venture out on such a street, Brew was annoyed. "No, some are the wives of store-keepers or miners, and a few are prospectors, staking their own claims. Do *not* make assumptions, Mr. O'Reilly."

O'Reilly apologized and carefully kept all his opinions to himself when they joined Sanders for a late dinner. As the senior officials chatted, he wondered how to describe Yale's exciting pandemonium in his next letter home. He decided to tell Mamsey that it was twice as chaotic as Dublin on market day.

A man hobbled over to their table and Brew introduced him as Jim Craigie, the new constable for Hope. The chief said later, "Although Craigie looks old, he's capable. Respect and listen to him, Mr. O'Reilly. His broken leg has almost healed, so he can manage fine on horseback."

After dinner, O'Reilly was directed to the government sleeping quarters. He tried going to bed, then got up, found his diary and, in the kerosene lantern's dim light, crouched over a rough table and wrote:

I have written Mamsey Letter No. 11, telling her of my new position. God grant that the dear ones at home are all well again. How I wish I will soon receive their letters. Cannot sleep because of being dreadfully annoyed by mosquitoes and some terrible large black flies that bite out a chunk of one's flesh.[2]

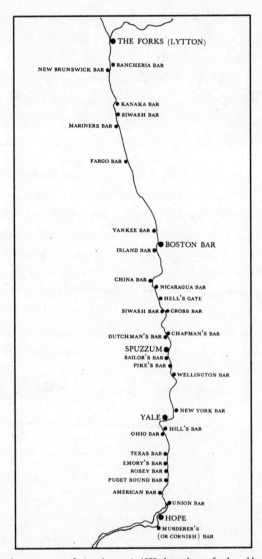

The Fraser River became a maze of miners' camps in 1859, the peak year for the gold rush. Men arrived from countries around the world to stand in cold water and shovel gravel, seeking their El Dorado.

MAP COURTESY OF LYNNE STONIER-NEWMAN

CHAPTER TWO

Gold Commissioner and Stipendiary Magistrate

The village of Hope quickly became O'Reilly's home, his tiny two-room rental a sanctuary. Improvised shelves held his books, chess set, fishing flies, the two riding trophies he'd brought with him and his precious letter box. In a corner of the clapboard walls, his cricket bats, fishing poles and rifle were crammed together, and his saddles and bridles hung nearby. He described all this at length to his mother. But when the mail sack arrived with no letters from Ireland, his homesickness would flare up and he'd spend the night fighting doubts about his wisdom in coming to British Columbia.

Within weeks of settling in Hope, O'Reilly met a pleasant Indian girl who became his housekeeper and companion through 1859's most hectic gold-rush months, September and October. Then, in early November, she left without notice. He was mystified as well as relieved. Though he had not told her so, he had realized he did not want an Indian wife. It would have horrified his family who, he knew, would not accept her.

Once his nearest neighbour, Edgar Dewdney, returned for the winter months, O'Reilly's deep loneliness lessened. Dewdney was an engineer and surveyor who was anxiously awaiting contracts to build roads. The two men became good friends, dining and playing cards together.

Deep frosts had claimed the Fraser, and most miners had departed. O'Reilly had little to do except write reports to Brew, who was in New Westminster. He was keeping order there while he directed the clearing of stumps for the construction of another small government building. Brew expected to be informed about what O'Reilly had heard and was most interested in any rumours of new gold finds in the distant Cariboo as well as around Lillooet, Fort Kamloops and the Boundary regions. However, there was not much for O'Reilly to relate once the miners stopped passing through Hope.

In early December, a letter came from Brew, formally notifying O'Reilly he was no longer on probation but a gold commissioner. The chief also told him he was to go to Victoria for December and January, where he would again supervise sorting paperwork, this time that of the past gold season.

O'Reilly told Dewdney, "I'm off probation at last, Ned, and assigned to oversee yet more clerical work! But in Victoria, where I can enjoy better food, chat with gracious women and lounge in deep hot baths. And have my boots resoled." Plus Tom, whose reputation was growing, could perhaps bring in more stud fees.

To O'Reilly's surprise, he was warmly welcomed in Victoria, as a gold commissioner, as the grandson of Major James Blundell of Ince Hall, Lancashire, England, and because demand for his stallion's services was as high as he had hoped. He was invited to many social events, including one hosted by Governor and Mrs. Douglas, and he savoured being in decent society again, where one's connections, dress and manners mattered. As his annual salary was now two hundred and forty pounds, a fifty pound raise, he also had a few more financial options in his tight budget. Though, as he wrote to his mother, while such an increase would have stood him in good stead in Ireland, it was still scanty in both colonies. A decent meal with a little wine cost two pounds and new boots, twenty-five pounds.

Many of his friends advised him to invest in property. At one dinner, Judge Matthew Begbie said that someone had to start the buying if either colony was going to develop, and that he was doing so himself. Another acquaintance, Joseph Trutch, an engineer who owned a house in Yale and had recently built a substantial home, Fairfield, on ten acres outside Victoria, suggested O'Reilly buy, even if only land.

O'Reilly had visited with Trutch earlier, when he was organizing a bid to build a section of the Cariboo Road, and decided that he respected most of Trutch's opinions. Since he longed to be financially successful, O'Reilly risked purchasing three inexpensive town lots in Hope. It was the first property he had ever owned, and he soon discovered an unexpected benefit: whenever he mentioned that he had bought property, he was considered committed to the colony's well-being.

After O'Reilly's stay in Victoria, Brew directed that he relieve Yale's gold commissioner, Ed Sanders, in February and March, and then, on Sanders's return, help him prepare for 1860's influx of miners. O'Reilly was relieved to be off probation and careful not to generate any further complaints. Despite his ongoing homesickness for his family and for Ireland, he shared it only with his diary, confiding he was again fighting his "blue devils"—his term for being depressed—along with recording his expenditures, weather conditions and who he had met with that day.

O'Reilly often compared his new position with his seven years in the Irish Revenue Police, aware of how much he preferred being a gold commissioner to having been a lieutenant. Assessing and collecting taxes on poteen (illegal, home-distilled whiskey) or seizing lands for unpaid taxes had been an unpleasant job, particularly as his senior officers were always bellowing at him or the other juniors. Here, he was impressed with the courtesy his fellow administrators regularly extended. Even when they were disagreeing with someone or fining or arresting a miner, they were invariably calm, firm and polite.

Although O'Reilly had only joined the revenue police because, as a third son, he lacked other choices, he had been devastated when it was amalgamated into the Royal Irish Constabulary. Two years ago, he had been given an honourable discharge, instead of the commission he had requested, and told he was too old to qualify, even though he had just turned thirty. This still stung. He had then accepted employment at one of Ireland's most prestigious stables and was responsible for keeping its pedigreed horses healthy. It was the career he had always wanted, and he dreamed of developing his own herd some day.

However, he had resigned after his father had brusquely pointed out that working in a stable was socially unacceptable for his family's status in Ireland. It might reflect negatively on his three unmarried sisters' chances. "Peter, insisting on being a stable boy may prevent them from making good marriages."

All those conversations echoed as O'Reilly stared out his tiny window, watching the leaden waters of the Fraser River through the ongoing spring drizzle. His longing to be with his large, extended family and, in particular, to be sharing a cup of tea and a cozy visit by the fire with Mamsey, was constantly with him, as it had been much of his life. Of the three boys and six girls, he was the only one sent to stay for months with his stern grandfather, to attend an English boarding school. He had become used to feeling like an outsider when he returned home to Ballybeg House each summer and had learned early not to talk about the headaches and blue devils he sporadically endured.

Those attacks worried him as he recognized that his father, Patrick, and all five of his powerful uncles, one of whom was a bishop, had become deeply glum men after the O'Reilly family's fortunes had deteriorated, first with the various religious edicts against Catholics, then with the potato famines. For the past two decades, the fields around Ballybeg in the Kells district, and all of County Meath, had been mainly fallow. Almost half of the farming families had died or emigrated to flee starvation, as had the weavers, after the sheep had been eaten.

Similarly, as Grandfather Blundell had so bluntly pointed out when he repeatedly advised Peter to emigrate, the wealth around Ince Hall and throughout Lancashire was also disappearing as Britain's depression deepened and the rich coalfields' harvest was sold for a pittance. O'Reilly had been born at his grandfather's residence on March 27, 1827, when Mamsey and his two sisters and two brothers had been staying with her father. That made him the only child of his parents not to have been born in Ireland at Bellybeg House.[1]

Perhaps that was why his mother had insisted that her father be allowed to supervise his education. Later, she'd been supportive when O'Reilly had decided to become a Protestant and joined his grandfather's church just before he went on to Trinity College in Dublin. She had said that, despite his father's disapproval, it balanced things: her own French Catholic mother, who had died when Mamsey was ten, had been allowed to marry a Protestant because her parents considered the wealthy Major Blundell a suitable catch.

Grandfather Blundell had been a big influence in O'Reilly's life, and when he again recommended that Peter emigrate, and had offered to pay his fare and the cost of shipping one horse, Peter had reluctantly agreed. After carefully weighing where to go, he had decided on British Columbia, because India's ongoing mutinies made it too dangerous, and the smaller British protectorates and island colonies would not provide a position with career potential. He knew little about the new colony on the distant Pacific, other than that Chartres Brew, whose mother was a friend of Mamsey's, was there, forming a constabulary. Major Blundell was pleased with O'Reilly's choice and arranged for impressive references from his own close friends; this had resulted in Governor Douglas hiring O'Reilly on his arrival.

Now, just over a year later, he was a property owner. He was aware that, even if one had little social standing or few family connections, becoming a large landowner here was possible. He began to realize how different his opportunities were, compared to the limitations in Ireland or England.

O'Reilly kept the government horse herd that he had assembled at Tom Glennie's ranch, just south of Hope, and Glennie's wife and stepdaughters often invited O'Reilly and Dewdney out for a social evening. That sometimes helped to alleviate O'Reilly's homesickness, but at other times he longed even more for his own sisters. In the spring of 1860, as he awaited the miners' arrival, he had little to do, and filling in time was a challenge. He went hunting and fishing with Dewdney, who was equally impatient, waiting to be hired for a survey or road contract.

By June, Sanders's total for mining licences was only about half of what had been sold in 1859. O'Reilly learned that Brew had told Governor Douglas that the Fraser gold rush was almost over, and worried about whether he would be let go. When he queried Brew, the chief told him to just keep busy, exploring and drawing rough maps of the Hope area. O'Reilly's loneliness and boredom grew. Except for his monthly journey to Fort Langley to hold magistrate's court, he had few official duties. As well, his social connections were decreasing; Hope was losing residents weekly, and Dewdney was surveying over in the Similkameen.

Begbie arrived in late July and told O'Reilly that the estimated number of gold seekers in all of BC was under a thousand—not counting the Chinese coming into the Fraser—and that most prospectors were heading into the Cariboo. Both knew that might sound a death knell for Hope, because the route to reach northern BC was up the Harrison, Anderson and Seton lakes to Lillooet. Men then hiked to Fort Alexandria and the rich creeks northeast of Quesnelmouth. Any prospectors heading into the lands around Fort Kamloops usually travelled up past Fort Colville in the American territory of Washington.

When O'Reilly wondered what he would do, Begbie advised, "Be patient. You'll be needed somewhere. Maybe even in the southeast. Douglas has to preserve our territory along the American border. He's directed Moody to have the Royal Engineers start surveying there."

O'Reilly brightened. "Maybe that's why Dewdney is surveying down there."

"Yes." Begbie took another mouthful of the fresh trout O'Reilly had cooked for them. He wondered aloud about how many Americans had already crossed into BC, fleeing their civil war, and how many more might come. Some were searching for gold in the creeks north of the border and finding it, he explained as he refilled their goblets with the white wine he'd contributed. Begbie believed, as did many upper-crust Englishmen, that necessities for one's travelling kit included good liquor, proper drinking vessels and sterling silver utensils.

When O'Reilly presented the berry pie that Jane Moir had sent in for him with Tom Glennie, her stepfather, Begbie was delighted. "Peter, how generous of you to share this."

O'Reilly was pleased that the opinionated judge, who had initially seemed overwhelming, was becoming a friend. During his last visit, he had insisted he be called Matthew. Then he had winked and said that of course if he was bested too often at chess, only "His Honour" would be acceptable.

Over brandies, the conversation returned to the colony's long border with the American territories. "Have you travelled in that area, Matthew?" O'Reilly asked.

"Only as far south as Okanagan Lake. It's large, like an inland sea. It's all rich land, ripe for the taking. In my opinion, Douglas is correct to worry about it being settled by Americans."

As they discussed BC's neighbour, O'Reilly asked, "How much is their civil war affecting our shipping to and from Britain?" and speculated that his long-awaited letters from home were being delayed because of it. Reports recently received in Victoria had predicted more naval battles.

"It might be delaying your mail. And it could drastically affect us. That is why the Royal Navy is adding ships to its Pacific fleet. But the greatest risk is for ships on the Atlantic routes, New York and south."

After Begbie departed, O'Reilly continued to roughly map the forests behind Hope, a lonely and tedious task. His isolation and the lack of letters from his family haunted him, and he suffered more attacks of the blue devils. When Brew arrived on the weekly river steamer in early August, he greeted him with relief, hoping that the chief finally had a new task for him.

Brew did. He told O'Reilly he was to leave in two days for the Boundary country. "You are to temporarily take control of the latest gold rush. It is at Rock Creek, quite a distance past Okanagan Lake. It's a long way from any settlements, and there are no services nearby on either side of the border." George Cox would be its official commissioner and magistrate, but until he could be located up in the Quesnelle Forks region, and get to Rock Creek, O'Reilly would be in charge.

"Yes, sir!"

"Rock Creek is almost right on the international boundary," Brew continued. His most recent information was that over five hundred miners were there, mainly Americans, and they of course took any gold they found back across the border. "If reports are correct about the quantities, BC is losing significant revenues, and your job is to ensure we receive our due. You and your constable will license all miners and maintain British law there."

"Yes, sir," O'Reilly repeated, elated that his long wait was over.

"You do realize that those miners will most likely not be co-operative? In fact, they may be quarrelsome, and they won't want to pay fees or abide by BC's laws. The job will require both tact and firmness," Brew warned.

The chief sat down at O'Reilly's desk, took out a map and outlined the route to Rock Creek, estimating it was more than two hundred miles east of Hope. He told O'Reilly he needed clothing for both hot and cold weather, as well as government forms and food supplies. "Take in enough for ten weeks, and Cox can use what you don't. Stop at John Allison's ranch. I am quite sure he will go in as your constable—he'll be glad to have the revenue."

As O'Reilly walked with Brew back down to the little side-wheeler boat waiting for him, they decided it would take his party at least ten days to reach Rock Creek. "And you must stay until you are relieved, Mr. O'Reilly. It's crucial to have a BC official there."

O'Reilly whistled as the boat left the wharf. Planning for his new duty, he decided to take the two sturdiest saddle horses from the herd he supervised, buy a mule, and leave his stallion with the Glennies. He strode to Hope's trading post and emporium, hoping to learn where he could get a mule, and to place his order for additional ammunition, flour, sugar, tea, lard, prunes, rum and medicines. He encountered Mrs. Glennie who insisted he come to dinner the next evening, and assured him, "Of course we will look after Tom."

Back at his cottage, O'Reilly stuffed six pairs of socks, summer and winter undergarments, an extra wool suit, shirts and a dozen white collars, his oiled rain cloak, his winter sheepskin jacket, his letter box, some favourite books and a collapsible fly rod into three small, watertight packs. Then he rolled two rifles and an extra blanket into his travelling bedroll and wrapped it with a tarp and ropes, which would also enable him to build a shelter.

For his goodbye dinner, the Glennies gathered sixteen friends around their big table, and they all asked questions.

"I might be there until late October or November, if Mr. Cox is delayed." O'Reilly explained that mining had to stay open until freeze-up.

Tom Glennie said, "Two things, my friend. The Civil War is changing Americans and the miners there will be from both sides. Don't even hint at a political opinion! And, secondly, Peter, the Boundary weather changes overnight. Be prepared. Get lots of wood in early, whether it ends up being used by you or by Cox. And buy more flour whenever you can and whatever the price. With five hundred men already at Rock Creek, peddlers will come up from Washington."

People around the table nodded in agreement. One man waved his left hand and said, "An early frost in the Similkameen mountains is how I lost these two fingers. Come back with all of yours."

CHAPTER THREE

Challenges and Rewards

The next morning before dawn, O'Reilly's little train left Hope and headed up the first long hill. He led his spare horse while Sam, his Indian guide, who was mounted bareback on his own pony, tugged the heavily loaded mule behind him. They followed the old Brigade Trail which wound up through the heavy forests to the Chituk'weyuk and Tulameen rivers and the tiny village of Princeton. Their progress was steady until dusk on the second night out, when a violent lightning storm hit. The mule panicked, shed his load and fled, and O'Reilly and Sam had to search all evening to find the animal.

When they reached John Allison's place in Princeton, O'Reilly asked the taciturn rancher to be his constable. Allison regretfully declined because of a previous commitment in New Westminster, but he recommended a man who lived on a new pre-emption a day farther on. When that man also refused, as his wife was about to have their first child, O'Reilly began stopping at each farm, and they were few and far between. He learned that it was harvest time, and getting the crops in was critical for the farmers' survival; no one was available. O'Reilly puzzled over what to do as they continued to the Okanagan Lake country. With five hundred miners to control, he certainly needed a constable.

He found the countryside very attractive with its many little lakes and sun-ripened pastures covered with dancing, golden grasses, and he spent most of his days picking out different locations where he might like to live. On their sixth day out of Hope, they turned down to the Sooyos area and he and his guide listened nervously for rattles, as Glennie had warned that rattlesnakes hid in the sagebrush or on the rock outcrops, and would strike out at a man or horse. At day's end, they followed a tumbling creek down to a lake and, to O'Reilly's great surprise and pleasure, encountered Governor Douglas, Colonel Moody and a small troop of the Royal Engineers.

Douglas was assisting with the survey of the area, analyzing its potential. "A rich area it is, and hundreds of families will live here in the future." They were also deciding on the best route to connect the Okanagan and Fort Kamloops. Hearing that O'Reilly was heading to Rock Creek, Douglas told him he had about three more days' travel, and that he'd heard miners were arriving there in droves.

Colonel Moody interjected, "Will you join us for dinner?"

O'Reilly agreed readily, helped his guide care for the horses and mule, cleaned up as best he could, then joined Moody and Douglas at a linen-covered table. During the lengthy meal, they discussed many topics, and O'Reilly asked, "Are there many settlers around here? Or Indian tribes?"

The governor said, "We remain unclear about the tribes. There are Okanagans both here and in Washington, but you may encounter the Kootenae tribe in the Rock Creek area." As they sipped after-dinner brandies and cracked nuts, Douglas warned O'Reilly the Rock Creek miners might be difficult.

"Yes, sir." O'Reilly wondered how he would manage without a constable.

"Commissioner, are you aware that wherever a staunch American northerner meets a staunch southerner, they frequently end up fighting?" Colonel Moody asked.

"I am, sir."

Douglas told O'Reilly that if he needed assistance, he was to send a messenger—his guide rather than his constable. When the governor realized that the gold commissioner did not have a constable, he summoned John Collins, an Englishman who was travelling with them, searching for property to pre-empt. "Collins is a most qualified man. He was the constable at Lytton until last month. Brew had to discharge him because most of Lytton's population has moved away," Douglas explained.

Collins would accompany O'Reilly on one condition. "My wife's sister's ship docks at Victoria in mid-October. She's marrying my best friend, and I *must* be at their wedding."

They left before dawn and O'Reilly was grateful to have a companion with interesting stories as well as an experienced constable. Collins recounted how he had managed the gold rush in the Lytton area and the difficulties he had encountered policing the miners and Indians there.

"It appears your experiences differ considerably from the annual summaries I've read about the Lytton region. Why? Did you not write those reports?" O'Reilly asked.

Collins chuckled. "I did, sir. But many of the little confrontations between, say, a cantankerous miner and an Indian were ongoing squabbles that never ended. I could not write those up because there is no category for continuing conflicts anywhere in the official forms."

As they rode, Collins and O'Reilly also talked about pre-empting. What factors were necessary for a property, besides the ideal climate and geographic location?

"My wife wants a place with short winters, good soil and water for fruit trees, and the potential for a community to grow," Collins said. "I need rich grass for about two hundred head of cattle to start, with plenty of room for expansion."

"Will finding neighbours be possible?" O'Reilly asked. The area seemed to have lots of water and good land but no settlers or Indians.

"Because I want a new area, no, not right away. But I have a list of folks waiting to know where I choose our land, and we will create a community."

The big man's quiet confidence made O'Reilly wonder if he should ask to be put on the list. He confided that unless conditions improved considerably in Ireland, he would have to stay in British Columbia. "Eventually, I would like to raise pedigreed horses, and this Sooyos and Okanagan country is appealing. But I will only do that if I cannot work for the government."

Collins had decided to pre-empt somewhere in the south Okanagan because of its longer growing season. "Finding land with good water is difficult. I want a steady, year-round source, above the fields so that we can use a gravity system."

On the afternoon of the third day, they reached Rock Creek and contemplated the sprawling camp from high ground above it. O'Reilly was shocked by its size and disorder. And as a pungent summer wind blew their way, he and Collins realized that the miners occupying the primitive shacks and ragged tents had not built proper outhouses.

"Ripe for an epidemic, aren't they, sir?" Constable Collins remarked. "As soon as we're settled, shall I supervise the construction of sanitary facilities?"

"Yes, do that, Mr. Collins. Though ensuring that miners buy a permit is our most important task."

However, no outhouses were built nor licences sold. The Rock Creek inhabitants were not at all welcoming and, in fact, became immediately threatening. When O'Reilly and Collins rode down into the camp, leaving their guide with the mule and spare horses, a crowd of miners gathered, impeding their passage. One man bellowed belligerently, "Who are you? And where do you think you're going?"

"I am the gold commissioner for Rock Creek," O'Reilly shouted, "appointed by the British Columbia government to organize this area. This is Constable Collins."

Many of the men surrounding them were obviously drunk, even though it was only mid-afternoon. They booed and yelled questions. One speaker roared above the noise, "British Columbia? Don't bother dismounting. Get out of here! Now!"

Collins nudged his horse close to O'Reilly, who was repeatedly shouting just as loudly, "I order you all to a miners' meeting. Here, tomorrow morning, eight AM!"

The miners blocked their way, and some snarled that they would chase the Brits out if they tried to stay. Completely surrounded by the mob, the gold commissioner and constable appeared to be in trouble, when suddenly, O'Reilly caused his horse to rear. He held it on its hind legs, letting the gelding's hoofs flail in front of the nearest miners.

As a path opened, O'Reilly nudged his horse into a gallop and led Collins back to the ridge where Sam waited in a grove of birch trees, well above the turbulent camp. He was instructed to keep three horses saddled and to dig a hole for a small cooking fire as O'Reilly and Collins watched the men milling below them.

The constable broke the silence. "Quite a horseman, aren't you, sir? Thank goodness. This heat, combined with whiskey, has them riled up. Did you hear Moody tell me this border area can be over on hundred degrees?"

O'Reilly smiled, hoping his nervousness and weariness were not showing. "Yes, this wind is like opening an oven. You and I should take turns sleeping, Mr. Collins."

"They are certainly a rough bunch," Collins commented. "Declaring this area British probably means nothing to most of them. The border's only a line on paper."

O'Reilly realized how true that was and worried about what to do. Could he and the constable gain control?

"Sam is leaving tonight, sir, and wants to be paid," Collins said.

O'Reilly nodded and undid the money belt under his vest. "Ask him where he is going, please."

"South. He has relatives down in Washington. I asked him to take a message to Douglas, but he said no."

The night passed without incident, though some miners were boisterous until dawn. As Collins had the last shift, O'Reilly awoke to the smell of coffee and to his constable's suggestion they start building a cabin later that day. "It will demonstrate our intentions, Mr. O'Reilly. And I can have us a shelter within a week."

O'Reilly agreed. After having coffee, they mounted and cantered down into the camp, their stirrups almost touching. As they neared the groups of men standing about, he called repeatedly, "All miners must come to the meeting at eight AM."

They rode to the centre of the clearing and positioned their horses head to tail, then waited, each erect in his saddle with his rifle loose in its scabbard. When about a hundred men had gathered, O'Reilly decided the missing ones were probably too drunk to understand much and shouted, "Good morning." He then briefly explained his and his constable's authority, and what each miner had to do. "You have to buy a gold licence from me now. You are not allowed to mine gold in British Columbia without one! No licence, no mining. And take off your Bowie knives and pistols. Now, boys, there must be no shooting, for if there is shooting, there will surely be hangings."[1]

The miners booed loudly. Some shouted that no one could stop them from mining or make them pay. A few crowded dangerously close to the horses, offering to take on the constable or the commissioner. By then, most of the other men had arrived, and they all jeered and stamped, a few even firing their pistols into the air. A self-declared leader jumped up on a woodpile and declared, "Not one of us will buy a licence! Or remove a revolver or knife! Not one! Or that man will have to deal with me!" Others joined his lead, ordering that no one was to obey O'Reilly and that anyone who did would wish he had not.

Realizing the situation was worsening, O'Reilly yelled, "Disperse, all disperse!" He signalled Collins to fall in behind him, then kicked his horse into a quick gallop, the big bay's size forcing men out of the way. Once they had again reached their camp, O'Reilly mopped the sweat from his brow. "That did not go particularly well, did it?"

"I have met more co-operative men," Collins said, equally dryly. "This is the most contentious group I've encountered."

O'Reilly thought the same and told Collins to prepare to ride out immediately. "Tell the governor and colonel that we need the Royal Engineers' assistance."

Collins balked and urged O'Reilly to go, but the commissioner refused. "No. If I leave, these men will think that they have won."

As his constable hastily filled a pack, O'Reilly scrawled a note to Governor Douglas:

Sir, these are mainly American miners who need to have a demonstration of the long arm of British Columbia's Law.[2]

Five long days later, Collins returned with the governor and the Royal Engineers, and O'Reilly was glad to see them. Even though the miners had not approached him as they watched him work on the cabin, he had slept little and had kept his rifle and axe at the ready.

· That evening, Governor Douglas, impressively official, his uniform heavy with gold braid, stood on a podium the Engineers had erected. O'Reilly was on one side of him, Collins on the other, and Colonel Moody and twenty red-coated, armed Royal Engineers were in formation below them. The governor requested Moody to have the Engineers fire a volley into the air, and the booming crack of those shots created an instant silence. The miners not in attendance rushed to the clearing to see what was happening.

Douglas ordered any man who did not possess a BC mining licence to buy one or leave before sundown the next day. "With our assistance, if necessary," he thundered. "You are welcome to stay and mine our creeks, but only if you buy licences. And only if you obey British Columbia's rules, as set out and enforced by Gold Commissioner O'Reilly. Or you must leave this territory immediately, and go back across the border."[3]

He then lectured them about BC's laws. He demanded that claims be filed correctly and honestly, and pointed out that when the gold commissioner declared mining was closed for the winter season, then, on that exact date, activity was to cease.

The next day, O'Reilly and Collins sold many mining licences. Only twenty men packed their gear and left, declaring that Rock Creek's gold was paltry, not worth the cost of a licence. Douglas, Moody and the Engineers remained for over a week, and their presence helped to demonstrate the British colony's power. The Engineers also directed the miners to build proper sanitary facilities and a deep water hole upstream, for clean drinking water.

Douglas seemed in no rush to leave. "He probably prefers a mining camp, or being part of Moody's surveying, to the complaints in Victoria or New Westminster," O'Reilly remarked to Collins. Since the end of the Fraser River's lucrative rush, he knew that the residents of both Vancouver Island and BC were demanding that the governor do something about the economy.

Douglas drew O'Reilly aside before departing. "You must continually ensure that all Americans or Indians arriving here understand this is British territory." As well as maintaining the peace, O'Reilly was to record details about the miners over and above the licensing information, and to make sure each man knew the colony welcomed immigrants who wanted to pre-empt land for farming or ranching.

"Yes, sir." O'Reilly was sure now that he had the governor's respect. In the following weeks, he oversaw Rock Creek without any more major incidents. He also discovered how little gold most miners were gaining in return for their long hours of wearisome panning.

By the time Gold Commissioner Cox came, in mid-October, there were fewer than three hundred miners left. One man's lament had summarized the general feeling. "This gold rush was a flash in the pan, and not a very lucrative one, at that."

Cox forecast that most miners would be gone before he closed mining for the winter and grumbled that his long trip had been for naught. This rush was over. He passed O'Reilly letters, one from Brew and three from Ireland. "What the chief's note says is that you are now to head to the Cariboo and report to its gold commissioner, Philip Nind."

O'Reilly scanned the chief's brief letter and tucked the letters from Ireland, two from Mamsey and one from his eldest sister, into his vest. Though he longed to be reading them, he continued visiting with Cox and asked if he knew how long he was to stay in the Cariboo.

"No, but at least for the winter. I believe Nind is taking leave."

"Is that area much colder than the Fraser canyon?" O'Reilly asked.

"Yes. Freeze-up starts at the end of September, Mr. O'Reilly, and lasts until May. There is so much snow, a horse can't get through the drifts by mid-winter." Cox added that Brew expected him to head for the Cariboo via Fort Kamloops.

O'Reilly was relieved to have his next posting. Surely the Cariboo would be preferable to spending another rainy winter in Hope. After he read the letters from home, especially the part where Mamsey thanked him for his detailed descriptions of his grand adventures, he whistled happily as he packed up his belongings.

Heading north, he began to feel a new affinity for BC. The pristine lakes, wide rivers, and trees blazing with autumn colour appealed to him, as did the sweet smell of sage ripening in the warm, sunny days. He even shot and cooked a delectable pheasant—Mamsey's favourite meat bird. After five days, he reached Fort Kamloops and was welcomed by Chief Trader Joseph McKay, who invited him to a dinner and dance that evening. O'Reilly danced enthusiastically with the three women attending.

ಌ ಌ ಌ

The next morning, he headed out in a storm, and the bitter winds and wet snow froze his beard within the hour. Six days later, when O'Reilly reached Alexandria, a tiny settlement on the Fraser River's east bank, across from the Hudson's Bay Company's old Fort Alexandria, he suspected his hands and feet would never be warm again. He was relieved to see a lantern glowing through the gloom.

Philip Nind welcomed him enthusiastically. "Brew sent you, did he? Meet my constable, William Pinchbeck, and sit here, by the stove, man. I'll get you a hot toddy." He waved O'Reilly to the only comfortable chair, near the barrel stove, and passed him a mug. "Well, Mr. O'Reilly, keep that stove burning as hot as you like. You have lots of wood." He explained that a pack train was leaving Alexandria in the morning and he would join it. O'Reilly's main task would be organizing last year's paperwork, listing and totalling the miners' fees and pre-emption payments.

O'Reilly hoped his chagrin did not show as he answered, "Yes, sir. I am experienced with paperwork."

Nind looked dreadful, his face even greyer than his moustache. Cox had described the Cariboo's terrain as exhausting, the prospectors and miners being spread out over hundreds of miles of creeks. O'Reilly didn't know if the gold commissioner was completely worn out, or ill.

"Except for a few pre-emptions and the small settlements at Quesnelle Forks and Quesnelmouth, Alexandria and Williams Lake—where the government building with my quarters recently burned to the ground—the Cariboo's population is scattered." Nind said that he would show O'Reilly his map detailing where most of the miners were wintering tomorrow.

After O'Reilly had consumed a second toddy and a bowl of beans, Pinchbeck took him across to a sleeping cabin with a miniature pot-bellied stove, a lantern stand and a narrow bunk. As the constable lit the fire, he said, "Nind needs a doctor, sir. He is in such pain. But when I've asked about it, he brushes me off."

"Is he the only government official in this whole area?"

"Yes—well, and me."

In the morning, Nind poured O'Reilly coffee. "Listen to Pinchbeck. He's a good man." The senior gold commissioner unrolled a rough map that showed the settlements and major mining creeks and began pointing out where the residents and miners were. "There are about four hundred in total, because when I closed all mining last month, I let some men stay on their claims. They said they were nervous about claim jumpers but, really, many of them can't afford the long trip out and then back in the spring. The men staying often have inadequate clothing for freezing temperatures, and I suspect they lack food. Flour is now over eighty dollars per sack. Hungry men can become sick or desperate."

"Will there be conflicts?" O'Reilly asked.

"Perhaps. Thefts, mainly, and Pinchbeck will sort those out as best he can. Travel will soon be difficult, and you will be able to get around only on snowshoes. My greatest concern is epidemics, particularly mountain fever, but there's not much one can do about that."

Nind asked O'Reilly if he had questions, then banged the tobacco out of his pipe and said he hoped to be back by late February. As he pulled on his fur-lined parka, he said, "Use my snowshoes. And start practising how to walk on them before you actually have to go somewhere."

By the time O'Reilly headed up to Quesnelle Forks and then on into the Keithley and Williams creek basins with Pinchbeck, he could cover many miles a day on Nind's snowshoes. They found the miners scattered in small groups and mostly in good spirits, passing the cold days by playing cards, making music, telling each other tall tales and arguing—usually companionably. All were also analyzing where the motherlodes were as they struggled to survive. Even the most cheerful admitted they were hungry, and O'Reilly found the majority of them looked as gaunt as the ruined potato farmers had in Ireland.

Hard as it was, he and Pinchbeck visited any man whose ailment kept him abed in a cold tent or log shanty. One, who had crushed his foot badly weeks before, was in agony, dying slowly of infection. Another had a jaw so swollen because of a rotten tooth that his right eye was closed. At a small camp, the nine men were all in shock. One cried as he related how their youngest member, a fine fiddler, had committed suicide the week before.

They snowshoed over miles of whiteness, and O'Reilly had to hold a magistrate's court only three times: he fined one man for infringing on his neighbour's registered property; decided that a thief owed three times the amount of flour to the man he'd stolen from; and dismissed the last complaint, a dispute between partners over use of their jointly owned tobacco.

After a month of freezing at night and eating bannock, bacon and beans, O'Reilly was coughing badly. When he and Pinchbeck finally returned to Alexandria, he found he had lost a considerable amount of weight. That perhaps was the reason he was feeling so unwell, he thought, though even more frightening for him was realizing he was having the blue devils, day after day. Pinchbeck and his wife, a kindly Indian woman, organized a community dinner for the nine local folk to mark the Christmas season, and O'Reilly attended, though he would have preferred to go to bed.

Pretending to enjoy the simple festivities was difficult for him. He longed for the traditional delicacies and cultured gaiety he knew his family would be enjoying at Ballybeg House, and when Pinchbeck asked him what Christmas would be like in Ireland, O'Reilly said, around the lump in his throat, "The usual."

By the New Year, he found that everything depressed him, even as he sat by the stove and sorted out Nind's confused paperwork. During the long, dark nights, as the wind howled against the cabin, he huddled in his cold bed and longed to be galloping across a green pasture in Ireland. His flour had weevils, he had run out of bacon, and he found that eating moose meat was not only monotonous, it disagreed with his system. Worst of all, he had received no mail since Cox had given him the three short letters from Mamsey in October. As he confided to his diary on January 27, 1862:

> I spent another miserable night and got up as cross as a cat. Bought a hind leg of a moose from an Indian, fresh. Also got another bundle of grass for the horses. Tried to read but I could only think of Mamsey so I reread her letters. Spent a wretched lonely day.[4]

The next day did not improve his situation:

> A deep frost and much snow fell overnight. Keep thinking of the dear ones at home and wishing I was with them. Or somewhere in Ireland. In house the whole day—no work to do. A regular attack of the Blue Devils, which I cannot shake.[5]

Nind returned in late February, looking much better, and told O'Reilly that he was to report to Chief Inspector Brew. He also said that

Governor Douglas had recently announced the construction of the long-awaited Cariboo Waggon Road.

"Brew said to tell you that Hope will be busy again and you'll be returning there, after your one-week leave in New Westminster. Now, the pack train I travelled with up from Lac La Hache is heading back tomorrow and you best go down with it as the trails are mucky. Lots of rotten ice. Tell me about the winter, pack up the paperwork and take it to Brew."

Eight days later, O'Reilly arrived in New Westminster, just in time for a mess dinner and dance at the Royal Engineers Barracks. Colonel and Mrs. Moody were welcoming Rear-Admiral Robert Baynes and the officers of his flagship, HMS *Ganges*.

Brew told O'Reilly that he was invited and reported that the guests included the newly appointed Attorney General Henry Crease and his wife, Sarah, Ned Dewdney and Jane Moir, Gold Commissioner and Magistrate Ed Sanders and his fiancée, Annie Moresby, Joe and Julia Trutch, John Trutch, and Judge Begbie. Vancouver Island Chief of Police Augustus Pemberton was also attending with Brew's sister, Jane, who was now his fiancée.

O'Reilly revelled in the evening and in wearing dress clothes again. All the guests were seated around a long table covered in starched white linen, the numerous candles reflecting on the silver serving dishes and cutlery. But he ate the delicious food cautiously, aware of how much his stomach had shrunk during the winter. The Engineers' musicians played until three AM, and O'Reilly danced often, appreciating being with ladies in colourful gowns again.

During the evening, he both asked and answered many questions. He learned that, although the Royal Engineers were now cutting a trail over Jackass Mountain as construction on the Cariboo Road proceeded, there was deep discontent about the mainland's growing financial instability, primarily because its revenues were being used to subsidize the Colony of Vancouver Island.

"Since the costs of governing both colonies keep growing, and the British Parliament has refused more subsidies for either colony, we British Columbians are nervous about the situation," Dewdney summarized.

O'Reilly immediately started to worry about his own stipend.

"It is a problem but, on the other hand, both Yale and Hope are regaining residents," Brew offered. Many road builders were arriving in the canyon, and another seven hundred indentured Chinese had been brought in to work the abandoned Fraser River claims.

"I suspect that brings it to about twelve hundred Chinese there," Colonel Moody said.

"Mr. O'Reilly will be soon telling us accurate figures because he is now responsible for Yale as well as Hope," Brew announced.

CHAPTER FOUR

O'Reilly Meets Caroline Trutch

O'Reilly spent the year in Hope and Yale, his weeks pleasantly full of duties. He methodically located all the Chinese miners now sifting the Fraser's gravel bars for any flecks of gold and sold mining licences to them. He also kept in close touch with the various Indian bands in the canyon, ensuring that they were co-operated with and not harassed by the road builders carving out the Cariboo Waggon Road.

The following spring, on Philip Nind's advice, the Cariboo goldfields were divided into two districts. Nind was moving to Richfield, near most of the gold creeks, and would manage that territory as Cariboo East; the balance of the vast district would become Cariboo West. When a former gold commissioner, Thomas Elwyn, turned down that post, choosing instead to reshape the government's gold escort freight service, Nind requested that Brew appoint O'Reilly.

In late April, Brew sent a message to O'Reilly. "Finish up in your district and report to me."

O'Reilly gathered up the prisoner in the Yale jail who needed to be transferred to New Westminster, completed all his reports, balanced his accounts and headed down the muddy, slippery road in the pouring rain. On May 5, 1862, he wrote in his diary:

> Arrived at Westminster at 9 AM. Prisoner Burke handed over to Prichard. Got my accounts all passed at the Treasury.[1]

He then reported to Brew, who, to O'Reilly's surprise, appointed him gold commissioner for Cariboo West. He would also assist with managing Cariboo East when requested by Nind. Knowing O'Reilly was off to Victoria, Brew told him to stay there until he had bought a dozen or so horses to take up to the Cariboo with him. As were most of the two colonies' officials, they were both going to attend the wedding of Judge Begbie's popular clerk, Arthur Bushby, to Governor Douglas's daughter, Agnes.

Pleased to be Nind's choice and happy to be on leave, O'Reilly noted in his diary:

> May 6, 1862
>
> Beautiful morning. Up at 4—arrived at Victoria at 9—Met Luard and Grant and executed no end of commissions. Called on the Governor, rode with him, Miss Douglas & Begbie to Cadborough Bay. Dined at Government House & went to a hop given by the bachelors at the Lyceum—very jolly party but the Ladies were not in proportion to the Gentlemen. Fire in the ballroom after supper, which might have been a serious affair & interfered with the dancing.

> May 8, 1862
>
> All bustle preparing for Bushby's wedding. Col. Moody & Brew arrived at 9. All passed off very nicely—stood as one of the best men . . . Long chat with the Governor who asked me to take charge of his nephew who is about to start for the Cariboo.

May 9, 1862

Long chat with the Governor & Young. Got at last my instructions & permission to buy horses for my journey to Cariboo.

May 12, 1862

Bought Stewart's grey horse for $120, also 4 horses with pack saddles for $150 each.

Bought two more for Nesbit & Armstrong plus one for Pemberton, each $125.[2]

O'Reilly was looking forward to returning to the Cariboo, particularly as it would be spring when he got there, and frequently realized how much his life had improved since his first hard months there. After the wedding festivities, he took two weeks to purchase a herd of horses and to hire drovers to help him move it up to the government pastures at Hope. There, after another goodbye dinner with the Glennies, O'Reilly removed his belongings from his cottage and rented it; that made three rentals he had in Hope. He also had a good visit with Ned Dewdney, who regularly returned to Hope to court Jane Moir. They celebrated O'Reilly's promotion as well as Dewdney's latest contract; he had done well on the Cariboo Road construction and was now returning to survey in the Similkameen region.

In mid-June, O'Reilly and the drovers moved the herd north. While travelling up, he called on businesses and new residents, as he described in his diary:

June 20, 1862

Issued spirit & trading licences. The country over which I passed this day is beautiful & well suited for farming & grazing. Camped at Lake La Hache—Mosquitoes more troublesome than I ever remember.

Past Felkers, passed a large drove of cattle & a number of men from Oregon . . . reached Wm Lake, place deserted.³

O'Reilly reported to Nind at Richfield at the end of June and was pleased to find the senior commissioner looking healthy and fit. Nind welcomed him, saying, "We have double the number of men here this early in the season as we had in 1861. It's going to be a busy year, Mr. O'Reilly." Nind inquired whether O'Reilly had heard anything about Alfred Waddington, who was apparently trying to build another route, a shorter one, to the Cariboo from Bute Inlet. It would go up the turbulent Homathko River's steep canyon and through the coastal mountains before heading over the Chilcotin tribal lands to Fort Alexandria.

"I have, though mainly from newspaper reports and from talking with Judge Begbie. He is concerned about it because he has talked with naval men and others knowledgable about the terrain and the Indians along that route. They all say it is risky." When O'Reilly and Begbie had recently encountered each other in Lillooet, Begbie speculated that Vancouver Island storekeepers were funding Waddington's exploration; they were desperate to limit their New Westminster counterparts's opportunities to supply the Cariboo gold rush.

"Does that plan seem feasible?" Nind asked.

"I don't know, but neither Begbie nor Joe Trutch seem to think so. Joe told me that from an engineer's perspective, it's unstable and that the Chilcotin Indians are fierce. Even the old Hudson's Bay brigade men were leery of them."

Nind stoked the stove and put the grouse O'Reilly had brought on to cook. "Perhaps everyone is too optimistic about this rush. I sometimes wonder if even the Cariboo Road will be able to produce the tolls projected for the next ten years. Gold rush revenues are hard to judge."

O'Reilly's next few months in the Cariboo differed radically from the depressing time he had endured when he first wintered there. During the summer of 1862, major gold discoveries were opened up and the new settlements of Antler, Williams Creek, Lightning Creek, Van Winkle and Barkerville were named to celebrate bonanzas. Barkerville quickly became the region's largest settlement, and prospectors arrived in droves. They hoped to duplicate Billy Barker's major find—he and his partners were taking out one thousand dollars a day from an eighty-nine-foot shaft.

O'Reilly spent most of his daylight hours on horseback. He travelled from Quesnel, as Quesnelmouth was now called, to Quesnelle Forks and Richfield weekly, keeping Nind informed about the latest developments. He also became quite innovative. When Nind was frustrated with how slowly the new Richfield courthouse and outbuildings were going up, because workers kept quitting to go prospecting, O'Reilly solved the problem. He sought miners who had previously been carpenters and suggested, "How about me bringing all your supplies in from Quesnel—flour, bacon, beans and alcohol—in exchange for you working on the courthouse one day a week?" Most of them agreed, as costs in Barkerville were prohibitive. When Begbie came for Fall Assizes, his courtroom had a watertight roof and he had a snug cottage.

O'Reilly came to know many of the miners, where they had come from, what they worried about and what challenges shaped their days. Since the miners found that he sympathized with their difficulties and despair, most co-operated when he inspected their claims and ensured that each had a current mining licence. Whenever it was required, he held magistrate's court to settle minor disputes and began to be addressed as "judge." Although he explained he should be called Mr. O'Reilly or Commissioner, the title pleased him and gave him a sense of self-respect he had never known before, except related to his expertise with horses.

He occasionally wrote in his diary about missing his family and Ireland, but the entries were now seldom gloomy:

August 13, 1862

Beautiful day—service in the New Church—took Communion—I walked up the Gulch with Kingston, Begbie, Wood & Walker. He and I went shooting birds later and dined together on a big grouse . . .[4]

When Nind declared the mining season closed at the end of November, he told O'Reilly to take the paperwork and report to Brew in New Westminster. "I am staying in Quesnel this winter. See you in the spring."

Brew greeted O'Reilly warmly and commented on how well he looked. "Come along, we will have lunch as you tell me about the Cariboo's gold season. And are you still planning to return to Ireland?"

"Not at the current time, sir. What I am craving is a good chowder. There's more choice of where to eat in Barkerville now, and more road-houses en route, but they only offer venison, moose meat, biscuits and beans."

Brew laughed. "Tedious." Then, over a steaming bowl of soup, he related his news. Governor Douglas had finally decided that Brew's primary duty was developing the BC Colonial Constabulary. Although he would continue to supervise the gold commissioners, the responsibility for the mining paperwork had been transferred to Victoria.

O'Reilly's bushy dark beard hid his smile. "Does that mean I am done with sorting paperwork, except for the Cariboo's?"

Brew said it did and confided that the gold totals for 1862 from the Cariboo were higher than the government's estimates, improving the colony's financial stability; they hoped this would continue next season. That would be O'Reilly's concern, as he would be the Cariboo's chief gold commissioner by then, the chief announced. Nind had decided to resign as of March 1863 and return to England, and O'Reilly would be senior, taking charge of Cariboo East and supervising the Cariboo West commissioner.

"Thank you, sir." O'Reilly was overwhelmed at the unexpected news and thought what a pleasure it would be to tell his family. Mamsey had been ill much of the winter, and learning of his success might cheer her.

"I haven't decided who will manage Cariboo West," Brew continued. He suspected it would probably be Thomas Elwyn, if the gold escort was discontinued, or perhaps George Cox. Although the government's insured freight service had functioned well, with few losses to robberies, it had not earned enough to cover the costs of running it, and he suspected that the legislature would decline to subsidize it further.

They finished their pork chops and sipped ale as each decided on dessert. Brew returned to reviewing events and asked O'Reilly what he knew about the smallpox epidemic among the Natives.

"I've heard there were considerably more smallpox cases than usual, but I don't know much more than that."

"We suspect thousands have died, but it is still too risky to send in constables to find out. If what we've been told so far is even half true, it's bad, very bad. We need freezing cold winter temperatures to halt the spread of the disease." Brew went on to describe how it had raged through the Indian camps on the outskirts of Victoria, then spread rapidly to the lower mainland and up the coast as sick Natives headed back to their home villages and infected them.

O'Reilly was stunned. "I had no idea. Thousands? In the Cariboo, we only had seven cases that I know of—three Indians, two breeds and two elderly white men. It did not spread."

Brew stroked his greying beard. "Many healthy young adults have died, along with children and the elderly, so who will have harvested and dried the meat, fish and berries? The Indians with long winters will have serious food shortages."

O'Reilly immediately understood the chief's worry. The colonies could not begin to feed the starving Indians, even if they could be reached.

How could the normally peaceful relationships between whites and most Indians survive?

As they walked back to Brew's office in New Westminster's recently completed government building, carefully avoiding the numerous tree stumps, the chief said, "If I'd lost most of my family, and the rest were starving, I'd take food from wherever I could find it. Wouldn't you? Travellers and isolated settlers will be at risk." In the office, Brew passed him a stack of government reports and told him to read them.

"I have a tough new assignment for you. You're to spend the next three months on Vancouver Island, buying horses and reporting at length to Governor Douglas and other officials on what is happening in the Cariboo. Oh, and I assume you are taking Tom, as Mrs. Douglas is waiting for him to service her youngest daughter's mare."

O'Reilly laughed and said he would call on Mrs. Douglas and arrange for Tom's appearance.

In the reports, as well as the estimates of smallpox deaths, O'Reilly read about how much bootlegging to Indians had increased. The growing numbers of conflicts between Indians and pre-emptors, fishermen, traders and loggers in the various coastal areas were of concern, and the Royal Navy had decided to supply two small gunboats, the HMS *Forward* and the HMS *Grappler*. They would arrive next summer, each equipped with two cannons and manned by a naval crew of forty. Brew's addendum to that report pointed out that as long as one constable or magistrate was aboard, policing actions were under civil authority rather than military. O'Reilly was aware that the Colonial Office was adamant about maintaining that distinction.

O'Reilly checked with the chief before his departure the next day, and Brew had one other request. "I want you to buy a sloop during your stay on Vancouver Island."

"A sloop? But, sir, I know nothing about boats."

Brew passed him the specifications and explained that with Moody and the Royal Engineers leaving next November, the constabulary needed its own water transportation. "I tried to have one built in New Westminster, but the boatbuilders are too busy. Find an advisor, Mr. O'Reilly, and look after it."

"Yes, sir."

When O'Reilly reached Victoria, he was shocked at how little remained of the bustle and gaiety he'd encountered when he'd first landed, almost three years ago. Now, as he rode Tom down Front Street, Victoria's busiest, he counted only seven people, three British seamen and four women. None of the men looked as if they might be miners, which surprised him because New Westminster was crowded with men escaping the Cariboo winter. And he saw no Indians: Brew had told him they had been driven away and their shanties and huts burned when smallpox had broken out. Victoria's residents were terrified that the epidemic would spread to them, and all the Natives were chased away, even the sick ones.

O'Reilly noticed that the chairs on the hotels' wide porticoes were now empty. He decided on the grand Colonial Hotel, pleased that he was now able to pay whatever its rates were, but his room cost less than half of what he'd paid at lesser hotels previously. He mentioned how quiet Victoria seemed, and the desk clerk, dressed in formal, pearl-grey morning attire, admitted it was. "But sir, this lack of activity is temporary. The riches being found in the Cariboo will soon be making their way down here, once the goldfields are closed for the season."

O'Reilly nodded, feeling sorry for the lad. He did not tell him that mining had been ended for over two weeks and the miners seemed to be wintering in New Westminster. It now had hotels, boarding houses, stores and services almost comparable to Victoria, and staying on the mainland eliminated the expensive boat ride.

Julia and Joe Trutch had invited O'Reilly to call on them when he was next in Victoria, so in mid-afternoon he rode out to their home, Fairfield

House, on an acreage east of Victoria. Joe greeted him warmly and invited him to stay for dinner. O'Reilly was pleased, mainly because he was lonely, but also because he was being welcomed by a family who were part of Victoria's elite.

Joe ushered him into his library, where his younger brother, John, also a respected surveyor whom O'Reilly had met before, was already ensconced in an Italian leather chair. The trio sipped brandy as they chatted about recent events and enjoyed the warmth from the massive fireplace. The brothers seemed to know a great deal about what was happening, both in the colonies and in the Colonial Office, and O'Reilly listened eagerly to the gossip.

They discussed the rumours that London investors were concerned about some of Douglas's decisions and what changes they might create, then moved on to the looming departure of the Royal Engineers. They agreed that the troops had helped to stabilize BC as they laid out its towns and built roads, although Joe pointed out, "On the other hand, think how their departure will increase opportunities for private contractors!"

O'Reilly became aware that Joe was hoping to benefit. He had recently bid on building a suspension bridge across the Fraser River.

"There are many possibilities already. The mainland is doing well and I'm overwhelmed by survey requests," John said. "Good thing, because the ones I used to get on Vancouver Island seem to have dried up." But he was afraid that the Indians who used to work on construction might have died in the epidemic and that those who had survived might not work for whites any more. He was also wondering if the anger Indians must be feeling might make it dangerous for isolated crews.

"I agree it could be risky," Joe said. "Do you know any men who might want to be guards, Peter? I'll hire them to protect the workers building my bridge, once I get the contract."

O'Reilly explained that most of the men he knew now had pre-emptions and families. They would work in their areas as special constables, when required, but they probably could not leave their crops or livestock during the summer.

"Do you realize how outnumbered we are, if the Indians start rebelling?" Joe asked.

"Yes. The estimates I've heard vary from fifty thousand to seventy thousand and I suspect our population ranges from five thousand to seven thousand, depending on how many miners there are in BC. From a defensive point of view, it would be difficult," O'Reilly replied.

Joe drank deeply. "To be blunt, the epidemic's after-effects may be inconvenient now, but not in the long term. From my perspective, these colonies have too many Natives. We need immigrants committed to our way of life, and they will want the lands along rivers and lakes that the Indians claim are theirs."

O'Reilly suddenly understood what Douglas and Trutch had been discussing at a dinner he'd attended in Victoria the previous winter. Douglas was adamant that the Indians be respected; he believed they were part of the colonies' wealth. Trutch had disagreed. Begbie had overheard the conversation and later commented to O'Reilly that he hoped Trutch would not become too powerful. He suspected the man might be a bad kind of colonizer, typical of a lad raised in a world where slaves ensured his family's comforts and wealth. Since Trutch had often lived with his maternal grandparents on a plantation in Jamaica, Begbie wondered whether he could begin to understand the governor's point of view.

"Joe, do you realize how harsh you sound?" John asked.

"If these Pacific colonies are to survive, better fewer Natives. Disputes over land between settlers and Indians will become the reality, if we are to prosper."

O'Reilly tried to hide his surprise, not wanting to disagree with his host. He had little experience with such issues because they did not interest him, and he was not sure what he actually believed. He found hoping for the eventual extinction of Indians a non-Christian idea, not at all acceptable. BC had so much land and water; could it not be shared with the Aboriginals? Yet he remembered how hard that had been during the Fraser River gold rush when nuggets were found in an area Douglas had reserved for Native fishing. As he listened to the Trutch brothers, he thought of Maria, his name for the Indian woman he had briefly lived with, and he was relieved when they were summoned to the dinner table.

After introductions, O'Reilly was directed to a seat beside Joe's and John's youngest sister, Caroline Trutch. He was so mesmerized that he found it difficult to eat. Her lacy attire, ladylike gestures, pleasant voice and dainty hands charmed him. When she later played the piano, he saw that those little hands certainly were not frail. She and the senior Mrs. Trutch, their mother, sang song after song, then insisted the others join in. O'Reilly had a strong tenor and did so enthusiastically, managing to stand by the piano, right beside Caroline.

Much later, after hot chocolate to end the musical evening, he cantered Tom back to his hotel and lectured himself: Mind your expectations, Peter. You are not at all of the quality to be a suitor for someone like Caroline Trutch. Enjoy the grand evening and all their warm hospitality, but do not forget you are without assets or future inheritances. Your only prospects are the ones you can earn for yourself! As he prepared for bed, he wondered again whether he'd been right to emigrate. Would he ever be able to afford a wife?

CHAPTER FIVE

Marriage and Two Governors

O'Reilly hoped he would encounter Caroline Trutch again, but he did not. He went about his business, trying to forget her, yet aware that he was continually watching for her. In early December, when he called on Jane Pemberton to admire her new baby boy, he found Joe and Julia Trutch there, sipping sherry. After they had visited for a while, Julia said, "Peter, we would be pleased if you would be our guest at Fairfield over Christmas and New Year's. Carry's helping to plan the festivities."

O'Reilly dropped his glass. Wiping up the sherry, he spluttered, "Yes, I would like that, very much." The gold commissioner felt as flustered as a youth and knew he'd turned red. He glanced at Joe, who winked discreetly. It seemed they had decided he was a potential and acceptable suitor for Caroline's affection after all. He wondered if he should tell Joe his financial situation, then decided perhaps it was premature.

He did so in February. And at the beginning of March, with all the Trutches' blessings, Caroline Trutch and Peter O'Reilly became engaged. Fairfield was fully decorated for the gala ball in their honour, and at midnight, Joe announced the couple's betrothal. When he invited the guests to the wedding, planned for mid-December, everyone thought they were well matched and that it was time for each to marry. Caroline—or Carry, as her friends and family called her—had turned thirty-two the previous September, while Peter was three years older.

After their engagement, they spent more time together without a chaperone, holding hands and exchanging chaste kisses. Carry had much more travelling experience than O'Reilly. She had gone to India to stay with a sister in Madras, although she didn't explain to Peter why she had made that trip. Joe was not as reticent. He confided she had hoped to be married to a childhood friend, but that officer, who was in her brother-in-law's regiment, had been killed a few weeks before she arrived. This was shortly before the mutiny began in Cawnpore, and O'Reilly asked her if she'd been terrified when the rioting broke out.

Carry reflected before replying. "We went on with our activities, Peter—church, visiting, arranging dinner after dinner in the English compound. I usually had a lump in my throat, and we were all jumpy, on edge. But I'm my mother's daughter and we carry on. Mother was raised around frequent rebellions in Jamaica, so that is in our blood."

O'Reilly knew that the five Trutch children had spent considerable time on their grandparents's estate in Jamaica, which her brothers remembered clearly, although Carry, being the youngest, did not. She had enjoyed unusual latitude for a girl. In England, as well as the normal training in handicrafts, household management, singing and playing the piano and harp, she had often sat in with her two brothers and their tutor, and received a classical education. When their father died, leaving Carry and her mother alone in London with inadequate funds, Joe and Julia insisted they visit Victoria and consider making Fairfield their home.

"Thank goodness you came," O'Reilly exclaimed. He had taken the afternoon off to go riding with Carry. Almost all his administrative obligations had been fulfilled, and he had managed to purchase thirteen horses, within

Brew's budget for ten. He had allowed Tom to breed one man's prize mare in exchange for purchasing two excellent horses for the price of one; that pair would become his personal mounts for the Cariboo. Tom would again be left behind, this time in lush pastures out past Craigflower Farm in Esquimalt. When Brew had heard about O'Reilly's engagement, he'd instructed him to stay on the island and buy more horses for the government.

They stopped to picnic on a flat, sun-warmed rock in the midst of fresh-smelling spring grass, yellow johnny jump-ups and tiny blue violas. After they finished their chicken sandwiches, Carry asked O'Reilly whether he was upset that it seemed none of his family would be at their wedding.

"No, Carry. When my letter announcing our engagement reaches Mamsey, she'll be relieved and delighted that I've found you." O'Reilly did not add that, other than an annual note from his two younger sisters, no one but Mamsey wrote to him anymore. His grandfather, now bed-ridden, had sent him a few lines, hoping he was making a stable life for himself in British Columbia, because there had been no improvement in the O'Reilly family's well-being. As he had all those years ago, attending his stark English boarding school, O'Reilly now felt apart from most of his family, but trying to explain that to Carry, whose family remained close, was not something he chose to do.

Three weeks after the engagement party, Augustus Pemberton, Vancouver Island's chief of police told O'Reilly that Brew had authorized his coming along on a naval expedition to Nanaimo and around to the island's west coast aboard the HMS *Devastation*. He would be investigating reports about bootleggers and increased Indian attacks on settlers, as well as estimating the effect of the smallpox epidemic on the northern Vancouver Island tribes. O'Reilly was pleased, glad of the opportunity to learn more about this colony, and appreciative of a break from all the socializing.

He had become weary of elaborate dinners and evenings shared with the same small group of people. He could now summarize what each person's concerns, opinions and recommendations were about the future of the colonies, the American Civil War, the possibility of Upper and Lower Canada uniting and whether or not future Indian wars on the west coast were a looming risk. As he stood on the *Devastation*'s afterdeck, watching Victoria disappear in the mist, he puzzled about why its residents had such little interest in what was happening in the colony of BC.

When Victoria's wealthy residents left for a holiday or a business trip, it was for a short stay in San Francisco or a long one in England, Scotland or Ireland. Few travelled to BC, not even as far as New Westminster. Many had decided, incorrectly, that mainlanders wanted affiliation with the American states and rejection of their British ties.

When O'Reilly tried to refute that, he had encountered disbelief and, twice, a lecture about loyalties. Although both colonies' governments expected the Colonial Office to order amalgamation eventually, it was never discussed; it was considered far too political a subject for dinner parties.

In New Westminster, almost everyone wanted information about what was happening in Victoria, perhaps because it was where Douglas and most members of BC's executive council governed from and lived. O'Reilly also realized, during the many dinners he'd attended with the Trutch family, that only a few people in Victoria were interested in his duties. They did not want to hear about the mud or mosquitoes or blackflies. Nor did they care about how he, and most folks in frontier regions, struggled to get food, be it slightly tainted meat, or flour with more weevils than wheat. On the other hand, they were curious about why very few miners were ever murdered, and surprised to learn that most upcountry deaths were from drowning, accidents, or diseases, often caused by unclean drinking water. They were also surprised when he said there were only a few Indians living in the Cariboo's mining areas.

O'Reilly enjoyed going around the island and, ten days later, when the *Devastation* returned to Esquimalt, he had gained a new understanding of BC's sister colony, particularly its coalfields, its huge trees and its impressive logging camps. He had also purchased Brew's requested sloop, with the amused assistance of the captain, who had conveniently offered that the *Devastation* could deliver it to New Westminster.

On O'Reilly's return to Victoria, a letter from Brew awaited him, ordering him to the Cariboo. He and Carry spent their last few days together, planning their wedding and preparing for O'Reilly's northern sojourn. As he told her just before his departure, "I still cannot believe that I am blessed with being your future husband."

She hugged him and laughed. "In December, not only do you get me, you officially become part of a big family again. Are you sure you're not marrying me for my mother, Mr. O'Reilly?" Carry was as delighted with him as he was with her.

"Mrs. Charlotte Trutch is an older version of her beautiful youngest daughter, and I am most grateful to have two new women in my life."

"Irish blarney, that's what you're blathering." Carry turned a pleasing shade of rosy pink.

When O'Reilly left the next morning, he had company. Joe Trutch had decided to travel with him as far as Yale, since he had just received the contract for forty-five thousand dollars, plus the rights to all tolls for a seven-year period, to build the suspension bridge. It was to span three hundred feet across the Fraser River at Alexandra, a few miles north of Yale. That bridge, the first of its kind in North America, would finally allow traffic to use the Cariboo Waggon Road.

In early July, Julia, Carry and Mrs. Trutch were also in Yale as they were spending the summer at Joe and Julia's home there and arranging the bridge's opening ceremonies.

O'Reilly had planned to attend, but the demands of managing the Cariboo's gold miners that season kept all the government officials working without breaks. The amount of rich ore coming out of the deep shafts was almost unbelievable, and the number of disputes between claim holders multiplied. As news of the Cariboo's wealth spread, con artists and thieves as well as prospectors were attracted.

O'Reilly found it easy to take charge. Although George Cox, who had been his superior at Rock Creek, was now his junior as the commissioner of Cariboo West, they worked well together. Settling the miners' conflicts was not difficult, and O'Reilly had no bouts of his blue devils. The Cariboo, particularly Barkerville and Quesnel, was changing. People came to open stores or provide services rather than to seek gold. When O'Reilly first visited the new lending library in Barkerville, he realized that it symbolized the arrival of civilization to him. He frequently attended community socials as an honoured guest, sometimes accompanied by Judge Begbie. Their friendship grew as the judge often stayed in his cabin at Richfield, not only for the spring and autumn assizes.

When the Richfield courthouse was finally completed, O'Reilly, Begbie, Cox, Elwyn and a number of other guests celebrated far into the night. The next morning, O'Reilly spoke for many of them, "I either have a larger head or an overly tight hat!"

On the miners' advice, O'Reilly took the innovative step of establishing an elected mining board. That helped create even more general co-operation, although outsiders continued to believe that there was much disorder in the Cariboo. On August 17, 1863, the *Colonist* reported:

> Everything is very quiet and orderly on the creek, owing in great measure to Mr. O'Reilly's efficiency and the wholesome appearance of Judge Begbie, who seems to be a terror to evil doers and a sworn enemy to the use of the knife and revolver. Crime in the Cariboo has been vigorously checked . . . The most prejudiced of foreigners on the Creek allow that a security of life and property exists which twelve months ago it would have appeared as useless to expect.[1]

O'Reilly and Begbie chuckled when the newspaper eventually arrived in Richfield. They agreed that twelve months earlier, there had been a surprising lack of "evil doers" in the area, probably because of the general lack of residents, Native or white, in the whole region east of the Fraser River, between Williams Lake and Quesnel. But by August 1863, the population had grown to over two thousand. Constable William Fitzgerald worked with Cox and Constable John Wolsey with O'Reilly, and only an increasing number of disputes over claims disturbed the general peacefulness. Even then, when O'Reilly or Cox made a decision, the miners usually accepted it.

When O'Reilly realized he could not leave to attend the opening ceremonies for Joe's Alexandra Suspension Bridge, he wrote to his future brother-in-law on July 21, 1863:

> I am busy seven days, every week. The claims are now beginning to pay well generally all down the Creek & large prizes are being won every day . . . 3,000 oz. per day. The Escort took down about $50,000 this trip. My impression is that next time, they will get as much as they can carry.
>
> Like yourself, I was much surprised to see Elwyn driving them, I did not think he would like to play Second Fiddle . . . By the time this reaches you, the ladies may be with you at Chapman's Bar, to take part in the celebration of opening the Bridge. How I wish I could run down & surprise you all, but that is impossible & I must put such a notion out of my head . . .[2]

He was particularly disappointed as he knew that Carry and her mother had been chosen to take the first official trips across the bridge, Carry riding sidesaddle and Mrs. Trutch driving a buggy. Many other guests were coming up for the celebrations, and he would have enjoyed being there, escorting his future wife. Every mailbag brought letters from

Carry, replies to the numerous ones he wrote to her. Many also came from Ireland. Notes from three of his sisters and an aunt confirmed that none of his family could be at his wedding, but Mamsey reported her complete pleasure at his approaching marriage and confirmed that she had shipped the belongings he had requested.

List of clothes O'Reilly sent for in his letter to Mamsey, Sept 29/63:

1 Suit of dress clothes, pants Peg top fashion & to be worn without braces

1 "also suit," country fashion, serviceable

1 suit—morning clothes

2 prs of hunting Windsor Cord unmentionables to fasten at the instep

2 Prs of long riding boots (best)

2 Prs of best shooting boots to fasten with hooks

1 Pr of Morning boots

2 Doz best pocket handkerchiefs

½ Doz Night shirts

2 Dress shirts (best)

2 Hats (not too narrow in the brim)

4 light coloured scarfs [3]

O'Reilly was surprised that he did not feel at all distraught. Instead, he was relieved that no one mentioned the one factor about the wedding he had worried might upset his family: their vows were to be exchanged in a Protestant cathedral. He was now grateful that he had converted, as Carry would not have been allowed to marry a Catholic.

After closing mining for the season and rushing down the new Waggon Road, he reached New Westminster on November 4, 1863, just in time to attend the goodbye banquet and poignant celebrations for Colonel Moody and the officers of the Royal Engineers. Within the week, they and their troops were sailing for England on the HMS *Chameleon*.

O'Reilly would miss the Moodys' friendship and, being a gold commissioner, he also would miss knowing that professional soldiers were available if the need arose; the presence of the Engineers had defused many earlier situations. Although a volunteer militia was being organized in New Westminster, the departure of the Royal Engineers left a big gap.

As well as attending the celebrations, he spent a week sorting through reports and discussing with Brew two complaints about his management of the Cariboo. He was then on leave and boarded the boat for Victoria. Anxious to be with Carry, he was pleased at how warmly they greeted each other, but the weeks before their wedding did not go smoothly.

His prized stallion, Tom, was unwell. O'Reilly spent hours with him every day and had to apologize to Carry continually, nervously explaining why he needed to stay with Tom rather than be with her at the many social events planned for them. Luckily, Carry understood, though when he was late for the celebration ball hosted jointly by the Royal Navy commander and Julia and Joe Trutch, she was miffed, until O'Reilly whispered, "Tom is dead," and his eyes filled with unshed tears. Then the normally dispassionate gold commissioner, stipendiary magistrate and high sheriff had to turn away from the dining-room table and blow his nose.

Carry patted his hand, murmured her sorrow and covered for him, answering all questions directed to him and firmly changing the subject from horses each time it came up. By the time O'Reilly had consumed the hot oyster soup, he was again in control of his emotions.

In addition to the pre-nuptial socials, O'Reilly had the duty of replacing Augustus Pemberton as Stipendiary Magistrate for Vancouver Island for the winter. He recorded in his diary on Monday, November 30, 1863:

Read My Commission as S.M. for V.I. and instructions to take Pemberton's duty during his illness. Went to Police office at 11 ½ and remained till 3 PM. Pemberton looking very ill, "Jaundice." Walked to Fairfield with John & dined there.[4]

The Trutch–O'Reilly wedding was the highlight of the social season. Many guests travelled long distances, enduring winter sailings from California, Oregon and British Columbia. But the day before they were to be married, Peter, who had been fighting a heavy cold, looked and sounded dreadful. Carry insisted he spend the day in bed but said that he could attend the groom's dinner that evening. While he sipped the hot beef broth she had delivered to him, Carry chatted about the wedding guests.

"Do you realize almost everyone we've invited is coming? Except, sadly, I just received a message from Matthew Begbie. He won't make it back in time. Mr. Brew is coming and most of the gold commissioners. I am glad the Miss Moirs are accompanying Dewdney. Of course, we have all the locals—Sarah and Henry Crease, the Helmckens, the J.D. Pembertons and Rear-Admiral John Kingcome and Governor and Mrs. Douglas and all their family." She then instructed him to have an afternoon nap and left.

As O'Reilly tried to get comfortable, he mulled over his new family. He considered himself fortunate that Carry Trutch would be his wife, but he was worried that being connected to her family might be overwhelming at times and was concerned about how his status in both colonies might be changed. The Trutch brothers were increasingly powerful, and O'Reilly did not want to be perceived as representing their interests, particularly Joe's; he had made enemies with his sharp business tactics. "As a gold commissioner and magistrate, I have to make my decisions at arm's length, without any bias or favouritism," he said to himself, then coughed several times. Joe reminded him of his dictatorial grandfather, whom he respected, perhaps even loved, but had often disliked when he'd been a controlling tyrant. His grandfather had not brooked any disagreement and had seldom conferred with anyone or asked a question.

Under British law, weddings were legal only if they took place in the morning so, just before noon on December 15, 1863, in Christ Church Cathedral in Victoria, Caroline Agnes Trutch, youngest daughter of Charlotte Hannah Barnes Trutch and the late William Trutch, became O'Reilly's wife. The *Daily Colonist* reported:

> In bridal array, she came with her brother, their carriage and horses were decked with long white ribbons and rosettes. Her gown was of white brocaded silk and she wore orange blossoms on her veil and tiny heelless white satin slippers . . .[5]

During the lengthy service and exchange of vows, the cathedral glowed with hundreds of candles. The pleasant smell of melting beeswax helped to mask the women's eau de cologne and the odours of the gentlemen's woollen suits, redolent of brandy, cigars and perspiration. The choir saluted the newlyweds with a selection of songs, but many listeners missed Carry's clear soprano. After the final blessings were given to the couple, the cathedral bells pealed as Mr. and Mrs. Peter O'Reilly and their guests filed out to their horses or carriages.

All were heading to Fairfield. O'Reilly helped Carry into the best Trutch carriage; as it was the bridal chariot, they had had its seat heaped with soft white furs. "Mrs. O'Reilly," Peter said, his wonder showing in his voice. "Look at the blanket of new snow and the sunshine breaking through the clouds. What a background for our new life together." He had a moment of panic about whether, with his slim finances, he would be able to give her the life he wanted to, but he firmly buried such thoughts in a long cough and lectured himself to reject any invasion of his blue devils. Since Tom had died, he had been suffering from them again.

When they arrived at Fairfield, the gentlemen formed an impromptu arch to honour the bridal couple. Laughing, Peter and Carry rushed through it and up the steps to the wide porch, which had been decorated for both the wedding and the Christmas season. Masses of boughs covered in red berries and tied with white ribbons hung everywhere. As they entered the crowded reception hall, the first person to welcome them was Carry's mother. Before embracing her radiant daughter, she gently hugged Peter and said, "Now you are officially my son."

The guests adjourned to the dining room for the seven-course wedding lunch, and the groom could hardly believe how many people had come to feast with them. When he rose to toast his bride, he managed, to his relief, to get through his speech without sneezing.

Ladies & Gentlemen:

I feel quite inadequate to the task of thanking you for the Kind feelings expressed for my Wife & my self & I need not say how gratifying it is on such an Eventful & happy occasion to find myself surrounded by so many old & valued friends. I sincerely hope that the feelings of friendship always subsisting between us in my Bachelorhood may be, if possible, further increased by seeing you all often. I again on the part of my Wife and myself, give our best thanks for your good Wishes & assure You that the kind sentiments expressed are appreciated.

In conclusion, I may perhaps express the hope that my Bachelor friends that I see around me, may at some future time be in a similar position & likewise to assure them that their Good Wishes for our happiness today will not be more heartfelt than our own for them on a similar occasion.[6]

After the meal, the guests visited with each other and awaited their turn to chat with the new couple. O'Reilly was moved when Chartres Brew, the only person attending who knew his family in Ireland, told Carry what a lucky man Peter was. "I recently received a letter from your husband's mother, who is my mother's dear friend. She asked me to personally welcome you into the O'Reilly family for her and I take great pleasure in doing so."

Brew and O'Reilly also had a private moment together. After the chief wished him much happiness and complimented him on his beautiful and gracious wife, he mentioned how sorry he was about O'Reilly's loss of his stallion. "What were the findings of Tom's post-mortem?"

"Worms, sir. The worst case of worms I've ever seen in a horse his age. He was infested and it affected his kidneys. I should not have sent him to that pasture last winter with all those Indian nags."

The chief inspector paused, then quietly asked, "Is it possible you're assuming too much? Do you know whether any other horses in that herd are doing poorly or have died?"

"No, sir, I do not," O'Reilly admitted, aware that he had probably gained another black mark in Brew's esteem—and at his own wedding! Although he knew he was doing well as the Cariboo's senior official, O'Reilly realized he was not always adept at saying the right thing. "Here I am again, being overly judgmental, and without facts."

Brew clapped his shoulder and said warmly, "Forget about it. Go and enjoy your party, man, and have a lovely wedding holiday with your dear Mrs. O'Reilly."

They did. He and Carry had chosen the Belmont Hotel beside the Gorge in Esquimalt and during their ten-day stay, his diary pages remained empty. On their return, they moved into the four-room apartment they had sublet in James Bay, and O'Reilly resumed his duties as Pemberton's relief.

As Pemberton had predicted, Victoria and the island remained law-abiding over the winter and O'Reilly was home most nights. When their busy social life allowed, he and Carry spent their evenings by the fireplace, reminiscing and sharing stories about their earlier years. He was content.

In the process of sorting through his belongings to move in with Carry, O'Reilly had reread some of his jottings before discarding them. They had shocked him, revealing how desperately lonely he'd been in Hope when the young Indian woman had moved in with him. He deeply regretted that now and knew he would never tell Carry about his brief liaison with the comely and trusting girl. In retrospect, he judged it his worst failure; she had left him and gone back to her people, not having told him she was expecting a child. The following spring, when he heard she'd had a baby, he knew it was his. O'Reilly sent an offer of support but received no response until his former housekeeper's younger brother brought a message from her. She had married, and that man would raise the baby girl as his own, on the condition that O'Reilly did not ever contact her or their child.

The more he and Carry discussed their earlier years, the more O'Reilly was awed by his wife's education and experiences. "Jamaica, India, Persia, Vancouver Island and British Columbia—you are quite a traveller, my little wife. And better educated than I am. Your brothers' tutor must have been a tough taskmaster." Sometimes, he found her knowledge disconcerting. After a dinner and dance given by Julia and Joe Trutch to welcome the officers of a recently arrived Royal Navy gun ship, he'd inquired what language she and the captain had been speaking.

"Why Peter, that was French with the Caribbean cajun twist. Do you speak French?"

"Only a little, and badly." O'Reilly was again aware of the differences between them. According to his bride, the main one was about managing their finances. She felt he was overly nervous about them, particularly when he knew how frugally she and her mother had lived in England.

∞   ∞   ∞

Governor Douglas was forced to retire as of April 1864, because the colonial administrators in London had decided that a governor for each colony would work better. Frederick Seymour was to be the new governor for British Columbia and Arthur Kennedy for Vancouver Island. Seymour was to be advised by the new Legislative Colonial Council of British Columbia, and among the appointees to that assembly were all BC's magistrates. Thus, Peter O'Reilly became a member of the legislature.

London had also directed that each colony had to become economically viable without British subsidies in the near future and O'Reilly continued to be apprehensive about the stability of his income. When Pemberton returned to duty on March 1, 1864, the O'Reillys moved to New Westminster and into a very small house.

They travelled to Hope in late March for the marriage of Edgar Dewdney and Jane Moir, much to Carry's pleasure. Among her husband's friends, Ned was one of her favourites and Jeanie, as friends had nicknamed Jane, was a lovely match for him. The Dewdney wedding was an intimate affair at Hope's new church, the first to be held there. At the grand party in the Glennies' decorated barn that evening, Carry and Peter danced almost every jig and waltz. The next morning they parted; she boarded the stage for Yale to join her mother and spend the summer at Joe and Julia's home there, while O'Reilly caught the river steamer back to New Westminster to rejoin the sitting of the BC Legislative Council.

Despite O'Reilly's private hesitations about his suitability, because previously he had been uninterested in politics, he enjoyed being a member of the council and found participating easier than he had expected. However, when his fellow members refused to ratify the nomination of Joseph Trutch to be the new surveyor general and commissioner of land, O'Reilly became increasing uncomfortable and said nothing as the furor grew. The colonial administrators in London had appointed Joe to be Colonel Moody's successor, but the BC legislators whom O'Reilly most respected would not accept his appointment. They charged that it was a blatant conflict of interest, and not to BC's advantage, because Trutch was also a member of the Vancouver Island Legislative Council. The consensus was that he could sit as a member of the BC legislature as well, but he could not be in charge of BC land and roads.

O'Reilly did not comment on the issue, not even to Carry, but he understood why Joe's appointment was being disputed. His brother-in-law expected to continue to collect the lucrative tolls from the Alexandra Bridge, though perhaps in John's name, and to bid for road surveys and construction contracts. Eventually, Joe said that he would sell the suspension bridge.

As the issue continued to be contentious, Begbie recognized what a dilemma O'Reilly was in and, when they lunched privately, asked, "Now that your Joe has offered the damn bridge for sale, even at an outrageous price, can you comfortably vote for him?"

O'Reilly grinned and commented that it was good Joe and Julia were about to leave for England and Europe. "I hope they return," and he confided that Joe had told the family that if his appointment was not ratified, they might just stay permanently.

On April 8, O'Reilly scrawled in his diary, "Joe will be officially approved, thank god."[7]

O'Reilly's next unexpected duty, while he was waiting for the Cariboo to thaw so he could reopen mining there, was to assess what was happening in the Fort Kamloops area and to investigate rumours of gold being found far to the east of the Shuswap Lakes. Brew needed to know whether there was a possibility of a gold rush there. "Do take your wife, Mr. O'Reilly, if she is willing. She'll probably learn as much as you, and it won't be as obvious that you are out there to do some snooping."

Carry was delighted, having a friend in Kamloops with whom she could stay while her husband travelled to the Shuswap region. As the O'Reillys stepped into the morning stage from Yale, she teased him that she just might gain more information than he did. They had a pleasant trip to Savona where, after an uncomfortable night in a cabin they shared with mice, they journeyed down Kamloops Lake in the Hudson's Bay Company's thirty-foot bateau. Carry was as taken with the area as O'Reilly had been the first time he'd seen it.

"Perhaps some day we will have a horse ranch here," O'Reilly suggested.

"A ranch, Peter? Live up here, this far away from New Westminster or Victoria?" Carry looked as startled as she sounded.

CHAPTER SIX

May Day Celebrations and the Chilcotin War

As the O'Reillys floated down Kamloops Lake in the bateau, it was much quieter than being in a stage-coach, and they could chat. "How will you know if a gold rush is likely?" Carry asked.

O'Reilly admitted it was a challenge, one that involved mainly listening to and trying to interpret rumours. As well, reviewing the recent claims and mining licences told him who was poking around in the creeks and hills. "Carry, a sort of grapevine exists in gold areas. Once one man finds enough dust or nuggets to file a claim, other prospectors arrive and start staking nearby." If enough men found gold, a gold commissioner had to be appointed for the area to ensure that the colony received its share from licensing miners and taxing that gold. If little gold was being found, assigning a commissioner was not financially beneficial.

"Would you like to manage the Kamloops area, Peter? I could live in the village there."

O'Reilly replied that he liked being the chief gold commissioner for the Cariboo as it was a senior position, even though he disliked having to be apart from Carry for months. He told her he'd considered whether she might want to join him in Barkerville. There were now more women and even a few children, but he had decided the primitive conditions were not at all suitable. He had to travel extensively during the season and could not always be with her, so she would often be alone there.

Carry nodded. She did not point out that living in New Westminster was also quite rough, and she would not be seeing him between June and November.

On their arrival back in New Westminster, O'Reilly reported to Brew that, although increasing numbers of prospectors were exploring far east of the Shuswap Lakes, he had not learned of any major gold finds to date. There was a tiny settlement called Seymour, which had had a considerable population the previous year, but, according to rumours, those miners had found their returns scanty and few planned to return. A similar situation was reportedly building up over in the upper Columbia River basin, but his informant could not recall that little settlement's name, only that it had very few residents.

Brew said, "That's a relief. Managing a new gold rush while the administration moves from Victoria to New Westminster would have been most inconvenient."

The O'Reillys had returned just in time to join in the celebrations to welcome British Columbia's new governor, Frederick Seymour. On April 22, 1864, he disembarked onto the long wharf as the band played and they, along with most of New Westminster's residents, cheered enthusiastically. They paraded after him to the former Royal Engineers' hall where Judge Begbie read the revocation of Governor James Douglas's tenure with great dignity and swore in Governor Seymour. Church bells rang out, the band played "God Save The Queen" and the New Westminster Volunteer Rifle Corps fired a seventeen-gun salute.[1]

That evening, at the dinner and dance for the second governor of the Colony of British Columbia, Brew presented O'Reilly and his wife to the governor. Seymour greeted them warmly, said he had many questions about gold mining in the Barkerville area, and immediately led Carry onto the dance floor.

O'Reilly confided to his diary that night:

> Seymour sworn in as governor by Begbie today. He seems pleasant, taken with Carry. He danced three times with her. Weather cloudy, no rain.[2]

BC's Legislative Council met with Governor Seymour the next day in its temporary quarters, the Engineers' former mess hall. The new governor's first speech assured members he was most optimistic about the colony's future and honoured to be charged with assisting this rich land to reach its potential. Later, however, he wrote a private message to his superior, Lord Carnarvon:

> I had not seen, even in the West Indies, so melancholy a picture of disappointed hopes as New Westminster presented on my arrival. Here, however, there was a display of energy wanting in the tropics . . . But the blight has come early.
>
> Many of the best houses are untenanted. The largest hotel is to let, decay on all sides, and the stumps and logs of the fallen trees block up most streets. Westminster appears, to use the miners' expression, 'played out.'[3]

Nor was Seymour impressed with the roughly constructed Government House. He asked why there were so many traps, and after learning that rats were a problem, he managed to say the place had potential. He decided improvements needed to begin immediately, including the addition of a ballroom. When the colonial treasurer questioned those unexpected costs, the new governor justified them by declaring that, for the general morale and for him to govern appropriately, the colony needed to have a proper place to hold dances and social occasions.

Seymour also decided to continue the annual May Day event for the Indians and ordered that messages be sent out to BC's Native peoples to come and celebrate their great mother, Queen Victoria, on her birthday. When he learned that former Governor Douglas had provided biscuits laden with molasses, he decided the menu had to be expanded to include cake with whipped cream. Although his advisors told him that it was important to keep the food simple, as nobody knew how many thousands of Indians would come to compete in the canoe races and sports events, he insisted it must differ from Douglas's hospitality.

When Brew, O'Reilly and John Trutch dined together a week after Seymour's arrival, Trutch asked Brew how he was finding the governor. The chief replied with his usual tact. "Hard to tell, so far. At our meetings, it appears he is more concerned with social events than with administration." His main concern was Seymour's apparent lack of interest in learning about BC's Indians, their history, and the differences among the numerous tribes.

"He needs to understand that some are co-operative and some are not, and a few are potentially dangerous," O'Reilly interjected.

"Yes. But he said that Native populations are the same, worldwide, and he has had much experience with managing them," Brew said dryly. "Perhaps when he has time to read the reports, he might ask questions."

When O'Reilly wondered whether Vancouver Island's new governor, Arthur Kennedy, had the same opinions, John Trutch replied, "Evidently he is astonished by the deteriorating conditions in Victoria. And he is unhappy with the administrators here and in London."

Although the ceremonies for Kennedy had been welcoming, one detail had been missed—appropriate housing for his family, who had come with him. Former Governor Douglas, who was en route to England where

Queen Victoria would bestow a knighthood on him, had always lived in his own house. Kennedy had recently asked how he could reach Joe and Julia Trutch, with whom he was acquainted, because he hoped to rent Fairfield temporarily. He had also insisted that Vancouver Island's administrators buy and complete the unfinished Cary House, outside Victoria on Rockland Avenue's rocky bluffs.

In the following weeks, the O'Reillys repeatedly heard rumours that Kennedy was reluctant to co-ordinate the governance of the two colonies, apparently because of his opinion of Governor Seymour. Kennedy was a senior British Empire administrator with a stellar reputation and good health while Seymour had few such attributes and a history of over-imbibing.

"What if Kennedy and Seymour can never work together?" Carry worried.

Her husband speculated that once the many problems of separating the administrations were worked out, relations would improve. In his opinion, the endless discussions about the declining economy and dissension over executive appointments had dominated and prevented progress in both legislative councils. "Carry, when some men claim residency in both colonies and say they intend to continue being loyal to both, it is difficult."

"Like Joe. Because his appointment as BC's land and works commissioner is controversial, it must be hard for you." Carry knew that Peter had been dismayed when her brother had announced that he expected to run again for the Legislative Council of Vancouver Island. Joe had told the family that if Victoria's voters wanted him to represent them for a third time, he would do so, and that he fully expected, at the same time, to be on the BC Legislative Council's executive as its land commissioner. After all, he reiterated, he did most of his business in one colony and lived in the other, so he had every right to serve both.

O'Reilly did not think that he could do both well but had not risked telling him that. After the controversial appointment was finally ratified, and Joe was the BC land commissioner and surveyor general, O'Reilly had asked Begbie, "Do you think people will question my suitability because I am Joe's brother-in-law, Matthew? Gold commissioners do make general recommendations and identify lands that are suitable for pre-emptions."

"Perhaps," Begbie had replied. "Be careful to make your reports and recommendations only to Brew or whoever the chief gold commissioner is. Never, ever, discuss them first with Joe. Although your duties actually have little to do with his rulings, accusations of bias are possible."

O'Reilly explained that was why he had not said much during the whole contentious legislative sitting. Except for answering questions related to the Cariboo, he had purposely been an onlooker.

"Well, you will be perceived as either deep or lazy! I understand you were again appointed BC's high sheriff, so that is some recognition," Begbie said.

౿ ౿ ౿

In mid-May, an agitated O'Reilly told Carry, "I have to catch the stage in two hours."

"Why? Are you going up to the Cariboo?"

"No, I'm off to the Fraser Canyon. There has been a dreadful massacre on Waddington's road, up above Bute Inlet." The Chilcotin Indians employed on the project had killed the other road workers—and, almost as shocking, it had happened almost two weeks ago. Governor Seymour had immediately feared it might be the first of many Indian rebellions and had asked for naval assistance, both to patrol the coastal areas and to investigate the massacre. He had ordered Brew to send someone up the Fraser Canyon because he had decided that the Fraser River should be blockaded at Hope. He also wanted all Indians informed that the May Day celebrations were cancelled.

Brew had convinced the governor that it would be difficult, if not impossible, to stop traffic from using the Fraser; there was no physical way to erect a barricade there. Nor, at this late date, would it be feasible to cancel the May Day festivities. The chief inspector then told O'Reilly to go to Yale and assess the Fraser region. "Find out what's happening there, whether those Indians are aware of the massacre. We need to know how many of them might be supportive of the suspects—and if there are any signs of organizing for a future uprising."

O'Reilly mulled the situation aloud to his wife as she packed his travelling trunk. "Carry, I do not expect all the Indians will revolt." He told her that the men most knowledgable about the colonies' tribes, particularly James Douglas, felt there was no possibility of all BC Natives joining together against the white population, because each group was an entity unto itself. Frequently, a band's nearest neighbours were their sworn enemies. "But there are other men who believe that although there appears to be no mechanism for a co-ordinated Indian attack, if one tribe successfully rids its territory of white men, others might follow their example."

He picked up his trunk and hugged Carry, telling her that he expected to be back the following week to help organize the May Day celebrations. "Thank goodness Brew sent Cox up to run the Cariboo. It will probably be weeks before I get up there."

As O'Reilly sat in the crowded stagecoach, squeezed between two other passengers on the narrow seat, he analyzed what he had heard about the Chilcotin territory where the murderers had probably fled. Organizing an effective search was more an illusion than a reality, with BC's small population and few men available. Seymour, Brew and New Westminster's recently formed militia were heading up to Bute Inlet the next morning to start investigating the site of the killings.

When O'Reilly left the stage at Hope to pick up a saddle horse, he encountered Edgar Dewdney. His friend was on his way to the Okanagan, unaware of the massacre. After he had heard the details, Dewdney said that capturing the Chilcotins in their vast territory was a ludicrous expectation, and he hoped the new governor would realize that. "Peter, a search like that could bankrupt BC."

"Ned, do you believe there is any chance of more uprisings?" O'Reilly asked.

Dewdney judged it unlikely and repeated what O'Reilly had heard from other credible men. The Chilcotins were an isolated and powerful group who liked to make war and were feared by smaller tribes, so it seemed unlikely they would receive any outside assistance.

When O'Reilly arrived at Joe and Julia's house in Yale, Mother Trutch greeted him warmly, then was horrified when he explained what had happened on the Bute road construction. She was immediately defensive about her Sto:lo workers and friends, and was sure they were trustworthy. They talked about it as she made tea, and then she remembered that Joe had left an envelope for him. O'Reilly discovered it contained reports and summaries of the 1862 smallpox epidemic; he sat at Joe's desk at the far end of the parlour and scanned them. The bound reports started with Royal Engineer Lieutenant Henry Palmer's record of his July visit to Puntzi Lake in the Chilcotin, describing the devastation. O'Reilly continued flipping through, reading bits and pieces of the various accounts, until he reached one by Robert McLeod, a trader he knew, who had written in October 1862:

... we again smelled it. Puzzled, we walked along the trail, and came upon a large Indian village of some twenty or thirty houses. No dogs appeared to warn the occupants of our approach, nor came any of the inhabitants to greet or question us. ... two heaps of earth looked much like a grave. But more demonstrative was a heap of brush piled over another Indian corpse, and beside this yet another partially wrapped one in a blanket, his face turned to the sky and his shrunken eyes drawn into the skull ... flies crawling over all those sightless and decaying bodies . . . Speechless, we realized this was Nancootlem.[4]

O'Reilly put the report back in the envelope, suddenly wondering if the devastation of the smallpox epidemics was related to the killings on Waddington's road. Had conditions since then been so bad that many Indians were just waiting to avenge their loved ones? After reading the usually taciturn McLeod's summary, O'Reilly understood what Begbie meant when he had repeatedly lectured his friend, "We are intruders, Peter. We cause change and will reap the consequences."

When a nervous and respectful O'Reilly called on every Sto:lo chief he could find in the Fraser Canyon area, he saw no cause for concern. Most said that they had not heard of the Bute murders, although knowing how quickly information flowed between Indian communities, he thought it seemed strange the news had not spread. He then visited the Nlaka'pamux chiefs farther up the river and concluded that no discontent was simmering. He had been greeted as usual and he'd sensed no guile. Most of the Indians were curious about why Governor Douglas had left and what the new one was like, and many of them reported they were coming to the May Day celebrations.

By the Queen's Birthday, O'Reilly was back in New Westminster, assisting Governor Seymour to welcome an unknown number of celebrants. He learned that the HMS *Sutlej*, a warship with five hundred and fifteen officers and men and armed with thirty-five broadside guns and a chase gun, had taken Brew and forty men up to Bella Coola. They were searching the coastal areas, then the chief inspector's party was to disembark and continue to hunt for the fugitives in that region of the Chilcotin territory.

Seymour said, "Brew and I decided that Cox will lead the searchers in from the Fraser River side. Best that you continue administering the Cariboo, though without an assistant for the present. We hope the searchers will apprehend the criminals within the month and Cox will be back before too long."

When O'Reilly asked when and where the search parties would rendez-vous, since they were starting out about five hundred miles apart, Seymour did not reply.

He reported that to Begbie when the judge came for dinner, as he did quite regularly. Matthew was as fond of Carry, with her astute analysis and her musical talents, as he was of Peter. After the meal, Begbie asked, "What is Seymour's reaction to the Indians coming for May Day and setting up their camps along the Fraser?"

China Bar Bluff on the new Cariboo Waggon Road was twenty-two miles north of Yale and typical of the roads Peter O'Reilly had to travel, either on horseback or in a stagecoach.
IMAGE A-03873 COURTESY OF ROYAL BC MUSEUM, BC ARCHIVES

"Amazed at the numbers, and impressed," O'Reilly replied. As the Indians arrived at New Westminster, each load of colourfully dressed passengers sang and chanted and, on the sturdier canoes, pounded their paddles on the sides in unison. Those from the interior carried at least six people while the large, ocean-going canoes held three times that number. Although the party did not officially begin for two days, an estimated thirty-five hundred Indians were already there, about half from the coast and half from the interior. Many were practising for the races, paddling up and down the mile-wide river in an impressive variety of canoes.

As camps were set up, members of each nation carefully grouped together, away from those they did not trust. Then, on the Queen's Birthday, after the canoe races, they all came to New Westminster for the games and white man's food, cake and whipped cream as well as the traditional molasses and biscuits. In one park, a large platform had been erected and decorated with what appeared to be every flag in New Westminster.

At noon, Governor Seymour, elegant in his dress red uniform, welcomed everyone in a lengthy speech. He assured the Indians he was honoured by their attendance, and by their trust. Then he prayed that all Indians and white men would have good relations with each other under his guardianship.

After the governor's speech, three senior chiefs from the lower Fraser Valley were invited to the podium to reply, and their interpreter read a speech, evidently developed with much editing and input from a priest, to welcome Governor Seymour:

Great Chief English, we the native Indians, are gathered here to welcome you, to show you we are of good dispositions ... We wish to
become good Indians and to be friends with the white people. Please
protect us against any bad Indians or any bad men. Please to protect our

land . . . that it will not be too small for us. Many are pleased with their reservations, and wish that their reservations be marked out for them. Please to give good things to make us become like good white men, as an exchange for our land occupied by the white men. Our heart will always be good and thankful to the Queen, and to you, Great Chief. We finish to speak to you.[5]

"Carry, neither the chiefs nor most of the Indians know what that interpreter has just said to the governor. Nor that he has claimed to represent all the Indians here—it's malarkey!" O'Reilly whispered. Finally adept at conversing in Chinook, he had discovered how different the languages were, and how few Natives could fully understand each other.

Various Native peoples gathered in New Westminster Park, waiting to be greeted by Governor Frederick Seymour on May Day.
IMAGE AA-00013 COURTESY OF ROYAL BC MUSEUM, BC ARCHIVES

And, although many Natives had only about twenty words of English, they often acted as if they could understand more.

O'Reilly visited at the campsites, welcoming the various bands on behalf of the governor. He also watched for any signs of discontent or for more than the normal number of weapons. He was wise enough not to ask questions, and he knew that the massacre was not a subject open to conversation, particularly with a white man.

Two days later, when O'Reilly reported to Seymour that he was leaving for the Cariboo, he found the governor in a huff, disturbed that the Indians had not left promptly at the end of the celebrations. Many continued to race canoes, to visit and to trade. O'Reilly said that was usual when the tribes gathered. Although the governor wanted them to leave and was debating ordering them to do so, the gold commissioner said, "Sir, when the Indians are ready to go, they will."

The governor was also upset because he had not heard one word from Brew since he and the searchers had been dropped off by the HMS *Sutlej*. "Why would the chief inspector not send a message?"

O'Reilly unknowingly repeated what many had already said. "Sir, Mr. Brew probably cannot, because sending one messenger would most likely result in that man's death."

A week later, when O'Reilly met Cox at Alexandria with the horses and supplies that the large, fully-armed troop of special constables was to deliver to Brew's group, he mentioned the governor's desire for more communication.

Cox was furious. "Two more men have recently been killed by Chilcotins. Even without having to take in a herd of horses, travel is risky. Doesn't the governor understand that the territory we're in is over fifteen thousand square miles?" Then he asked, "Who will replace me in Cariboo West?" and reported that the number of new prospectors and returning miners was well above projections.

"No one. I will oversee both districts while the search is under way, and once the fugitives are caught, you can probably assume those duties again. It's up to Brew."

The summer passed quickly. Having to be gold commissioner and magistrate for the whole Cariboo territory kept O'Reilly on a horse from dawn until dusk; then he did paperwork during the evenings. Except for the newspaper accounts Carry forwarded, which told him little about what was actually happening in the Chilcotin, and the occasional rumour, O'Reilly did not learn much until late August. Then he received a message to meet Seymour in Williams Lake where the governor, with a force of thirty men, had just returned from a meeting with Brew and Cox at Puntzi Lake.

When O'Reilly showed up with the carriage the governor had demanded for his tour of the Cariboo, Seymour related what had happened. Both Brew and Cox were frustrated and no longer expected co-operation from any Chilcotin. Friends of the fugitives would pretend to arrange a rendez-vous, then lead the searchers into a maze of sloughs, lakes and forests, and abandon them there. Both groups were worn out, particularly Brew and his men, who had been short of food for weeks.

Disturbed, O'Reilly asked, "Does Chief Inspector Brew believe they are close to apprehending the suspects?"

"No, but I ordered them to continue at least until the snow flies," Seymour said.

The governor wanted to see the boomtown of Barkerville and the gold being extracted by the major mining operations. "I also expect to meet all the important residents and miners throughout the area." Since Seymour disliked riding horses, O'Reilly had rented an elaborate, red-velvet-cushioned carriage from a madame, who had said that it best be returned in immaculate shape. O'Reilly climbed in and sat across from Seymour, wishing he were on horseback like the group riding behind them, despite the dust the carriage was raising.

When they arrived at each little Cariboo settlement or mining area, everyone welcomed the governor like royalty. Barkerville hosted a grand party in Seymour's honour, and O'Reilly was amazed at how well most of those attending had managed to get the pervasive mud off their clothes. The governor found the area and activity interesting. He told O'Reilly that the quantities of gold coming out of the deep mine shafts made him optimistic about BC's future, despite the horrendous costs of what he was calling "the Chilcotin fiasco."

"It is shaping up to be a good season, sir. We have more men in here than ever before. The only difficulties are disputes over claims between the syndicates. Digging deeper shafts costs much more, and when men cannot handle those expenses, they find a financial backer and start a syndicate," O'Reilly explained.

In late September, news came that the Chilcotin war was over; the Bute Inlet massacre suspects were finally in custody at the small Quesnel jail. O'Reilly immediately rode over and went looking for Brew. The chief inspector looked dreadful, and when O'Reilly said he looked much thinner, Brew admitted he'd lost over forty pounds and said it had been a difficult four months. He remained distraught about the situation and now distrusted Cox, who had not followed Brew's orders about how the arrests were to be made and might have even jeopardized the trial. Brew confided that when Begbie came, he intended to confer with him before writing up his summary and returning to New Westminster to report to the governor.

"Do you expect Mr. Cox to be replaced as the Cariboo West's gold commissioner?" O'Reilly asked.

Brew shook his head and predicted that Seymour would decide to keep him, since most British Columbians would consider Cox a hero. The residents of Quesnel were hosting a celebratory dinner, but Brew had declined. "I claimed ill health because I do not believe the way the long hunt ended is an occasion for jubilation. I have allowed Mr. Cox to attend."

O'Reilly asked if Brew felt like joining him for a meal in the government quarters. While they ate, the chief explained his concerns. During the negotiations with the Chilcotins' representative, Cox had warranted through an interpreter that each suspect would be given rights as a prisoner of war. Then, when the fugitives had accepted those terms and had presented themselves at Fort Chilcotin, west of Puntzi Mountain, Cox had not sent for Brew as ordered but immediately imprisoned the eight men in chains. He had neither conformed with nor acknowledged the prisoner-of-war terms he had offered but instead, had charged each suspect with murder.

O'Reilly was unable to contain his dismay. Both he and Brew understood how much civil law differed from military-based regulations. They also knew that the Indians could justifiably accuse Cox of having spoken with a forked tongue and that his action could negatively affect future interactions with all officials. Under Douglas's governorship, first during the fur-trade and then the colonial era, the Queen's men had prided themselves on their honesty.

"This is a new situation," O'Reilly acknowledged, knowing how upset Brew was that one of his men, a gold commissioner and magistrate, had been blatantly untruthful.

The Chilcotins' trials began, heard by Judge Begbie. As all had expected, guilty verdicts were quickly returned by the jury. After Begbie had the death sentences reviewed by the BC Executive Council and Governor Seymour, as he normally did, Klatsassine, Tellot, Tahpitt, Piell and Chessus were hanged on the morning of October 26, 1864, as their fellow Chilcotins and residents from Quesnel watched.

Since O'Reilly was BC's high sheriff as well as the senior gold commissioner for the Cariboo, he organized the details of the hangings. He also had to attend, to ensure that all went properly. Later, he wrote in his report to his fellow legislators and to Governor Seymour and BC's executive council:

. . . a crowd of about 250 people had attended the public hangings and remained quiet, well-conducted.[6]

A month later, O'Reilly closed the Cariboo's mining for the winter and returned to Carry and New Westminster. He told everyone, including his wife and her family, that he was unwilling to discuss anything about the Chilcotins' arrest, trial or hanging.

CHAPTER SEVEN

The Forced Amalgamation of the Colonies

Shortly after O'Reilly was back with Carry in their cozy home, Joe and John Trutch came to New Westminster for a visit. The colonies' faltering economy became the main topic. Aid from London was mandatory, Joe and Peter agreed.

John asked why, as he had just returned from the Kootenays where he had been since May, unaware that British Columbia's financial problems had become urgent. Since Joe managed all the details of their business partnership and paid his brother a salary, John was indifferent to what was happening politically.

The other three took turns explaining why things were unstable in both BC and Vancouver Island. Joe blamed Britain's deep cuts to subsidies while Carry said it was problems with Indians and O'Reilly filled John in on the Chilcotin war. He then asked Joe about the *Kingfisher* incident; he was confused about what had happened up the coast while he'd been in the Cariboo.

"A black affair in my opinion," Joe said. "It was costly and unwise." In August, the *Kingfisher*, a small sloop trading seal oil, had burned and sunk, with all its crew. Rumours reached Victoria that it had been attacked by Indian pirates. Governor Kennedy had contacted Rear-Admiral Joseph Denman who had fourteen ships in BC waters; the Royal Navy's Pacific fleet had been increased to protect all British ships in the Pacific Ocean from rogue Yankee cruisers, Confederate raiders and Chinese pirates.

Denman had considered Kennedy's plea for assistance at length and decided that the Natives needed to see British strength. Then, before any ship sailed north, reports came that various Ahousat and Clayoquot bands on Vancouver Island were harassing settlers and traders, and that there might have been more deaths than those of the *Kingfisher*. Denman ordered his flagship, the HMS *Sutlej*, along with the HMS *Forward* and the HMS *Devastation*, to head north. Governor Kennedy, a magistrate and other officials were aboard to take control of the situation.

"What happened?" O'Reilly asked.

"Nine Indian villages and sixty-four canoes were shelled by the ships and destroyed, and at least fifteen Indians killed. Because the *Kingfisher*'s effects were found in many villages, all those who occupied them were considered guilty."[1]

O'Reilly was shocked. "Gads, Joe! They were all considered guilty? But the Indians who had raided the sloop would have quickly traded whatever they stole, for wives or canoes."

"Denman and Kennedy were evidently in full agreement when they ordered those villages be razed," Joe said. "They used the English law, 'possession of stolen goods is a punishable offence.'"[2]

"How awful. They killed even the children? Now our isolated settlers and fishermen will suffer," Carry murmured.

Joe continued discussing his concerns, which included how Kennedy had mismanaged relations with the Songhees tribe. At a recent gathering, he had assured them that they were secure in possession of their lands in Victoria and all their fishing rights.

O'Reilly interjected, "But Henry Crease told me that Kennedy requested his executive council to remove the 'intemperate Songhees Indians from their reserve in Victoria Harbour.'"[3]

"It isn't the first time that Kennedy's been saying one thing and doing another," Joe judged.

When the Colonial Legislative Council of BC sat again in January 1865, they had to come to grips with the horrendous costs of the Chilcotin war, estimated to be over eighteen thousand pounds, which was more than the colony's annual revenues. Not only was the stability of the colony's administration at risk, each member of the council was nervous, wondering about the reliability of his annual stipend.

After Frederick Seymour was sworn in as governor of the Colony of BC in November 1864, the First Legislative Council met in the former Royal Engineers' mess hall. The colony's appointed representatives, which included Peter O'Reilly, gold commissioner and magistrate, outnumbered the elected members.

IMAGE A-04736 COURTESY OF ROYAL BC MUSEUM, BC ARCHIVES

"I voted for deep cuts to public expenses, but most reluctantly. If the Colonial Office refuses to increase our subsidies, BC is on the brink of financial disaster," O'Reilly confided to Begbie. He did not add that his own meagre savings would hardly cover his domestic expenses for three months. Those had been diminishing rapidly since his marriage, and his property in Hope was becoming worthless as the economic depression deepened. He was again suffering from the blue devils at night, though he pretended to Carry, when she questioned his restlessness, that his back was bothering him.

In June 1865, O'Reilly and Arthur Vowell, his constable, went to Wild Horse Creek in the isolated East Kootenay. Although O'Reilly had been reluctant to leave the Cariboo because it was much closer to Carry, who was expecting their first child, John Haynes, an inexperienced gold commissioner, needed help with the latest gold rush.

After days of hard riding, they reached the mining area and quickly established control. Hundreds of the predominantly American miners had refused to buy mining licences and had been threatening Haynes; the situation was reminiscent of Rock Creek for O'Reilly. After he threatened to burn down Fisherville, their shacktown, they quickly became cooperative. O'Reilly became the East Kootenay gold commissioner and Haynes departed. Brew had sent a message, directing him to investigate the Upper Columbia.

On O'Reilly's return home in early November, he discovered that neither the colony's finances nor relations with the Indians had improved. There had been some favourable developments—the construction of the Collins telegraph and the long-awaited extension of the Cariboo Waggon Road to Lillooet—but annual expenses far outstripped revenues, despite the impressive returns from the goldfields. Britain itself was suffering severe financial problems and a depression loomed, so the question of what the Colonial Office would next refuse to subsidize became a popular topic. Businesses were closing weekly, and destitute men were begging for a meal or a job on the main streets of New Westminster and Victoria. Residents in both colonies began to accept that a union between them was inevitable.

"BC may benefit," Begbie said, when he went out for dinner with Brew and O'Reilly. He agreed Britain had to force unification, but he thought they would be subsidizing the colony for years. "They have to back the large investments they've made here. And some of those have good returns, though gold is not a stable revenue."

"It isn't proving to be very profitable at Wild Horse Creek," O'Reilly said. "And what is found is being taken south."

"Even Barkerville's output might be lessening," Brew stated. "I heard many hard-luck stories there this autumn." He also worried that the disputes between mining syndicates might worsen in the next season, which would certainly decrease production.

As the three ordered a cheese tray, they analyzed what was happening in the various areas. "I believe the Indian situation will deteriorate," Begbie said, "both on the island and here, because of the Royal Navy's punitive actions and the Chilcotin war. If I were a potential settler, I wouldn't rush in to take up a pre-emption. I would wait for things to stabilize."

Brew said ruefully that if Seymour was the governor of the united colony, it could take years. He had heard that BC's governor, who was in London to be married, was also lobbying his relative, Lord Carnarvon, to be chosen for the job.

Another concern of the two senior administrators was that if Victoria became the capital of the joint colony, it would put the powerful islanders in control.

"Are you saying that amalgamation might cause more problems than it resolves?" O'Reilly asked.

"No, it will have benefits. Except possibly not for me because there *cannot* be two chief justices. For you officials, it will eventually create increased stability," Begbie replied. Brew nodded.

O'Reilly was somewhat relieved, though he knew that when the colonies were united next summer, it would not change what he would be doing. He expected to be back in Wild Horse Creek. When he had forecast two thousand or more miners for the next mining season, Brew had informed him that he would be the commissioner there again. For the first time in his career, O'Reilly was considering asking the chief to send someone else, though he was hesitant to do so. Yet if he could return to the Cariboo, and Carry and their baby spent the summer at Yale, he would be able to visit them regularly.

After Brew left, explaining that his arthritis was taking him to bed, Begbie returned to wondering whether he or Vancouver Island Chief Justice Joseph Needham would be appointed senior judge. He recognized that Needham had powerful connections and asked O'Reilly if he expected to ever return to Ireland, then confided, "I am unsure if I could live in England again."

"No, not since Carry married me, Matthew. Now that we are about to have a child, it seems most unlikely. My mother has all my brothers and sisters looking after her since my father died. I do worry whether BC will eventually be a stable home for us, but where would I find a job that pays this well?"

The next morning, he and Carry boarded the boat for Victoria. They were spending the festive season at Fairfield and Carry would remain there until their baby arrived. As she endured the choppy passage across the Strait of Georgia, O'Reilly thought about the previous night's conversation, and about the fact that gold rushes did run out. Combining two administrations meant competition for government positions, but he knew that as long as there was gold, he would be a commissioner. After that, perhaps he would have to pre-empt and start his horse ranch.

When the Trutches and O'Reillys shared breakfast the following day, Mother Trutch said, "We should congratulate ourselves. We are all doing reasonably well, despite these unsettled conditions."

"Yes, it has not been too bad a year and, if we're cautious, the coming one will be better." Joe sounded hopeful.

O'Reilly and John were relieved to hear that, as Joe's connections were extensive and often enabled him to make astute decisions. They suspected he was becoming a wealthy man.

Carry, well-rounded with the child to be born in late January or early February, bantered, "Just a moment, my dear husband and cherished brothers. Do you not think your achievements pale compared with mine?" All the family was anticipating the baby's arrival, the first member of the Trutch clan to be born in this new world.

O'Reilly was delighted that he was about to become a father, despite his nervousness about the future. He felt surprisingly well and had not had one attack of the blue devils since the previous spring. His abilities were being recognized and he was more often expressing an opinion as a member of the legislative council. As well, he had received an unexpected raise before being sent to control Wild Horse Creek and, as he had told Begbie, BC had become home for him and for Carry. Even when letters from Ireland were slow to arrive, he no longer grew anxious.

In fact, instead of replying to Mamsey's latest as he'd planned, he decided to ride into town and pick up Carry's presents. Although he had given her a ruby ring the week before to mark their second anniversary, he had also splurged on her Christmas gifts. He had ordered silver brushes and was having them engraved, and had bought her an elegant, fur-lined white robe. That would keep her warm and comfortable through the next few weeks of waiting for their baby. It was not easy for him to spend on such items, but O'Reilly had learned to accept Carry's need to give and receive gifts; it was as important a part of the Trutch family's traditions as the elaborate decorations for every celebration.

Whenever men gathered during the holidays, they discussed what London might dictate and what the consequences would be. Many were concerned for their own well-being, and O'Reilly overheard Joe say repeatedly, "As land and works commissioner for British Columbia, I believe our very survival is threatened if we don't unite. If we want to attract settlers from overseas, we need to promote a clear, single identity." Joe's voice was so full of confidence that few questioned him.

During one such conversation, John asked O'Reilly whether any of the men coming to search for gold in Wild Horse Creek might decide to stay. "What's that community like?"

"Fisherville is the usual primitive mining village," O'Reilly answered. "It's unattractive and a muddy mess when it rains. But the East Kootenay has lovely rolling pasturelands, groves of trees, and pretty streams and lakes. The miners come mainly from the States, mostly from its interior territories, but they are of many nationalities. That tends to make them clannish and edgy."[4]

Caroline Trutch was a talented musician who spoke a number of
languages and enjoyed being part of a large extended family.
IMAGE G-09394 COURTESY OF ROYAL BC MUSEUM, BC ARCHIVES

"Do they get along?" John asked.

O'Reilly explained that the Italians disliked people from Russia or the Balkans, the Brits were often shunned, and American southerners and northerners were still fighting the Civil War, despite its cessation. He judged that, once the gold was played out, few would stay. The region was too isolated, and the lush and more temperate Oregon Territory to the south was also trying to attract settlers.

Joe interrupted to tell the guests how Peter had spent the American Fourth of July celebrations at Wild Horse Creek. Recalling what Carry had read him from her husband's descriptive letter, he said O'Reilly had been awakened at dawn as miners rang anvils to celebrate their Day of Independence, and he then had to review a long and disorganized parade.

"It was quite a day, especially as it was scorchingly hot," O'Reilly said. "After the parade, I was directed to sit under their big Stars and Stripes flag, and I spent the rest of the afternoon listening to other people's boring speeches and saying a few words myself. That evening, I went to Galbraith's Ferry to be a judge at the races."[5]

Henry Crease asked, "Were the miners at Wild Horse Creek generally peaceful?"

O'Reilly replied that they were, if one did not count fisticuffs, as they were usually surly with each other. "That keeps my constable, Arthur Vowell, and me on edge, since we are far away from any back up."

He told the group about the season's largest brawl. When an inebriated miner had declared that the killing of Abraham Lincoln had been beneficial in some ways, he had enraged another man and his pals. In the subsequent fracas, over a hundred men had pounded on each other. There were three broken arms and many black eyes and banged-up noses. No charges were laid, O'Reilly explained. "It was a dust-up. Vowell and I seized five pistols and many knives, and gently used a cudgel to keep it from getting too rough, but laying charges wouldn't have accomplished anything."

Crease asked if O'Reilly had encountered Edgar Dewdney on his return trip and how the road he was building was progressing.

"Dewdney expects that the route between Hope and East Kootenay will be complete by next July." O'Reilly had spent a night at the road camp, and when Ned had heard Carry was having a baby, he had announced that he and Jane would be the child's honorary aunt and uncle.

A few days later, Joe waylaid Peter, led him to the den where John was waiting, and, barely able to contain his fury, said he had just learned that Rear-Admiral Denman had sent a derogatory letter to Lord Carnarvon. "He has judged the united colony will be of little potential benefit to Britain and he wrote that 'They best allow us to join the United States!'[6] And he considers himself our friend!"

John and Peter were astounded. Although both knew that some of Vancouver Island's legislative members had lobbied London, requesting that they be given the right to consider whether it would be best for Vancouver Island to become an American state, this was different. Having Denman, the Royal Navy's senior admiral in charge of the Pacific region, offering such opinions was disheartening. "British Columbia has to remain British," all three agreed, but they decided not to join in any protests against Denman's action.

Joe then said, "British, for now." To the amazement of the other two, he speculated that once Upper and Lower Canada and the Maritime colonies united and became a Dominion in the British Empire, British Columbia would eventually join.

"Joe, you cannot be serious. What possible benefits could there be for us? Affiliations over three thousand miles make no sense," John said, and O'Reilly was of the same mind.

Joe was adamant it could happen. Then he changed the subject and asked whether either John or Peter had heard the rumour that the Russians were considering selling Alaska to the Americans.

Both had. They wondered why Britain was not bidding and decided it was probably not financially feasible. Britain was at a low ebb and some of its politicians were blaming its stagnant economy on the continual expansion of the British Empire. But all three wished that, somehow, Alaska's vast lands could be tied to the colonies. They would rather not have American territories on both sides.

On the other hand, the Trutches and O'Reilly welcomed other recent developments. Progress had been made while the colonies waited for Britain's announcement as to when, and how, they would be united. New Westminster had been connected to Seattle via the telegraph in early 1865, and communication within most of the settled areas of British Columbia was now possible via the Collins Overland Telegraph. The Cariboo Road's numerous potholes and collapses had been repaired, a new road was being built along the Thompson River to connect the Fraser and Cariboo with Kamloops, and the completion of the Dewdney Trail had been funded. As well, a steamboat-navigation system for the Kamloops and Shuswap waterways had received preliminary support.

O'Reilly had voted for all those improvements and he was becoming increasingly influential in the legislative council. He liked having his opinion valued because of his knowledge of many of the colony's distant areas, but being Joe Trutch's relative was something he had to continually downplay.

In early January, after promising Carry he would return to Fairfield weekly and would be with her when their baby was due, O'Reilly boarded the ferry for New Westminster. Before the first session of the 1866 BC Colonial Legislative Council, he met with Henry Ball, a fellow gold commissioner, and Begbie. They agreed that cutting expenditures was the priority. O'Reilly said that he would advise his fellow members not to overestimate gold revenues, and he knew Nanaimo's representative would be requesting similar caution for the coal industry. Worldwide, the price of coal had fallen significantly and, startlingly, the price of gold was also declining.

As O'Reilly listened to the legislators acrimoniously debate the colony's finances, he realized that he and Carry were at the same stage. She had begun questioning, somewhat tartly, his plans for their future. She believed it was time to buy a house, and had recently cited their previous agreement to do so when their first child was born. He argued that they had to continue renting for at least another two years; he reminded her that one of his rental houses in Hope had sat empty during the past year, and the rent for the other was half what it had been two years ago. Investing in more real estate did not seem wise.

"What if we sign for a mortgage, Carry, and the property depreciates? We'd end up owing more than it's worth," O'Reilly lectured. She had reluctantly decided that they could delay until autumn.

The O'Reillys' son, Francis Joseph O'Reilly, arrived on February 9, 1866. Carry came through her ordeal well and Frank, a big, healthy baby, delighted his father and mother. However, O'Reilly could not remain with them for long; Carry would stay at Fairfield until Frank was at least six weeks old, but he had to return to New Westminster. The steps toward the unification of the colonies were being voted on in the legislative council.

At a session that O'Reilly missed because of Frank's birth, Colonial Secretary Arthur Birch had read a memo from Governor Seymour. It included a copy of the report of The London Committee for Watching the Affairs of British Columbia which recommended the immediate union of Vancouver Island and British Columbia. This lobby of powerful men represented the interests of the Hudson's Bay Company, the Bank of British Columbia, investors in British Columbia bonds, the Colonial Office, the

Treasury, the Foreign Office and the Admiralty. Because of their approval the union of the two colonies became a given.

Seymour's message from London was a jubilant note to Attorney General Henry Crease, written on February 11, 1866:

> We shall be in a position to dictate our own terms. The constitution will be that of British Columbia—with some alterations . . . Capital N. Westminster . . . and retaining British Columbia's tariff acts.[7]

O'Reilly was relieved that the location of the capital for the united colony had been decided and pleased that BC's representation in future legislatures was to be greater than Vancouver Island's, because of its greater revenues. As he prepared to leave for Wild Horse Creek in April 1866, he told Carry that they would buy a house in New Westminster on his return.

When O'Reilly returned to the East Kootenay in mid-May, he discovered that he and Constable Vowell had fresh new quarters. Fisherville had been washed away in the spring flooding and the miners had had to build a new village, which they named Wild Horse, after their gold-bearing creek. Thanks to Vowell, who had stayed over winter, this camp was much better organized than the previous, smelly shantytown. It was set on higher ground beside the roaring creek, and the nearby snow-topped mountains were a picturesque backdrop.

Brew had directed O'Reilly to explore more of the Columbia River valley north of Wild Horse this season, wanting particularly to know what creeks entered it, and where. Two weeks after his arrival, the commissioner left Vowell supervising the camp and headed north, accompanied by his Métis guide, Anton. They travelled for a hundred miles up the Columbia valley, past the mud flats crowded with flocks of ducks, geese and swans, and into the mountains. They were surprised at how many bears they encountered, including two big curious black ones which came much too close to their camp, and how numerous the herds of deer and elk were. They met few people: only one group of five Indians, who said they were Ktunaxa people, and two old prospectors.

When O'Reilly asked the pair about the country farther up, neither had been there, but one man, whose hands were badly crippled, repeated the rumour O'Reilly had heard earlier: "It is a rich land, up in those mountains—nuggets as big as my fist."

It sounded like one more prospector's myth, Anton said later, and they continued to follow the Columbia up to the northern region of the East Kootenay. As Joe Trutch had asked O'Reilly to draw maps wherever Land and Works might eventually be able to release land for settlement, he selected a number of areas along the river or creeks which looked fertile and appealing to him. On their return to Wild Horse, Vowell reported that the season was not going well; most miners were disappointed with the quantities of gold and many had already left to return to the United States.

O'Reilly said, "The new colony's administrators will be disappointed." He was glad that he had cautioned them earlier that their projections for revenues from Wild Horse were too high.

CHAPTER EIGHT

Point Ellice House Becomes Home

A snowstorm hit Wild Horse Creek during the third week of October. O'Reilly immediately closed mining for the season, and by noon the next day, he and Constable Vowell were headed home. O'Reilly was anxious to see Carry and Frank, and he was expected in New Westminster in time for the return of Governor Seymour and the new Mrs. Seymour from England. The celebrations were being combined with the formal declaration of the union of the two colonies, and as high sheriff of British Columbia, he was a participant.

He got home with two days to spare and was welcomed warmly by Carry, but not at all by his son; Frank would not go to him. While Carry prepared lunch, she filled him in on what had been happening. On August 6, 1866, Queen Victoria had finally given her royal assent to the British Columbia Union Act—which, Carry reported, everyone was now calling "the shotgun marriage"—but the administration of the new colony was in chaos. Because the edict authorizing union had been expected in May, most decisions had been delayed until it was signed; when New Westminster finally received the legalities and details, the expected directives of how the amalgamation was to be carried out were not included. Sorting out the confusing logistics of having two of any official services was left to the colonial government.

"Who is to stay in a position is still undecided and the administrators just keep on paying two men," Carry said. "It's ridiculously expensive as only *one* is now required." She told him she had to leave after she fed Frank because she was one of the main organizers of the festivities to welcome the Seymours. Her group was determined to make New Westminster's celebration for them special, to help make up for slights they had apparently endured. "The mayor of Victoria only gave Seymour a thirty-two-second welcoming speech," she fumed.

Joe had told her that some of Vancouver Island's powerful residents faulted Seymour for what they called the partisan terms of union and for the cancellation of Governor Kennedy's appointment. Seymour was to become governor of the united British Columbia at an indecent annual salary of four thousand pounds. Joe had said that Vancouver Islanders assumed he would favour mainlanders, and he predicted that the islanders would not be co-operative in the future.

O'Reilly followed Carry into their small bedroom as she began to feed Frank, and she blushed with pleasure when he told her how lovely she and their son looked. "Do you know, Peter, the most contentious issue is the new capital? The union agreements did not name either New Westminster or Victoria."

"What! New Westminster was announced as the capital before I left. Henry Crease read a letter to the legislative members—Carry, now what will we do about buying a house?"

☙ ☙ ☙

When Governor and Mrs. Seymour landed in New Westminster, they were greeted enthusiastically. Church bells rang, the artillery fired a salute and residents cheered, then they followed the parade with three bands to the Seymours' reviewing stand. That evening, the formal ball included a serenade to Mrs. Seymour by the Orpheus Glee Club, arranged by Carry, a member of the club.[1]

At noon on November 19, 1866, eight years to the day since British Columbia had become a colony, the high sheriffs of the former colonies, Peter O'Reilly in New Westminster and C.S. Nicol in Victoria, simultaneously proclaimed the union. The Colony of Vancouver Island was now amalgamated with the Colony of British Columbia, as the new entity was officially to be called.

At a family party later that month, Joe Trutch again predicted this was only the first union and that the next one would be with Canada. All the family, including Julia, found his opinion most peculiar. "Especially since the lobby to join the Canadian Confederation is headed by Amor de Cosmos, whom you have previously, and quite vocally, not admired," John said.

Joe had publicly and repeatedly said that de Cosmos had created his own pulpit, *The British Colonist* newspaper, to spread dangerous misinformation. For Joe to now be helping him to organize the movement for Confederation with Canada startled his family.

Peter listened to Joe expound and realized he would never risk stating his beliefs as openly. He was more like John, either moderately agreeing with an issue, or quietly disagreeing, whereas Joe was convinced that it was his obligation to lead, and he could become quite melodramatic about his opinions. O'Reilly had learned not to question any of those, even when he knew more about a subject than Joe did.

After all, he rationalized, Joe was generous to Carry and himself, helping them out in various ways. O'Reilly found it almost automatic to be loyal to Joe and the family, even as he wished that his opinions were more valued by his powerful brother-in-law. "Joe, wouldn't Canada have even more control over us than the London office? More rules and fewer subsidies?"

"Not if we negotiate strong terms of union, Peter."

Since O'Reilly hoped to be promoted from magistrate to county court judge, he wondered what would happen to him if BC did join Canada. Like most of his fellow commissioners and magistrates, he had no legal background. He had heard that Canada had many lawyers, and a strong and increasingly exclusive legal profession, and it seemed improbable that anyone without similar training would be considered suitable.

When the enlarged legislative council convened at New Westminster in January 1867, O'Reilly and his fellow magistrates again sat as government appointees along with the elected members, four representing Vancouver Island and five representing BC. As in the previous year, the economy was the primary subject. The exodus of miners, even from Barkerville, was expected to continue and the council was shocked at how small a sum the gold export tax had yielded in 1866. Similarly, its members were dismayed that the Collins Telegraph Company's project to connect Russia with the United States had recently been abandoned, leaving fifteen hundred men unemployed.

The most debated issue, however, was the location of the united colony's capital. Seymour had not legally designated New Westminster, as he had agreed he would; he continued to delay his decision, which affected many people, including the O'Reillys.

Carry's patience was stretched by living in their inadequate rental house, and when Frank became ill with a dangerous chest infection, she started looking for better accommodations. She found a two-storey house with a fenced yard and a pleasant view of the Fraser which appealed to her, but when she tried to rent the place with an option to purchase, the agent said no. Joe suggested he finance a mortgage on it when he heard about it from Mother Trutch.

O'Reilly balked. He was suffering from a headache and feeling cross. "Carry, I do not want to buy yet. Nor will I accept your brother's generous offer." He pointed out that such a mortgage could easily be considered a conflict of interest by the public.

"Well, Peter, we cannot stay in this house," Carry said firmly.

"What if Victoria becomes the capital? Selling a house here will be hard and we'll lose money."

Seymour continued to avoid deciding on the capital, hoping London would. It was well known he wanted it to be New Westminster, but many also understood his hesitation; some of Victoria's wealthiest residents were planning to leave the colony if that city was not named the capital.

The Joe Trutches, the Creases and the O'Reillys were invited to join the Seymours for an informal dinner. During dessert, the governor said that he believed New Westminster made the best sense, as Victoria's location on an island would necessitate ongoing and expensive dependence on ships. "However, offending the island's residents is too risky. Better let London do it."

Everyone nodded politely; no one urged the governor to stop debating with himself and decide. Later, Carry told Peter she'd had to bite her tongue not to do so.

The next evening, O'Reilly decided that they could live in Victoria. Even if the legislature remained in New Westminster, it was only a trip across the strait, and he would be able to spend much of each winter with Carry and Frank.

"Really?" Cary asked, with some disbelief.

O'Reilly said that since Victoria's society was more firmly British, which he wanted for Frank, they should move there, and he asked her if she could put up with their current house until the following year. Again, he preferred to rent for a year or two in Victoria before buying, so they could assess the neighbourhoods and see which had the best future potential.

Carry hugged him. "Oh, yes! I've made good friends here but I miss the sunshine, the gardens, the picnics and the musical evenings in Victoria—and my family and friends there."

Seymour finally passed the decision-making about the capital on to the legislative council, and to his chagrin, on March 29, 1867, its members voted for Victoria, thirteen to eight. When the dejected governor complained, no council member, including O'Reilly, would discuss the matter further. Nor would anyone tell Seymour who voted for which town, much to his annoyance.

The governor then refused to ratify their decision and sent that on to London in hopes that administrators there would reverse it. As the issue remained stalled, the general discontent grew and the governor's credibility was again lessened.

In the summer, a small faction began promoting union with the United States. Its members, mainly islanders, were adamant that if the capital were not Victoria, it would be more sensible to become part of the United States, but Joe Trutch and Amor de Cosmos loudly dissented. Even though Canada had just become a legal entity on July 1, 1867, they were convinced that BC would benefit by eventually becoming one of its provinces.

When Joe asked for O'Reilly's support, his brother-in-law hesitated.

"Peter, it is inevitable, if we want to maintain ties with Britain. I do. Don't you?" Joe admired many of the American relatives he'd gained when he and Julia married, but he did not want to be a US citizen. "Have you considered what losing a British connection might mean for you and your family?" He then switched to describing how impressed he had been when he'd met with Sir John A. Macdonald, Canada's first prime minister, in Ottawa and Toronto. He also mentioned that Macdonald was a staunch supporter of BC's eventually joining the Dominion.

"I cannot support you at this time," O'Reilly decided. Although he was against any connection with the United States, Confederation did not seem viable to him. He could not assist with Joe's lobby anyway, since he would be leaving soon for the Columbia and Kootenay regions. This year, at Joe's direction, as well as supervising the miners throughout the vast territory, he would be opening up a few areas for pre-emption.

As soon as he could return in the autumn, the O'Reillys were to move. Carry was expecting their second child in December, and she was looking forward to being settled in a suitable house in Victoria before the baby arrived.

O'Reilly rode alone to Wild Horse, which he enjoyed. He decided all the political debating seemed irrelevant, once he was on the back of a good horse. His responsibility was to ensure that BC got its share of gold revenues from its goldfields, and that work suited him just fine.

Five hundred fewer prospectors and miners had appeared by mid-July, 1867, about fifteen hundred compared to the previous year's two thousand.[2] Again, Constable Vowell was left to supervise them while O'Reilly and Anton headed north. They travelled all the way to the Columbia River's Big Bend and met many fewer prospectors than they had expected. They also learned that not many had staked claims, judging that the returns would probably be too low because the mining was difficult and the region was far from any services.

The migraines which had plagued O'Reilly during the unpleasant disputes within the legislative council, and had been aggravated by Carry's discontent over their housing, had completely disappeared. He felt well, slept deeply in his tent, despite mosquitoes about the size of hummingbirds, and liked riding in such wild and varied country.

Letters from Carry awaited him when he returned to Wild Horse. She and Frank were staying with Mother Trutch at Fairfield, since Joe and Julia were in Ottawa. She described her life as pleasantly busy, and whenever she felt well enough, she socialized. In one six-page letter, she wrote:

September 2, 1867

Victoria

My own beloved husband,

When you see the date of this you will at once consider me delinquent of the deepest dye, but I must at once protest for I have a great counter charge to make, you have treated me very shabbily. This time, only a little scrap from Sooyos & I have had such a long & anxious wait & now, at last, there is news from you, you only send me a note, not a letter . . .[3]

Carry wrote that affairs in the Cariboo were unsettled, and she was afraid he might be ordered to Barkerville in the coming winter. A dispute between two mining companies, the Grouse Creek Bed Rock Flume Company and the Canadian Company, had escalated to almost a war.

She had rented what she'd judged to be a most suitable house for them as of the beginning of December, and explained how she was paying for drapes and other necessities, for the nanny and the many other expenses, including outfits more suitable for Victoria and her condition:

> You will wonder where I got the money but I found on going to the Bank that there was a large amount, I think $1500, so I ventured to draw for these sums . . .
>
> On Thursday week, we had a grand dinner party & it took all day to arrange my dress & I believe I looked very well . . . Sir James & Mrs. D., the Elliotts, Mr. & Mrs. Gureschi, the new American people, Capt. Liddell & Williams & Mr. McKay from the "*Zealous*." I sang . . .[4]

Carry's letter also related that she had joined Governor and Mrs. Seymour's party for an outing to San Juan Island on the governor's personal cruiser, the *Leviathan*. It would have been considerably more enjoyable for her if the governor had refrained from racing the steam launch from the HMS *Zealous*, which frightened her badly.[5]

∾   ∾   ∾

When O'Reilly returned a week earlier than planned, Carry was pleased. She told him that of all the goings-on, the most interesting was that Seymour had received the long-awaited reply from London. He had been directed to accept the legislative decision and to ratify Victoria as the capital of BC. The Seymours were in the process of moving to Victoria, and Mrs. Seymour had been out to Fairfield for tea. She had confided that she and the governor were unhappy about the move, as he had still expected the capital would be New Westminster and they both preferred it to Victoria. She was not looking forward to living in cold, damp Cary Castle.

Carry and Peter were relieved that they had chosen Victoria and that they were about to move into the ideal house she'd rented. Sadly, their move did not go as expected. When Peter had to go to Yale to hold court, he received a frantic message from Carry via special messenger, and a clipping from the *Colonist*:

> The splendid residence, formerly occupied by the Rev. Mr. Cridge and owned by David LeNeveu, Esq., was totally consumed by fire between 12 and 1 o'clock this morning. The house had been rented to the Hon. Peter O'Reilly.[6]

Her note directed him to come immediately but not to bring any of their boxes and furniture from New Westminster; he had been going to do that on his return from Yale and they were to move in immediately. When he reached Victoria, O'Reilly tried to get Carry to accept the Trutches' offer of returning to Fairfield, but she was adamant. "No. Moving to Fairfield would not be fair to Julia. She is unwell and longing to have her own child.

Peter, you'll soon find us somewhere suitable. I want this baby born in our own home."

O'Reilly scurried around Victoria but finding anything to rent was a challenge in BC's new capital. After two days of frustration, he encountered Begbie and spilled out his woes, hoping his friend might know of more houses.

Begbie did not but insisted that O'Reilly meet him for dinner later, when they could consider the problem. As the pair walked into the Colonial Hotel's dining room, they encountered Captain William Grant. Begbie introduced O'Reilly, mentioned the family's housing dilemma and asked if the captain knew of any possibilities.

"What would you think about buying a little house out on the Gorge, Mr. O'Reilly?" Grant inquired.

"Are you selling one? Is it empty? You see, we need to move in immediately," O'Reilly blurted, hoping he did not sound as desperate as he felt.

"No. It belongs to John Work, the son of my old neighbour who died recently, and it's unoccupied." The captain explained that the elder John Work had had the house built for one of his daughters, Kate, and his son-in-law, Cam Wallace, when they had married, but they had encountered difficulties and moved out.

"Captain, would you happen to know how much Mr. Work is asking for it?" O'Reilly tried to sound logical and gracious, despite his hurry to get Carry settled. Although buying a house still seemed premature, if this property had desirable land, it could be a good investment, as long as the mortgage was manageable.

Begbie interrupted. "More important, what can you tell us about the house, Will? How big is it and in what condition?"

Captain Grant said that he had never been in it but it appeared to be a pleasant little place, somewhat bigger than a cottage, set about two hundred feet above the Gorge. "It is on Point Ellice, near where I have my fishing fleet moored."

O'Reilly asked if Captain Grant would introduce him to the owner in the morning.

"Certainly. Come about ten o'clock."

Later, after O'Reilly and Begbie had savoured steak and kidney pies, the judge offered to accompany his friend, if he wanted a second opinion.

O'Reilly immediately accepted. Not only was Begbie much more knowledgable about what to assess when buying, Carry would be relieved. He said, "Matthew, according to my wife, I'm not astute about housing. So far, she has lectured me about flooring, stoves, windows, water supply and suitable neighbours."

The next morning, they rode out to the Grants. When O'Reilly saw the cottage-styled bungalow, he immediately liked its gables, its gracious lines and the big windows overlooking the Gorge.

"It has charm, Peter," said Begbie. "Carry will like it, even though it needs work, a considerable amount. It is a very acceptable address, and that could be important for you, down the way." As they went to the Works, he advised that because money would be needed for repairs, perhaps a smaller down payment would be acceptable.

Work greeted them warmly and insisted they take time for tea before going to tour the cottage. He told O'Reilly he could offer a mortgage on it, since the previous owner had signed a quitclaim deed. As well, the legalities of dividing the house and an acre of land from the main property were in progress. Having been told about Carry's situation by Captain Grant, he assured O'Reilly, "If you want to purchase the house, you and your family are welcome to move in immediately." He handed him the key and invited him to go and view it with Judge Begbie.

As soon as O'Reilly walked into the front hall, he said, "This feels like home."

There were five rooms, and the two men agreed that Carry would like most of them. Extensive cleaning needed to be done before the O'Reillys could settle in, but some rooms could be made livable. There was a good-sized living room overlooking the water, the master bedroom was of reasonable size and each had a well-built fireplace. The two other bedrooms were small but adequate, O'Reilly decided. The nanny could use one and Frank would have his own room which could double as a guest room.

He said to Begbie, "The problem is this kitchen. Small and dark, isn't it? The stove is adequate, though, with a big oven."

"It is a small oven, Peter, and Carry will need a new stove soon. But she will like this house," Begbie reassured his friend before asking whether O'Reilly had noticed there was no running water, the well's casings having completely collapsed. "The wood looks rotted and it will have to be replaced."

"No, I missed that. It will have to be fixed next spring. For now, do you think storage barrels and water delivery will do?" O'Reilly asked, watching a canoe pass by on the Gorge. He realized that even his grandfather would approve of a location like this and decided that, whatever the cost, he wanted the property.

By noon, Peter O'Reilly owned his family's future home, certain that his dear wife would be as pleased with it as he was. Finally, they could have the gardens they wanted, Frank would have room to play, and O'Reilly would be able to keep at least one horse, maybe even two. Once he had managed to control his anxiety about assuming debt, negotiating the contract for the purchase was easy. Work asked for a twenty-five hundred dollars down payment and offered to carry a mortgage of eleven thousand and five hundred dollars at 4.75 per cent, a reasonable interest.[7]

O'Reilly was relieved, as he had expected the price to be higher. He shook Mr. Work's hand and made the arrangements. When he filled Begbie in on the financial details as they returned to Victoria, Matthew congratulated him.

Carry could hardly believe it. Her frugal and sometimes financially insecure husband had actually purchased a house that he was delighted with, in an area she knew and liked. During her first years in Victoria, she had often canoed, ridden horseback and picnicked out on the Gorge. "What a lovely place to raise our children," she exclaimed, as she asked questions and repeatedly stated that she was fine with the water situation and the kitchen.

When her husband offered to rent a carriage and take her out to see it, Carry demurred. She expected the baby to arrive soon, so perhaps it was best that she make only one trip, when they moved out there in four days.

"Four days?"

"Yes." Carry started giving him instructions. He was to hire two men and one woman to clean, then go to Fairfield and borrow one of Joe's carriages to take the cleaners out, and to ask her mother to supervise the task. He was then to go to New Westminster and return the following day with their furniture and belongings.

"Carry, are we not rushing things?"

"No, Peter." Carry did not share her concern that the baby might be arriving before the due date in three weeks.

On December 12, O'Reilly tucked Carry and Frank into a Trutch carriage, complete with their personal belongings, and took them to their new home. He wrote in his diary that night:

Drove to our new house, got two rooms ready . . . and TOOK POSSESSION.[8]

On December 31, 1867, at one PM, Carrie gave birth to a baby girl in Point Ellice House's master bedroom. The proud parents christened her Charlotte Kathleen O'Reilly—although her father immediately nicknamed her his wee Puss.

CHAPTER NINE

Indian Protests and the Genesis of Confederation

Despite the outdoor privy and the lack of water on site, the O'Reillys quickly determined Point Ellice House would be their permanent home. Their land delighted them, even in its January hibernation, as it was high above the Gorge and none of its rich, loamy soil could be soured by salt tides. They spent hours studying plant books and catalogues as they chose which annuals, perennials and shrubs they would plant in early March, intending to create a park-like garden.

O'Reilly decided that he would not buy the horse he'd been looking at, as owning two when they needed a water system did not seem right. The quantity of water needed to do laundry and care for the family amazed him, as did the cost of hauling it to fill their three barrels. With their tight budget, repairing and decorating the house had to be their first priority.

Little Frank was as happy with his new sister, a new home and the Gorge as his parents were. They all spent hours watching boats and canoes pass as well as the ducks, geese and herons which often came up onto their lawn. At night, they saw raccoons and deer in their yard and heard, which was worrying, the occasional shriek of a cougar.

Frank was an ongoing responsibility as the toddler loved exploring and was much too interested in the water for his own safety. A sturdy lad now, he suffered no more bouts of bronchitis after they moved. Similarly, baby Kathleen thrived, a happy infant, though her father proudly declared that she had the loudest bellow he had ever heard from a baby.

Mother Trutch disputed this. "I suspect her mother could have outdone her at this age, Peter. We always said the early exercise of Carry's vocal cords is why she has such a lovely singing voice today."

Carry regained her strength quickly, but caring for a new baby and a two-year-old, cooking on a smoky stove and doing a little gardening was exhausting her and she needed more help. Although O'Reilly's duties were in New Westminster, where the administrators were still trying to sort out how the united colony was to be organized, he worked hard every time he came home. As well as cleaning up the yard, he looked after the children. He was surprisingly capable, Carry discovered, probably because he had come from a large family.

O'Reilly's search for household help was perhaps hastened by this growing list of tasks. They were trying to hire a nanny, a housemaid and a gardener but so were many of Victoria's new residents. Servants were in short supply, and finding a nanny who would agree to work away out on the Gorge was difficult. Finally, an old Chinese gardener said he would work for them but on one condition: If they didn't like his advice about what to do in the garden, he would not stay. Two weeks later, as O'Reilly's departure for the summer season neared and he hadn't found additional help, he hired the gardener's young cousin, Lee, as Carry's house boy. He apologized to her because the man had almost no English, but pointed out that as Lee had looked after many younger brothers and sisters, he could be responsible for Frank, who wasn't speaking much English either. During one of the Trutches' many visits out to Point Ellice House, O'Reilly confided to Joe, "Looking after a two-year-old is considerably more challenging than sorting out gold miners. My son wearies me."

His brother-in-law laughed and said he had not yet had that experience. O'Reilly nodded in acknowledgment, pleased at the sudden intimacy between them. Previously, Joe had never made reference to his and Julia's longing for a child.

John Trutch often stayed at Point Ellice House when he was not away surveying and was an adept helper. Carry had nicknamed her brother "Uncle Teddy Bear" as he was patient with and able to soothe his nephew and niece. He could also make the stove work better than anyone else. Carry found that amusing and suggested to Peter, "Perhaps you and John can adjust your schedules so one of you is always home with me."

By mid-March, O'Reilly had to leave for the legislative council, and Carry told him not to worry about them. Everything would be fine, particularly as they had finally found a nanny. On their last night together, they strolled around their property, comfortable with the knowledge that he would be returning soon. This year, O'Reilly expected to be back for a few days each month because, once the council session ended, he would be relatively nearby, working as the county court judge and assistant land commissioner for the Yale and Lillooet districts.

By the statutes uniting the two colonies, O'Reilly and six of his fellow stipendiary magistrates and gold commissioners had been named county court judges: George Cox in Columbia and Kootenay, Warner Spalding in Nanaimo, Henry Ball in New Westminster, William MacDonald in Victoria, Thomas Wood in the Victoria district and Chartres Brew in the Cariboo. These appointments gave the new colony experienced men, each knowledgable about a specific area.

The second session of the United British Columbia Legislative Council[1] began on March 21, 1868, and the expenditures for containing the Grouse Creek confrontations in the Cariboo in 1867 became its most frustrating subject. The budget shortfalls caused deep concern for BC's government as further subsidies were unlikely. The worldwide depression was deepening, and Britain's administrators were struggling to balance costs against declining revenues.

Chief Inspector Brew was not in attendance to discuss his terse reports about what had occurred between two mining syndicates in Barkerville. He sent Thomas Elwyn, the gold commissioner assisting him in the Cariboo, to represent that region and to explain that the chief had decided he needed to stay to continue tight control when mining reopened in the spring.

It was only one of the reasons he did not come, O'Reilly learned from Begbie: Brew was also reluctant to rehash in the legislature how he believed the situation had been mismanaged by Governor Seymour's costly and inept intervention. That sensitive subject, and how to pay the debt BC had incurred during what was generally referred to as the Grouse Creek war, was being discussed as much outside the sessions as during them.

County court judges Peter O'Reilly (left) and Henry Ball (right) with Chief Justice Matthew Baillie Begbie.

When Begbie and O'Reilly went out to dinner with Henry Ball, the gold commissioner who had been in charge of the Cariboo when the syndicates started battling over a twelve-foot strip, he related what had happened. "The Canadian Company claimed that a rich, twelve-foot strip had not been staked while the Grouse Creek management claimed it had, and accused the Canadian Company miners of being thieves. They both hired more supposed miners to increase their forces, and both sides began swinging shovels and picks at each other. I recognized it was too many men for us to control and sent to Brew for help." Brew's telegram replied that he and a force of special constables were being organized and would arrive within the week.

O'Reilly asked how Governor Seymour had become involved. "His arrival was unexpected and his untrained men were not helpful. The fighting had escalated and we only regained control when Brew and the special constables arrived later that week," Ball replied dryly, looking as worn out as he sounded. "Once that happened, the chief sent me down to take over New Westminster and announced to the governor, and the directors of both the syndicates, that he would be assuming all supervision of the Cariboo."

O'Reilly sympathized, said that he wouldn't have been able to maintain control of the miners in that situation either, and assured Ball he'd done all he could. He then changed the subject and asked how they thought the budget shortfalls could be made up. "What perturbs me most is that our governor and executive do not seem to understand how unreliable gold revenues are. When a mine goes dry, it's done."

Begbie said that he believed most people knew that but chose to ignore it. "Perhaps of necessity, because what other resources does BC have?" His own concern was that the colony still had two chief justices, an expensive and untenable situation, and he was considering what he would do if he had to leave.

O'Reilly's own situation had improved as he was now a county court judge for BC, a step up from being a magistrate and gold commissioner. It gave him a title recognized within the British Empire's legal system, although his responsibilities remained the same as they had been. The one exception was that he would now also supervise the new stipendiary magistrates who were to be appointed when an area developed to a certain population. They would handle cases of relatively small importance or financial disputes under twenty-five dollars.

County court judges heard cases of greater importance or larger financial amounts while one of the two chief justices, Begbie or Needham, would continue to hear all serious cases—offences and prosecutions usually requiring a jury—at each region's spring and fall assizes.

After dinner, Ball asked, "Have you heard that county court judges might also be appointed assistant land commissioners? I'm worried about the inherent conflicts of interest. How can we assign land one day and then switch hats and sit as a judge, when our decision is challenged?"

O'Reilly concurred. He'd found that a problem when he'd acted as a temporary land commissioner on occasion, dictating where boundaries went and assigning water rights, then as a magistrate, having to sort out the disagreements caused by his decisions. But he was not too concerned about it, compared to the issue of Confederation with Canada. "I cannot support it. But it's a contentious subject for me because of my relationship with Joe, and I will not be able to participate in the legislative debates at all." When Joe Trutch asked the members to agree to further investigation, O'Reilly knew that he best not disagree publicly with his brother-in-law.

Begbie believed Joe was right on the subject. Without other affiliations, BC would not survive when the London office inevitably withdrew all colonial subsidies. "I suspect that will be sooner rather than later, Peter. Becoming either an American or a Canadian seems to be the choice and I have trouble with the idea of being an American. Perhaps more than you do because you're Irish and you probably have mixed loyalties to Britain and the Crown."

Like Begbie, the majority of the legislative members eventually felt that being tied to Britain was better than to the United States, and a committee was formed to take the first investigative steps.

The next difficult issue on the sessional agenda was Land and Works Commissioner Trutch reintroducing a motion from the previous sitting. He wanted the authority to reduce the size of Indian reserves. As he had the year before, Trutch argued that it made no sense to leave BC's lands underutilized. If well-qualified settlers were to be attracted to the colony, the members had to revalue its prime agricultural lands and the related water rights. When the legislative members were split on that issue, Trutch stressed that the revisions to be done this year were only on reserves in the lower Fraser area and the Yale-Lillooet district, and the executive would authorize him to proceed.

Five days later, on March 26, 1868, the Honourable Amor de Cosmos, Trutch's new supporter and keen partner in lobbying for Confederation, moved:

> That His Excellency the Governor be respectfully requested to lay before the Council a Return showing the population of the Colony, distinguishing between Whites, Chinese and Indians; and setting forth the estimated population in each District represented in the Council, distinguishing between Whites, Chinese, and Indians.[2]

It was carried unanimously.

Although the census was to be used as a first step toward Confederation negotiations, O'Reilly knew how jubilant Trutch was when de Cosmos's motion passed. The count would show how the number of Indians had been reduced since the Douglas era, and that would validate the need to reduce the acreages assigned to them earlier.

"Ten acres per family will suffice," Trutch lectured his listeners at every opportunity.

While O'Reilly readily agreed that some prime pasturelands needed to be regained from the Indians, he refrained from speaking on the matter, knowing how many problems it would create in his district. When the legislative members forwarded the motion to the executive for a decision, eliminating the possibility of members speaking against it, O'Reilly was relieved that he'd not had to vote. Although the legislative council's elected members—Amor de Cosmos, Dr. John Helmcken, Joseph Pemberton, John Robson, Robert T. Smith, George Walkem and Francis Barnard—represented the voters, they were outnumbered by the appointed members, which included all the county court judges. Those appointees, including O'Reilly, voted as directed by the executive which, although supposedly advised by the governor, was actually governing BC.

The executive consisted of powerful men: William Young, acting colonial secretary and presiding member; Henry Pellew Crease, attorney general; Robert Kerr, acting treasurer; and Joseph W. Trutch, surveyor general and chief commissioner of land and works. However, many knowledgable people, including O'Reilly, believed it was two men who made most of the decisions: Henry Crease and Joe Trutch. They had roomed together in their school days and remained close friends, and they chose the legislation they considered beneficial for the united colony.

In a move unique to BC, the executive appointed all county court judges to also be assistant land and works commissioners, giving them broad powers, separate from and not as regulated as their court authorities. They were to be directed only by Land Commissioner Trutch as they ensured that settlers' needs were accommodated and Indian reservations reshaped as necessary.

When Ball and O'Reilly discussed this latest legislation, they knew that trying to enforce it within their districts would be challenging. Ball speculated that he would probably have fewer difficulties in the New Westminster area, where settlers had already taken over considerable land, than O'Reilly would encounter in the Yale and Nicola regions.

O'Reilly admitted that he was concerned. His district had many more Indians than settlers. How could he expect the chiefs and band elders to accept the changes? Explaining that the government had decided that the land and water, which he or former Governor Douglas had assigned them in earlier years, were not theirs anymore was not going to be easy.

When the budget for 1868/1869 was brought to the floor, the members found it a sad summary of BC's troubles; it had no allocations for public works. Even the ten-year tradition of inviting Indians to New Westminster and Victoria for races and picnics on the Queen's birthday celebration had been cancelled. All the members voted for the ruthless cuts with little discussion; it was the only way to keep the colony going for another year.

∞   ∞   ∞

When O'Reilly returned to Point Ellice House after the session, he said to Carry, "I have decided Joe is right. We should actively support union with Canada."

"Mrs. Seymour thinks so, too. She visited me last week and said that the governor has another bout of dengue fever because the colony's financial stress is weakening him so much." Carry didn't concur with her husband's opinions about what the governor's alcohol consumption was doing to him, believing Seymour suffered from ill health. O'Reilly was certainly not a teetotaller himself, but he disliked those whose loss of control or overindulgence affected others.

O'Reilly left for Yale and the first county court circuit of his district the following week. He'd decided to separate his two hats as much as possible and planned to simply investigate what land commissioner duties would be required of him in the coming season while he was fulfilling his judicial duties. Then, at a later date, he would enforce the land issues. Reducing the size of established reserves and challenging an Indian band's use of land and water would be touchy, and their protests would most likely become a problem. Assessing penalties, as a judge, for any protests about his decisions as an assistant land commissioner would be very awkward. Separating the times when he made them might help.

He hoped that two factors might help him. Some Indians respected him for his ability to diagnose and treat their horses, and he had done so, whenever requested. Also, the training he had received in the Irish Revenue Police had given him the skill to issue unpopular orders firmly, which might help alleviate some of the difficulties that he expected.

Perhaps his hardest task would be to recommend new pre-emption areas. Joe expected him to regain some of the frontage used by Indians on the Fraser or Thompson rivers, as settlers were seeking such locations. Before O'Reilly left, he'd discussed the problem informally with Joe as they sat on the Point Ellice House wharf. He pointed out that one thing in their favour was that many of the Fraser's small fishing areas, which Douglas had designated as Indian land, were no longer identifiable; the boundaries had been marked by a big rock or tree which had since been washed away.

Another issue O'Reilly had queried was how to estimate the quantity of water in a lake, river or stream because that varied greatly with annual rain and snowfall. "What figures am I to use? Should I reduce water rights using the amount available in the driest years or in the average years? And what about those old fishing areas?"

Joe considered at length and decreed that averages would have to be used for the water rights and that attempting to identify Douglas's designated areas for Indian fishing rights was a first step. "Most of those will have to be preserved for the Indians, but not all."

As O'Reilly travelled north, he mulled over that conversation. The previous year had been extremely dry, and some creeks and lakes had almost dried up by the autumn. Some settlers took all the water available, even if they were upstream from an Indian community. A few Natives had taken matters into their own hands, removing the dams and breaking the flumes that were taking their band's water or what the salmon needed to get upstream to spawn. Men on both sides of the disputes had appeared in O'Reilly's court, and he had decided against the white settlers in some cases and against the Indians in others. Overall, most had accepted his judgments. He hoped that would continue.

CHAPTER TEN

Assistant Land Commissioner and County Court Judge

By August 1868, O'Reilly was weary. He was getting more protests from Indians than he had expected and many settlers were trying to claim lands, or expand an extended family's holdings, before those areas were available for pre-emption. There was also confusion about which disputes or charges could be heard by the newly appointed magistrates and which required a county court judge; O'Reilly often made a long trip, only to learn that the issue was one that the local magistrate should have handled.

Because much of his vast district was accessible only on horseback and travelling was slow, he had not had time to return to Point Ellice House since mid-June. However, knowing his family was settled in a house they owned was an ongoing pleasure for him as were Carry's letters. They were happy, full of how the children and garden were thriving.

She wrote that she was singing with her former church choir and that the tea table, which O'Reilly had placed under a canvas canopy on the lawn overlooking the Gorge. They used it almost daily, sometimes for breakfasts as well as for teas with friends and family. Because Carry was a Trutch, she was again welcomed into Victoria's upper circles, and O'Reilly would be on his return.

Her interest in gardening grew and as O'Reilly travelled, he gathered clippings from his friends' gardens in Yale, Lytton, Cornwall and Kamloops, carefully packing them in wet moss or towelling. After receiving one such shipment, Carry sent him a parcel of little pots and a note, delivered by Begbie:

Peter, Sarah [Crease] suggests you pot all the slips you are collecting and either keep them in Yale or bring them home with you on your next trip down. They have to be kept wet. She recommends we should not plant them until September and she said when Henry brings her a plant, he sketches the full grown one. So would you please do that?[1]

When O'Reilly met Begbie in Yale, the judge reported on his recent visit with Carry. "I am to tell you the roses are in full bloom and how amazing they look. And that Puss is now crawling across the grass, even though she does not like the feel of it."

O'Reilly was glad that Carry and Matthew's friendship continued to grow, around their mutual interests in theatre and choral performances. He was also relieved that Begbie appeared content again. Needham had notified Governor Seymour he would be leaving BC in a year or two, and that had resolved the issue of two chief justices.

O'Reilly told Begbie he was working long days, either trying to resolve confrontations or in the saddle, and he wanted to hear what was going on elsewhere in the colony as he was poorly informed. He knew that a convention about joining Canada was to be held in Yale in the fall and said he expected the next steps toward Confederation would be achieved by its delegates. "Do you still think we should join, Matthew?"

"Yes, I do," Begbie said. "Now what I want to know, have the Indians in Lillooet settled down? The newspaper articles make it sound like a rebellion there."

"Those blasted reports are mainly fictitious, you know, not at all accurate." Although all the bands were furious with Trutch's revisions, particularly those at Bonaparte, Savona's Ferry, Upper and Lower Nicola, Kamloops and Shuswap, they were not threatening anyone physically, as far as he knew.

O'Reilly found the numerous disputes over land and water wearying and confusing. Many settlers and a few Indians brought them to his court but they were not usually legal issues; they required his decision as the assistant land commissioner. His biggest concern was water; it was drying up even more quickly than it had the previous summer and most disagreements were about its use.

"Any opinons about whether the Indian protests will escalate?" Begbie asked.

"The chiefs are powerful and these bands are well-organized. Dangerous, if they choose to be, but compared to some coastal tribes, they're still peaceful." O'Reilly added that at a recent meeting, all the chiefs and councillors of the Kamloops and Shuswap Indian Reserves had bluntly told him how angry they were, having recently learned about a *Gazette* notice in New Westminster on October 5, 1866, revising their reserves' boundaries. Joe, as commissioner of land and works, had published it; O'Reilly unfolded a copy from his notebook and read:

The Indian Reserves above described [Kamloops and Shuswap] will be exactly surveyed and staked off immediately, and the remainder of the land hitherto claimed by Indians along the north bank of the South Branch of Thompson River will be open to pre-emption from the 1st January, 1867 . . .[2]

As he refolded it, he said, "So, officially, they've had almost two years' notice that changes were about to happen. But only in that *Gazette* notice, and that's a very ineffective method of informing them."

"Yes, it is, Peter. What's happening now?"

"First I have to revise the boundaries, and that's difficult because experienced assistants are hard to find, and I don't know much about surveying." O'Reilly knew he was not revising the reserves as quickly as Joe expected but, considering the opposition that he and his acting surveyors had encountered, he was pleased with what they had achieved so far. After defining new boundaries for the bands in the Lillooet and Nicola areas, O'Reilly had proceeded to designate Secwepemc reserves at Deadman's Creek, at Bonaparte and up the North Thompson River. Once he had made his decision about those reductions, quite drastic ones in some instances, and his team had placed the new marker pegs, they became official. He also forwarded notification and description of the land he had removed from each reserve to the colony's surveyor, Edward Mohm, who listed it with the pre-emptions available for settlers.

O'Reilly changed the topic and asked Begbie, "Will you be in Yale during the convention?"

"No." As a judge, Begbie had to remain at arm's length from the subject.

O'Reilly had been told by Joe to be in Yale, as backup to maintaining order when the convention started on September 14, 1868. Representatives of all twenty-six of BC's districts were attending to discuss the pros and cons of joining Canada and, if most found the concept favourable, to decide on the initial terms of Confederation.

On August 19, 1868, before departing for the Kamloops area, where various tribes were gathering for trading, games and feasting, O'Reilly wrote to Trutch:

> I undertake the adjustment of the reserves . . . and am [determining] the extent of the land to be included in each . . . as a general rule . . . an allotment of about 10 acres of good land should be made to each family . . .[3]

Perhaps neither O'Reilly nor Trutch understood what they were doing by expecting ten acres of interior land to sustain a family. Trutch's concept of what ten acres could produce had been developed in Jamaica and Victoria while O'Reilly's had been formed by what he had grown up with; ten acres of land was considered adequate in Ireland or England. Yet both believed that a settler's plea for more land was credible—necessary for his well-being, and for creating the colony's future stability. Trutch regularly approved extra grants of five hundred acres so a rancher or farmer could expand.

O'Reilly arrived in Yale just as the convention started and enjoyed hearing about it daily. The delegates quickly agreed to go forward with Confederation, if all BC's conditions were met, and they began discussing the primary resolutions. In exchange for becoming a province of Canada, the colony wanted a representative government, an efficient and less costly civil service and a reciprocal trade treaty with the United States, ensuring that BC lumber and other raw products be allowed to enter duty-free.[4]

By the time they had developed those demands, O'Reilly was on his way north. He and Begbie decided to go up after they learned that Barkerville had been razed by a devastating fire on September 16, 1868. As the telegraph system had been destroyed, Chartres Brew had no way to summon help. After a bone-jolting, dusty trip, they found the village a blackened rubble and Brew directing the many people clearing the charred timbers. He looked surprisingly fit, considering his poor health, but admitted quietly to them that he had been astride his big sorrel for hours and would appreciate O'Reilly's assistance with dismounting.

When the three sat at a table outside Brew's small tent, he told them that the first estimate of loss, seven hundred thousand, was low. Everyone had basically lost everything. Barkerville's residents were anxious to learn what support they would receive from Victoria, as they had to rebuild quickly, before the beginning of winter.

Brew described how, when the fire started, it created a hot wind which rushed down the narrow valley, spreading the flames and burning the whole town within hours. "There was no water to fight it, because the creek is almost bone-dry this year." His first concern was that no rebuilding be undertaken without conforming to the new town plan. Although most people good-naturedly planned to do that as they cleared debris, a few did not; Begbie's and O'Reilly's help would be useful.

Within an hour of their arrival, O'Reilly was prescribing how streets were to be laid out, ensuring that each was wide enough to allow two wagons to pass, while Begbie informed landowners that every new building must have a sidewalk attached to its neighbours, and at the same level. The steep, flimsy stairs, which had connected one building to the next before the fire, were no longer allowed.

"We couldn't stop Barkerville's hodgepodge construction initially but, this time, let's impose some order," Brew said repeatedly, back atop his sorrel.

A week later, as O'Reilly and Begbie prepared to leave, Barkerville again had a framework. Two boarding houses, one hotel and five saloons were already under construction, and many owners predicted their buildings would be finished before the snow flew.

∞ ∞ ∞

O'Reilly stopped briefly in Yale on his way down to New Westminster. He quickly completed his reports and was finally able to return to Point Ellice House, arriving the day before Carry's extended family was coming for a croquet tournament and one more picnic together before the weather grew too cold.

At the party, Joe reached for a second slice of Carry's lemon cake as he told the family about his meeting with Prime Minister John A. Macdonald, in Ottawa in July. He'd had Governor Seymour's and the London colonial officials' blessings to discuss Confederation with the prime minister. "John A. believes in it for BC as much as I do, but he is also aware of the opposition developing here."

"Is that because Vancouver Island and the mainland were forced to be one colony?" his mother asked.

"That, and the general distrust about Seymour's ability as governor."

John Trutch knew O'Reilly was anxious about his own position after Confederation and asked Joe, "Assuming we do join, won't it take years to sort out who is responsible for administering what?"

"If Canada is putting money into BC," Mother Trutch interjected, "they will be managing it."

Her eldest son laughed. "Mother, you could be John A.'s mouthpiece."

O'Reilly continued to worry about what would happen to his income. He judged that since he was now over forty, starting a different career was probably not an option.

When Sarah and Henry Crease visited shortly after the Trutch family gathering, the men discussed Confederation. "I agree with Joe," Crease said. "We will have to join." He predicted that the next election might be a fifty-fifty split, creating a new difficulty. Dr. John Helmcken and Montague Tyrwhitt-Drake, both well-respected men, were running on an anti-Confederation platform, against Amor de Cosmos and Dr. Israel Powell, who were supporting it.

Crease stretched out his legs in front of the fire and asked, "How was your season, Peter?"

O'Reilly admitted it had been a hard year in his district. He told Crease about a recent conflict in the Bonaparte valley where about a hundred Secwepemc, counting men, women and children, had claimed miles of the Bonaparte River. Their land ran along it and, annually, when the salmon came, their many relatives who did not have river frontage came to fish for their winter supply.

The settlers there had sent a petition to Commissioner Trutch, explaining that their pre-emptions needed extensive water rights on the Bonaparte. Meanwhile, some Indians had blocked the settlers' access to the river and removed one settler's flume as they thought it might interfere with the salmon run. The settler had laid charges, and they all ended up in O'Reilly's court.

"Even the salmon are struggling to get upstream in the low water," he explained to Crease. His decision had given some additional frontage to the settler who had lost his flume, though less than half of what he wanted. He had left most of the Bonaparte with the Indians, recognizing that the salmon caught there fed a considerable number of people. He did not add that Joe had recently criticized that particular decision.

O'Reilly expected to be home most of the winter, to his and Carry's relief, as the next legislative session would be in Victoria. After the Sixth Session of the Legislative Council opened on December 17, 1868, O'Reilly told his wife he had been impressed with Governor Seymour's address because it made the future seem positive.

"Peter, when we join Canada, will you have to be elected to be a county court judge?"

O'Reilly laughed. "No, my dear, certainly not. As long as I'm paid by the government, I can never run for election, thank goodness. Campaigning and kowtowing do not appeal to me at all." He suspected that he would not do well at figuring out how to attract voters. He needed a lot of solitude, and escorting Carry gave him all the interaction he wanted. His wife was now an established chatelaine in Victoria and much in demand socially. She reported to Peter that she'd had to refuse as many invitations as she accepted for the holiday season.

To O'Reilly's surprise, he was enjoying the festivities as much as Carry was; both were pleased to be celebrating their first year in their home. Point Ellice House was decorated with cedar boughs, holly, red satin bows and a large, elaborately trimmed tree. On Christmas Eve, when Peter lit its candles, Carry glowed in the soft light as she held Puss and Frank.

∞ ∞ ∞

Some of the subsidies the colony received from London expired at the beginning of 1869 and members supporting Confederation had gained a slight majority in the recent legislative election, so the terms of the Yale Convention were passed. Then came the motion to join Canada, to be forwarded to BC's executive council and governor for action:

> The principal resolution [was] British Columbia's immediate union with Canada . . . Another demanded British Columbia be given representative, responsible government, like that enjoyed by the Canadian provinces. A third demanded real government economy, chiefly by dismissing some civil servants and reducing the salaries of others . . .[5]

After the session prorogued, O'Reilly became increasingly concerned about his own situation, because many at the Yale Convention believed the civil service had bled the united colony dry. They had asked that the cost of each official be reconsidered and recommended that Governor Seymour's stipend be halved. O'Reilly asked Joe what the governor might do.

"He'll be gone before that resolution can even be brought before council, Peter. I've heard that London is planning to replace him with Anthony Musgrave, the current governor of Newfoundland." Joe said that the new governor was expected to get on with the negotiating. BC's second requirement, after the year-round wagon road or railway to connect the west to the east, was that public positions had to be protected or pensioned off.

O'Reilly did not want a pension; he wanted to remain a county court judge. He believed a year-round route across the Rockies was a naive expectation—he had been there, after all, and few of the negotiators had—but he did not say that to his brother-in-law.

When he returned to Point Ellice House from a trip in April 1869, O'Reilly was feverish and anxious to be in bed, but a message from Attorney General Henry Crease awaited him. The Royal Navy was transporting Crease and other civilian officials to investigate reports of four headless bodies of white men on the beach near a Hesquiat village in Nootka Sound, and O'Reilly was to join them. The dead men were assumed to be the crew from the *John Bright*, a small lumber-carrying freighter which had disappeared the previous March.

O'Reilly asked Carry to help him repack, but she declined, pointing out that he was far too ill to go. She'd already sent for Dr. Powell.

"Hurts to breathe, Peter, doesn't it?" The doctor examined him, then ordered him to stay in bed for at least a week and forget about work. He added that, in his opinion, everyone was overreacting to the four headless bodies. "Probably not caused by Indians at all, but by rocks or fish. I'll mention that to Crease, and tell him you cannot go—we're at the same meeting tonight."

On Crease's return from Nootka Sound, he visited the slowly improving O'Reilly and said that the naval surgeon's report, made after extensive examination of the dead men, agreed with Powell's assumption. "He found no evidence that the decapitations had been done by humans."

"The newspapers didn't report that. Most of the stories are about the captain's missing wife, and some editors are demanding that officials rescue her." O'Reilly asked whether they had learned anything about the woman.

"Nothing." Crease said that they had tried to ascertain whether she'd also drowned and had had all the nearby shoreline searched. He had talked with the Hesquiat chief and elders and decided they had no knowledge of her. But, because of the growing public furor, Governor Seymour had just requested Commander H. Mist of the HMS *Sparrowhawk* to make a second voyage with civilian officials so they could search the Hesquiat village for the woman. "I have to leave for Spring Assizes in Barkerville so I'm not able to join them."

When that group and the *Sparrowhawk* returned with prisoners, the newspapers reported that a witness had been found who swore the woman had been killed by seven Indian men. On his testimony, the Hesquiat suspects had been arrested and brought to Victoria for trial, along with the witness.

"Peculiar that there is just one witness," O'Reilly said to Carry, after he had thoroughly read the reports in both the *British Columbian* and the *Colonist*.

"Yes," she commented distractedly and again read out the invitation list to their May Day luncheon. When Governor Seymour had reinstated the annual celebrations in New Westminster and Victoria, Carry had declared that since Point Ellice was an ideal place to watch the canoe races on the Gorge and to hear the Royal Navy band concerts, they would host a lawn party.

O'Reilly was not as enthusiastic. "Carry, maybe only a few canoe teams will come to compete this year. The Hesquiat arrests might keep some of the coastal Indians away."

CHAPTER ELEVEN

Musgrave Becomes Governor

Hundreds of Indian canoes began to arrive a week before the races; officials soon realized that the usual number would come and that the same camaraderie existed among all the competitors, whether Native or white. Who had the best chance to win the various races became the main topic of discussion and many men wagered on the results.

O'Reilly was trying to help Carry prepare for their May Day party; after working with her to supervise the extra gardeners she'd hired, he pointed out that she was overdoing the occasion. He complained that he was beginning to feel like a corporal in the midst of manoeuvres while Carry was the impatient general. The guest list had become overly large, he thought, and the luncheon was now extravagant. Two bakeries were supplying tarts, scones, cakes and cream puffs while butchers were providing sausages, pies and other meat dainties. He was concerned that Carry was going to be exhausted as she had also arranged to borrow Julia's cook for the day before, to help her make some of the Trutch family recipes, including the popular curries from India. Although he admitted to her that he was pleased with how many Royal Navy officers and leaders of Victoria's society planned to attend, he did not like the chaos and expense.

When O'Reilly received a telegram from Chief Inspector Brew, ordering him to come up to Quesnel immediately, he did not hesitate. He found Carry on her chaise longue in their bedroom. "I am sorry, my dear, but a telegram was just delivered from Brew and I have to leave tomorrow."

Carry was stunned. "Miss our party? You cannot be serious, Peter. Why, even Governor Seymour and Joe are waiting until Monday before they sail north."

"I must go," he repeated, and explained that the miners going into a gold rush in the Omineca, an isolated wilderness far up in northeastern

(imprint of British Crown)

VICTORIA ANNUAL
GRAND REGATTA
MAY 25, 1869

Under the patronage of
HIS EXCELLENCY GOVERNOR SEYMOUR

A Grand Regatta will take place on the above date,
at the Gorge, Victoria Arm, to commence punctually
at 1 o'clock p.m.

1st Race - The GOVERNOR'S PURSE for four-oared boats, not outrigged, not exceeding 2 ft Keel. Entrance, $5. Prizes, $30. Long Course

2nd Race - Sculler's Match, wo pair of sculls. No coxswain allowed. Entrance $2.50; $15 added. Long Course

3rd Race - Open Race for four-ared boats, not ou-rigged. Entance $5 $.00 added,
Long Course

4th Race - Sculler's match, single pair of sculls. Entrance, $2, $$15 added. Short Course

5th Race - Whitehall boats, paid of oars. Entrance $2, $15 added. Long course

6th Race - MRS. SEYMOUR'S PURSE - $20; for four-oared reacing gigs and outriggers. Entrance, $5. Long Course

7the Race - For Canoes, with Indians. Prize $10

8th Race: - Tubs, single man, with paddle or shovel. Prize $10. Course to be fixed by Umpire

9th Race - For boys; four-oared boats. Entracne, $1, $10 added. Short Course

10th Race - Hunt the Duck. Not to exceed half an hour. Volunteers to draw.
Prize $20.

Excerpt from an ad that ran repeatedly in May 1869, in *The Daily Colonist*.

BC, were fighting with each other as they passed through Fort George. O'Reilly was now the gold commissioner for that rush and he reminded her that when Brew ordered, "Come. Situation urgent," he meant now.

Carry said tartly, "Oh, go! Luckily, I have brothers who will help. They can fill in for you as host." She offered her cheek briefly and told him to pack warmly. Then she put on her hat and left their bedroom, saying she had errands.

O'Reilly decided that he might as well leave right away, packed his wooden travel trunk and saddled his horse. His frustration with Carry's lack of understanding grew. Comparing her brother's and Seymour's journey, an attempt to sort out Nass and Metlakatla mission problems, with his trip was unfair. Conflicts between those Indians and the mission had been going on for years. Brew would not have said immediately if he did not need help immediately.

He caught the boat to New Westminster and wrote in his diary that night, "A stupid day, my head aches."

Early the next morning, O'Reilly boarded the stage for Quesnel and his meeting with Brew. Lonely and upset, he tried not to think of Carry's party and reviewed what little he knew about the Omineca. He had been told that only a few Indians chose to live in that country, far up above Fort George, and one old prospector he had visited with at a roadhouse had said that the Omineca was like nowhere else. Its numerous rivers and streams tumbled down the steep mountainsides with such power that they cut through the rock as if it were butter. He had also lamented, "Too far for me to go now. If I could, I know I'd finally find my bonanza."

Brew met the stage and told O'Reilly that the confrontation in Fort George had ended so he might as well stay in Quesnel to complete his preparations for heading north. "I've been trying to find better maps and descriptions of the Omineca." He told O'Reilly to take over questioning men who had been up there, to learn about the routes.

"Where do you want me to go?" he asked the chief.

"Probably up to Germansen Landing, but it depends on where you find the greatest number of miners. You'll have to figure out what's the best base." Brew said he'd never been that far north and the only maps he had were inadequate.

Before O'Reilly left Quesnel, he received a bulky parcel from Carry, filled with newspaper articles about Joe's and Seymour's departure as well as the Hesquiats' trial. She had also written a lengthy letter about the children, the garden and Victoria's latest gossip, then abruptly announced her startling news. Their family would be expanding again, in November.

O'Reilly wrote her immediately, saying how sad he was about the way they had parted and how happy he was with her news.

Among the many clippings Carry sent was one from the *Daily Colonist*, dated May 26, 1869:

Governor Seymour, with his secretary, M. Lowndes and Lands Commissioner Joseph Trutch boarded the *Sparrowhawk* the morning after the May Day celebrations to go up to Metlakatla, William Duncan's northern Christian village.[1]

She added a note that Joe had been reluctant to go, as he felt there was no chance of lessening the ongoing conflict between the non-missionary and missionary Indians but, of course, he had no choice.

As O'Reilly was sharing Brew's quarters, and both were sitting near the stove, O'Reilly read him the excerpt and Carry's comments. They thought Seymour's chances of resolving Duncan's concerns were slim, and Brew asked for news about the Hesquiats' trial. O'Reilly passed over the articles and editorials which reported that although the lone witness's evidence had been suspected by some of being dishonest, Justice Needham had found two of the seven men guilty of killing the woman missing from the *John Bright*. He directed officials to transport the convicted murderers to their Nootka village; gallows were to be erected on the beach and the two men were to be hanged with all the villagers forced to attend.

⌒ ⌒ ⌒

O'Reilly left the next morning and had a cold and tedious journey up Stuart Lake, north of Fort George. When he returned five weeks later, he told Brew it appeared that fewer prospectors were going in than projected, and they were so scattered that creating a base made no sense. The chief decided the area did not need a gold commissioner yet, and after telling O'Reilly to return to his Yale district duties the next day, passed him a pile of mail.

That evening, O'Reilly read his letters from Carry:

I am feeling unwell and our nanny has suddenly left to be married, no replacement is to be found at the wage you wanted to pay . . . I engaged Lee for garden . . . and at a generous wage, and you may be cross I hired him . . . the work you instructed to be done in the garden finally is.[2]

O'Reilly sighed. Carry still sounded annoyed with him. Yet with their family about to expand again, she did need more help. He knew that having a third child was an event he welcomed more than she did.

When O'Reilly reached Yale, a telegram from Joe Trutch ordered him back to Victoria; Governor Seymour had died. He caught the next stage and arrived home the day before the funeral to discover that Ned and Jane Dewdney were staying at Point Ellice House for a few days. To his relief, Carry welcomed him warmly.

That evening, O'Reilly and Dewdney went to the Esquimalt Naval Hospital where Seymour lay in state to pay their last respects. The largest ward had been completely draped in black cloth and white satin, and tall silver candelabra burned at the head and foot of his elaborate mahogany coffin.[3]

O'Reilly was an honorary pallbearer, along with the aged Sir James Douglas, Chief Justice Matthew Begbie and most of the colony's other dignitaries. They walked behind the carriage at the head of the long procession to the Naval Cemetery. Even those who had regularly questioned Seymour's abilities agreed that he had been a gracious gentleman, and everyone, especially Carry, was grieving for Mrs. Seymour. She had decided to return to England without making any formal goodbyes.

After the funeral, the Trutch, O'Reilly and Dewdney families gathered at Fairfield for dinner. Joe told them how ill Governor Seymour had become aboard ship, up near the Skeena. "It was a hard trip from the beginning. Before we sailed, I received a confidential communication from London saying that the colonial secretary was in the process of recalling Seymour."

"Would he have known that?" O'Reilly asked.

"Perhaps." Joe then told them that BC's future governor, Anthony Musgrave, had been instructed to make extensive changes within the colony and that he would arrive in August. Musgrave had been in London when news of Seymour's death reached there, and he had been sworn in immediately.

"Julia, you've met him, haven't you?" Carry asked.

"Yes. I've even danced with him. He's a pleasant, dignified man, a widower with two almost-grown sons. He's engaged to an American woman."

Victorians welcomed Musgrave on August 23, 1869, though some had reservations, as it was rumoured that he had been appointed to force BC into Confederation. Those fears were quickly confirmed when the new governor announced in his first formal speech, "My primary directive from the Colonial Office is to take British Columbia into the Canadian Confederation."

Civil appointees worried about how and where Musgrave would wield a sharp axe to reduce colonial costs. Begbie told O'Reilly, "It is inevitable, as it is the only way to begin to balance the excessive expenses. I've already informed Musgrave that one chief justice must go and he has to choose." Though Needham had announced earlier that he was leaving, he had not set a date.

O'Reilly hoped that there would be no reduction of county court judges.

An editorial in the *British Colonist* on August 24, 1869, summarized what BC was hoping for from Musgrave:

> Well; he has a great work to do; a large Colony to be populated; immense and varied resources to be developed; an empty exchequer to be replenished; important public works to be undertaken; a declining commerce to be restored; withering confidence to be revived; new political machinery to be constructed and last, though not least, a bloated Civil List to be reduced.[4]

Because of another confrontation between Indians and settlers, O'Reilly was in Kamloops when the new governor arrived and Carry sent him an eight-page letter describing the Trutches' dinner for the Musgrave family. She had liked the governor and had also met his sisters: "The older sister is amusing in the tart way which older spinsters can develop while the other one is quite charming."[5]

Her most interesting news was about John and the younger sister. Though Zoe Musgrave was much younger and there were many single men in Victoria, it seemed she was attracted to John. He had been attentive to the shy and gentle young woman whom the governor treated more like a daughter than a sister. "Peter, perhaps my dear staid brother is not a confirmed bachelor after all."

Musgrave announced that the legislature would not be recalled until late fall, as he needed to see and understand more of BC to govern it effectively, and he and some of his executive headed for New Westminster. He was accompanied by Philip Hankin, still the colonial secretary, and by Joe, who had recently had his appointment confirmed as Musgrave's surveyor general and the land and works minister.

After weeks of trying to resolve conflicts over the shortages of water in the Kamloops and Nicola areas, O'Reilly reached New Westminster at the same time as Musgrave and his advisors. At the formal ball that evening, Joe introduced him to the governor, humorously listing him as his brother-in-law, Carry's husband, county court judge, gold commissioner, assistant lands and water commissioner and assistant Indian commissioner before giving his name. "How did you do in the Nicola district, Peter?"

Musgrave listened closely as O'Reilly reported he had been firm with both sides of the dispute between the chiefs of the Nicola Indians and some new settlers. He had ordered them to share the water, having found that one of the Nicola band's protests was valid: one settler's large flume was taking too much. When O'Reilly ordered its removal, the man became belligerent, saying that his pre-emption was unworkable without the flume and he would probably move on. Since O'Reilly suspected that the chap would continue to cause trouble, he agreed and suggested that he and his extended family do so, soon. He explained to Musgrave and Trutch, "They had claimed three acreages, prime land. I hope it will be taken up by more suitable pre-emptors."

"What do you think of Musgrave, Peter?" Trutch asked when he and O'Reilly met for an early breakfast before Joe had to join the governor's tour of the logging camps along Burrard Inlet.

"I suspect he is everything Seymour had hoped to be but was not. Musgrave will do what he intends to, and with little fuss."

Trutch chuckled and told him that was an astute overview. He then asked whether his brother-in-law realized how well his skills at assessing and managing people were developing. "You're now almost as good at reading an individual as you are at judging a horse."

O'Reilly replied that he still usually preferred horses. "Will Musgrave make deep cuts to the civil list?"

"Yes. He is furious about the number of men being paid by the colony and says he has never seen such waste." According to Seymour's rough estimates, and not counting the Indian or Chinese people, BC had fewer than nine thousand residents. Musgrave was mystified that the former governor had expected the colony's future revenues to cover its expenses.

"Only nine thousand in both colonies? I thought it was more," O'Reilly said.

Joe piled marmalade on his toast. "I suspect even that figure is padded. Now, Peter, Carry told me you are nervous that Musgrave will discharge some county court judges, but that's most unlikely. So if you have been getting headaches, stop worrying," he ordered unsympathetically.

"Thank you. Please pass the butter."

Joe cleared his throat and broached a subject which he knew would be unwelcome. After meeting O'Reilly, Musgrave had requested that he join his tour of the Fraser district and the Cariboo. Trutch had had no choice but to agree and then decided O'Reilly was the ideal person to go on ahead and make arrangements. The governor needed to meet co-operative men who represented BC's business people, settlers and Indian chiefs, and his party required suitable accommodations.

"Joe, Carry expects me on today's boat. My family is waiting," O'Reilly protested.

"I know, and she is not well, but this will only take another two weeks or so. Musgrave needs to understand what's been achieved in British Columbia in its first ten years. He should see the Cornwalls' new water system—you can arrange all that easily whereas I cannot while I'm on the tour. And thinking of the Cornwalls, do stress that the governor will not be able to stay with them long enough to ride to the hounds or go to a dinner and dance. Invite them to the ball in Clinton."

O'Reilly nodded reluctantly. Although becoming better acquainted with Musgrave was probably good for his career, he hated having to send Carry another telegram, cancelling his arrival. Her latest letters had often seemed a confusing scrawl and lacked her usual perceptive comments and humour. She wrote frequently about how ill she felt and how overwhelmed she was at the prospect of managing three children. He was worried about her.

O'Reilly telegraphed his wife, telling her how bleak he felt at the delay, and then boarded the steamer for Hope. By evening, he was in another world, sitting in a freight canoe and heading up to Yale. As the Fraser flowed beneath the rhythmic strokes of the six paddlers, he realized it had been ten years since he had come to BC. His longing for his native country and his family had become faint, ever since Mamsey had died in her sleep the previous year. Carry, Frank, Kathleen and Point Ellice House were now his home. He expected to visit the old country in future years, though he and his family would probably spend more time in England than in Ireland, as he and Carry wanted their children to go to a good British school.

The head paddler asked, "Judge, are you getting out at the Trutch house or the village?"

O'Reilly chose the house, about a mile south of Yale. After being dropped off on the rocky shore, he carried his trunk up the path to Joe and Julia's two-storey cottage, which he called his second home. It was set two hundred feet above the Fraser, and the Cariboo Road passed between house and river. Its gardens were in sweet-smelling bloom, which made him think of Carry. They had often sat on the porch and savoured the magnificent view of the mountains and the narrow, winding river valley; it was especially pleasing when they could watch a full moon rise, creating mysterious shadows on the rock spires across the way. Carry always said the Fraser's rushing waters sounded like a symphony, O'Reilly remembered, wishing he was with her rather than up here.

In the morning, after finalizing the details for Musgrave's visit to Yale, O'Reilly boarded the stage. He was only going as far as Lytton where he hoped to find Adam, an old Nlaka'pamux chief he had known since the Fraser River gold rush. As he walked a block in Lytton to stretch his cramped legs, he encountered a striking Indian lad.

"Mr. O'Reilly, remember me? I am Pov-hallak. I used to help you with the government horses in Hope. My father is Pa-hallak," the lad explained in precise English.

O'Reilly greeted him, recognizing from his accent that he had been one of Mrs. Glennie's students. He asked after his mother and his father, a Nlaka'pamux senior chief who would also be ideal for Musgrave to meet. Perhaps even this articulate young man would do, O'Reilly thought, and asked, "Could you meet me here in three days, Pov-hallak? I want to introduce you to Governor Musgrave."

"No, thank you, Mr. O'Reilly. I cannot because my cousin is waiting for me over at Savona's Ferry."

O'Reilly then went looking for Adam, his first choice of a chief to introduce to Musgrave, and learned he was away at a daughter's village, celebrating the arrival of a new grandson. He sent an interpreter with a message, "Be in Lytton in three days' time to meet the Queen's new head man," and hoped the chief would return. Trutch had met Adam and judged him to be a smart man and had said, "Impressive, considering he is an Indian."

O'Reilly borrowed a horse and spent the rest of the day riding up to the Cornwalls' roadhouse. They welcomed the idea of Musgrave's visit and he stayed overnight, then rode out for Clinton at dawn. Most of the residents there were in a tizzy; entertaining the new governor was an honour that had to be done right. Not only were the village fathers hosting a dinner and dance, they wanted their arch, made of evergreens and flowers woven around a welcome sign which would stretch across the Cariboo Road, to be even more elaborate than New Westminster's had been. And when O'Reilly reached Barkerville, he discovered that many of its residents were preparing even more than the people in Clinton.

Brew said that all the activity was providing him with more amusement than he'd had in years. "Musgrave's visit is giving our fire department a reason to strut about in their new uniforms—and no, Peter, I didn't even ask them, 'Instead of uniforms, why not buy another hose wagon?' They wanted gold braid." Barkerville's firemen, probably among the most subsidized in the colony, were spending enthusiastically on their personal arch to welcome the governor.

"How many arches will there be?" O'Reilly asked.

"There is so much secrecy that no one is sure. Isn't it lucky that Barkerville's main street is so long?" Brew explained that after some hot disagreement about the first arches proposed, which were criticized as not representing the diversity of the Cariboo, he expected there could be quite a few.

By the time Governor Musgrave arrived, there were five arches for him to be driven under: One had been erected by the Chinese community and the other four by various English-speaking groups. The first said "Welcome," the second, "Union Forever," and the third, "Success to the Dominion." Then there was the one saying "welcome" in Chinese and, last, but certainly not least, the Firemen's Arch. O'Reilly later wrote to Carry that even Musgrave was speechless as he passed under it:

The Firemen's arch was festively draped with a wealth of buckets and hoses plus two long ladders. Honour guard, fifty firemen in red uniforms . . .[6]

By mid-October, Musgrave and all his officials were back in Victoria, and O'Reilly was finally home at Point Ellice House. Carry's face, feet and little hands were badly swollen, although the baby was not due for another month. The next day, deeply concerned and realizing how exhausted she was, he asked, "Would you like me to arrange for Puss and Frank to stay at Fairfield?"

"Certainly not! They need time with their father. And if you are really staying at home, we can manage."

O'Reilly prayed that nothing would demand his presence elsewhere. When Governor Musgrave received a dispatch from London and directed that the legislative members meet to consider its consequences, O'Reilly sighed with relief. Now he would have to stay in Victoria and could continue to help the new nanny with the children, as Carry's doctor had ordered her to stay in bed.

The dispatch was actually to all British Columbians from Lord Granville, informing them that the new Parliament had voted unanimously for British Columbia to become part of Canada. That news was startling, but the next clause was even more so. Parliament had also voted to cease subsidizing BC, if it chose not to join Canada. The colony could no longer be a cost to Britain:

> This is the colonials' official notice of a change in status. Within a time frame to be specified shortly, British Columbia would no longer receive assistance, financial or otherwise, from Great Britain.[7]

The Granville Dispatch was published in all the colony's newspapers during the week of October 20, 1869. Shocked residents organized townhall meetings to discuss Britain's dictatorial edicts and usually resolved, to Governor Musgrave's puzzlement, to reject them. Most non-official British Columbians did not—or would not—believe the urgency for, and inevitability of, Confederation. Then a Vancouver Island group decided that annexation by the United States would be preferable to joining Canada, but that fizzled out quite quickly, once it was put to a vote. Even most of its original adherents marked "No."

O'Reilly was impressed as the governor began to shape BC's opportunity to demand one-time Confederation grants from Britain. Musgrave expected each council member to listen to any ideas or opinions presented both within and outside the legislature, and he himself visited with many groups and organizations in Victoria, Nanaimo and New Westminster. He repeatedly asked, "What assets and responsibilities should BC retain? How can we gain maximum benefits in our future partnership with the Dominion?"

Joe and Julia hosted an informal dinner for the Musgraves, since Zoe Musgrave and John Trutch appeared to be seriously interested in each other. Carry insisted that Peter leave her bedside, where he now spent most of his evenings, and join the party. On his return home, after he had reported that Zoe and John were indeed courting, she wanted to know what was being said about joining Canada and when that might happen.

"Maybe as soon as late next year," O'Reilly speculated.

"Well, it seems as though we are not only going to have a new baby, we're going to have a new country."

CHAPTER TWELVE

Reluctantly Canadian

An accident interrupted British Columbia's progress toward Confederation. On November 2, 1869, Governor Musgrave was thrown from his horse and received crippling leg injuries which kept him in bed for months. As his doctors argued about whether to remove his leg, his wedding to Jeanie Field had to be delayed. The governor's main concern was who could best replace him for the final negotiations with Britain and Canada. This was a difficulty, because some of the colony's most respected and astute men had accepted the inevitability of Confederation only due to his leadership.

His choices included Joe Trutch and Amor de Cosmos but he was aware that many British Columbians questioned their credibility. Eventually, Musgrave decided that Trutch would be the head negotiator and de Cosmos his replacement if required. Two more men were needed to complete the team, but several who were approached declined.

During this uncertain period, the O'Reillys' second daughter, Mary Augusta, was born at Point Ellice House on November 23, 1869. The fragile baby fussed day and night, despite Dr. Israel Powell's attempts to bring her relief. As Carry was unwell, not recovering from the birth easily, Peter often rocked the infant through the night. That gave the nanny some relief but left him worried and weary. When Begbie called with a large bouquet for Carry, O'Reilly admitted, "Matthew, I have never felt as bone-tired in my life."

Begbie sympathized, and then, when they went for a stroll, he asked what O'Reilly knew about how the terms of Confederation were developing.

"The members are enjoying hearing themselves argue." BC was to be given funds to assist as it went from being a subsidized colony to a Canadian province, but the conditions were quite complicated. O'Reilly attended the legislative council most days and found it interesting, perhaps because his fellow members' opinions were preferable to the wails of an unhappy newborn.

The next day, when Edgar Dewdney, who was the elected representative for the District of Kootenay even though he lived on his ranch in the Cariboo, complained about how tedious the morning's agenda had been, O'Reilly said, "Ned, compare this work to my being a gold commissioner or you out surveying in miserable weather. We're not bug-bitten or hungry, no one has threatened to shoot us and we haven't been exposed to smallpox or mountain fever."

His old friend laughed. "No, Peter, and neither am I worrying about ranch expenses or trying to avoid being gored by a bull. I take your point."

However, O'Reilly began to dislike sitting in the stuffy legislative quarters, and by the time the session ended in mid-April 1870, he was more than ready to return to the outdoors and his circuit duties. Carry's health had improved enough that he was comfortable leaving home, especially as Mary was, against all odds, surviving.

When O'Reilly reached Yale and reviewed his schedule of court dates and the list of Indian reservations he was to reshape within the Fraser River, Nicola and Kamloops districts, he knew that he was going to be working long hours. He learned that a number of residents had left their pre-emptions, because of the declining BC economy or because the last winter had been cold and difficult. Yet in the Shuswap Lake country, people were taking up pre-emptions, perhaps because that was where the future railway would go.

In mid-June, O'Reilly reached Fort Kamloops and encountered Begbie. They greeted each other warmly, glad of an opportunity to toast Chartres Brew. He had died in Barkerville on May 31, 1870, and Begbie had fortuitously been there in time to share his last days. "I ordered his headstone with these words," he said sadly as he passed O'Reilly a card.

A man imperturbable in courage and temper, endowed with a great and varied administrative capacity: a most ready wit, a most pure integrity and a most human heart.[1]

They sat in silence for a few minutes. "Brew shaped my life, you know, Matthew. In 1859, if I'd been in charge, I probably would not have granted me a second chance after I stupidly offended a riverboat captain and then incorrectly taxed him. Luckily, the chief was more generous."

Begbie asked if Brew's decision had been wise.

O'Reilly considered for a moment. "Yes—because of his supervision and his patience. He nudged me along. Those expressive eyebrows of his. If he raised them when he said, 'Mr. O'Reilly,' I was immediately worried. Hard to imagine, but I was terrified of him during my first years here." He asked Matthew how he was feeling, knowing that losing Brew was hard.

"I keep putting one foot in front of the other, Peter. Even though Needham's resignation has solved the problem of two chief justices, I'm still not sure whether I should stay. What will my role be? Are you worried that Canada will eventually take over the BC judiciary and bring all our judges in from Ontario?"

"Yes, but less than I was last year. Since I've been so fearful for Carry and the baby, I have had no time for my other worries." But now that Carry was regaining her health, he was concerned about his career and whether his appointment as a county court judge would continue.

"I expect all judicial positions will be kept as they are for the first five years, but I'm considering the longer term. And I am deciding whether I want to become a Canadian." Begbie had choices, as he was well-qualified, but he was aware that O'Reilly had not completed a university degree, let alone the usual qualifications for a career in law. He suspected O'Reilly and the other county court judges and former gold commissioners would be part of Canada's legal system only for the transition period. They would then be shuffled elsewhere because the eastern law associations were powerful and adamant: judges had to be lawyers first.

"Before Joe left for Ottawa, he told me that if and when my appointment as county court judge ends, I will have a generous pension, and so will all the others in my position," O'Reilly volunteered.

∞   ∞   ∞

Musgrave's deputies to Ottawa, authorized to finalize the negotiation of the terms of Confederation, were an unlikely trio: Commissioner of Land and Works Joseph Trutch, Dr. R.W. Carrall from the Cariboo, an ardent and long-time supporter of Confederation, and Dr. John Helmcken, who until very recently had actively lobbied against BC joining the Dominion. He was an honest man and a respected doctor who had finally agreed to join the team, much to Musgrave's relief. The governor's shattered leg was not healing well, and he could not have gone to Ottawa in May 1870 nor continued on to London when a preliminary agreement had been reached.

Joe was positive about the outcome. Just before he and his two colleagues left for Ottawa, he reminded his relatives how they had scoffed at him when he had said only four years ago that BC would join Canada. Peter was not able to attend the goodbye dinner Julia had arranged so Carry reported on it in her next letter. What had surprised her was how outspoken John was becoming; he'd said, "Yes, and we might scoff again at your next idea, Joe. But I'm glad you're representing us."

When O'Reilly returned home for a weekend visit, Julia, who was about to leave to meet Joe in England, read them parts of Joe's latest letter. "We have almost reached preliminary agreements with Canada for all of BC's terms and conditions. London of course has the final say."[2]

Pop, as O'Reilly had nicknamed Mary, was having a fussy week and Carry moved her to her other arm. "I have been so tied up with family and health matters, I don't understand the sequence of what is to happen. I know that becoming a province means we will sever most of our ties with Britain and I feel sad about that. And I'm unclear about the terms of Confederation that BC is requesting."

Julia admitted she was almost as perplexed as Carry, though Joe would be horrified to hear that. Yet the terms did not seem real to her. After all, saying a road or a railroad must be built was fine but she questioned the feasibility. "Don't you agree that the Rocky Mountains are a massive barrier?"

Carry said she certainly did, and asked, "Peter, aren't the people on the prairies mainly Aboriginals? Who will be using the railway if Canada manages to build one?"

Sipping his tea as he watched a fisherman in a rowboat drift by, O'Reilly considered their opinions. He acknowledged that the decreasing numbers of residents, both in BC and in the other Canadian provinces and territories, was one of his hesitations about the potential success of Confederation.

"And why do Musgrave and his negotiators expect that Canada will give per capita grants for more residents than BC really has?" Carry continued.

O'Reilly said he did not know. Begbie had told him that the number to be used for BC's population, which Britain would subsidize, was much higher than its actual total of residents. He had speculated that the population was being inflated for future purposes, perhaps for attracting settlers or for fundraising for the railway.

O'Reilly was spending the season in the Fraser and Kamloops regions, relieved that he had not been sent up to the Omineca. When he returned after his first month, Carry declared that she, her mother and the children would be travelling back up to Yale with him and would spend the summer at Joe and Julia's cottage. Although that meant they would miss the parties planned for the newly married Governor and Mrs. Musgrave when they arrived from New York, Carry hoped that the change of air would be good for her sickly, seven-month-old infant.

O'Reilly's return trip to the Fraser became a jumble of luggage, women and children, its movement firmly directed by his wife. After two days of helping the family settle in, he said that he was expected by a band up the canyon and then had to cut across to the Nicola to meet with various bands there. He was still adjusting reserves to conform to Trutch's ten acres per family and sorting out settler–Indian disputes. He asked Carry to telegraph the Kamloops constable and government agent, Johnny Ussher, if she needed him. Then he hugged her gently and kissed the little face in the bundle she held. Each time he left their frail baby he wondered if he would ever hold his Pop again.

"We'll see you in a month or so, my dear," Carry said.

Mother Trutch, four-year-old Frank and two-year-old Kitty, who no longer wanted to be called Puss, walked him up the hill to the stable. After tying his bedroll and bags behind his saddle, O'Reilly embraced his children and his mother-in-law. He thanked her for being the loving support she was and said that she should also feel free to send for him.

Six weeks later when O'Reilly returned, he found his family thriving and even Pop seemed healthier. Carry had a stack of newspaper reports as well as Joe's and Julia's letters waiting for him, and he learned about the progress in London. The railway issue continued to be the term causing the most confusion; British parliamentarians, newspaper editors and potential investors questioned the sanity of building a railway across an empty continent. Trutch wrote repeatedly that he was frustrated, as some colonial officials had not even read his carefully prepared projections.

When editors began forecasting that British Columbia would join Canada on July 1, 1871, Carry and Peter accepted it as inevitable, agreeing they were still mystified about how it could work. As Canada was not going to replace any of the subsidies that Britain currently provided, they wondered, as did most members of BC's civil service, "Where will the money come from?"

Carry asked regularly, "When will you hear whether you are to remain a county court judge? And do you believe it will be at the same salary?"

O'Reilly reassured her with more certainty than he felt; he was developing headaches again, if he started pondering those issues in the middle of the night. Land and Works and the constabulary were to remain provincial responsibilities while Canada would take over all Indian affairs and the judiciary. It was confusing.

Joe had told him before he left for Ottawa, "Peter, if the Dominion replaces the county court judges with lawyers right away, those men won't do anything beyond holding court. Your services will always be needed because you can switch from being a judge to a land commissioner to a gold commissioner."

There was another subject much more interesting than Confederation within the extended Trutch family: John Trutch and Zoe Musgrave were considering marriage. Although the governor was not delighted with his young sister's choice of a husband—John was twenty years older—Zoe was adamant he was right for her. Carry and Mother Trutch tactfully hid their amusement as John was by turns proud, flustered and overwhelmed. Musgrave, acting for his sister, had demanded to know John's financial worth and his assets. But these had been tied into Joe's enterprises for years, and John had never bothered analyzing what percentage of a venture was his and what his holdings would be worth separately.

He wrote Carry, confiding that he was unsure about what to tell Musgrave and wanting her advice. O'Reilly was home, and as they sat in front of the fire after the children had been settled, she read some of her reply:

> John, your letter arrived by canoe Monday morning . . .
>
> I must tell you that you don't treat me quite fairly. You ask me for my opinion and yet you don't tell me a word as to whether you have come to any understanding with Joe as to what you are entitled to out of the Road and Bridge Contracts, but I conclude that it is satisfactory . . .
>
> You must tell Zoe, with my love, that I shall welcome her as your wife with the utmost pleasure and give her the place of a dear sister in my heart . . .[3]

O'Reilly put another log on the blaze, glad of the warmth on the brisk October night. Mother Trutch had left for Victoria when O'Reilly returned to hold court in Yale, and he and Carry were enjoying being at the cottage together. In two weeks, they return to Point Ellice House.

Carry was anticipating helping with all the social activities around John and Zoe's wedding and, more than anything, reassuring the bridegroom. O'Reilly was often amazed by his wife's closeness to her brothers. Using her skill and wit, she could lovingly take them or himself to task and, unlike him, without any mulling over what to say.

Although minute details about her attire or which china was best for which occasion could worry Carry, she was the best organizer he knew. Her many friends, both women and men, regularly sought her company or asked her advice. In his lengthy absences, he appreciated how she managed their home and the gardens, two boisterous children and a cranky baby—even if she did give Kitty and Frank too much leeway in O'Reilly's opinion.

Zoe Musgrave married John Trutch on December 8, 1870. Although there were neither formal bridesmaids nor groomsmen, their families stood up with the couple and included Mrs. William Trutch, mother of the groom, and Mrs. Peter O'Reilly, his sister. The bride's sister, Miss Agnes Musgrave, and her new sister-in-law, Mrs. Anthony Musgrave, attended her. The *Daily Colonist* reported:

> It was a formal affair with Governor Musgrave accompanying his sister, Miss Zoe Musgrave, attired in a corded white silk dress, long tulle veil and orange-blossoms exquisitely wrought into a wreath. His Excellency

A family visit on the lawn at Fairfield, *ca.* 1870. Julia Trutch is helping Frank to play croquet while his mother looks on, Mrs. William Trutch is seated and John Trutch is looking after Kathleen.
IMAGE C-05218 COURTESY OF ROYAL BC MUSEUM, BC ARCHIVES

wore the full Civil Service uniform. John Trutch, the bridegroom, was attired in an ordinary English morning suit.[4]

The wedding created interesting ties in terms of BC affairs. Joe Trutch and Peter O'Reilly, senior administrators of the colony which Musgrave was charged with governing, were now his relatives by marriage, and he could no longer consider them at arm's length. On the other hand, the new relationship only added to the affinity that the Musgraves and the Joe Trutches had developed since they had returned from London. Julia and the governor's wife had quickly become best friends.

During the celebrations around the wedding, Confederation dominated social chit-chat. Trutch, Helmcken and Carrall were all at the wedding, and the guests were very interested in their personal perspectives on how negotiations had gone. Standing in the reception line, Peter asked Joe, "What do people in Victoria most want to know about the union with Canada?"

Joe sighed. "That I ensure Esquimalt becomes the terminus of the future railway." He said he had now learned to nod his head in a circle, meant to confuse.

"Really? Do they expect the trains to use a bridge or a tunnel?"

Joe chuckled, relieved to be with someone who also recognized how unrealistic the demand was.

Later, when Carry was on her chaise longue feeding Pop, and O'Reilly told her about that, they laughed together, and Carry suggested maybe the trains could grow wings. He then became serious and asked about her expectations of joining Canada, other than their strong hope that he would continue to be a county court judge.

She thought for a moment as she burped Pop. "I want to still feel connected to England. Being a Canadian means nothing to me. I have not even been there."

For Christmas that year, the family gathered at Fairfield. Joe was pleased with what he and his fellow negotiators had achieved as there was now a workable draft for the terms of Confederation. Agreed to by London and Ottawa, it next had to be passed by BC's Legislative Council when its session began in early January. The three negotiators would then return to Ottawa and London.

"I'll be meeting Joe again in England," Julia announced. "He says he wants my help representing us British Columbians socially." Her family laughed. They all knew that their dear American relative was capable of appearing as upper crust as most royalty.

When O'Reilly joined Trutch in his den, Joe asked, "Do you know what's happening in the Omineca? I've been told considerable gold was found up there, Peter, and I'm puzzled about who we can send to be its gold commissioner next season. It needs to be someone with your qualifications and experience."

"Not me, Joe," Peter blurted.

"BC needs that revenue. Who else can do the job as well as you?" After Brew died, Trutch had temporarily taken over managing mining as well as Land and Works.

"Who will supervise the gold commissioners and the BC constabulary after Confederation?"

"I'm still not sure about the goldfields. The constabulary will become the BC Provincial Police because keeping law and order will remain a provincial responsibility. Musgrave expects its manpower to be expanded and the constables' duties to be clarified. They're too broad right now." Joe paused and refilled their port. "Peter, if you end up having to go to the Omineca, you could take in two constables, if you wanted. That might make it easier."

O'Reilly stared into the glowing coals. "How can I go away up there? Carry's still struggling with our baby and we don't know what will happen, Joe. And who could replace me in my district? Surely someone else can go." Although the need to administer the Omineca was months away, as no one could get into the remote area until the ice went out in late May, he was getting too old for that kind of endurance. He had chronic headaches and other problems which the constant travelling, poor food and uncomfortable living for seven days a week could only worsen.

"Well, who do you recommend?" Joe asked. He understood how O'Reilly must feel about such a trip; he himself was often bone-weary these days, and they were near the same age. He told O'Reilly to figure out who was experienced enough to control a new gold rush and he would be glad to send that man instead.

It turned out O'Reilly could not recommend anyone. Most former gold commissioners were either even older than he was or were in areas where it was best to leave them. Also, as his district was relatively quiet, it could easily be covered from New Westminster. He finally announced that he would go north. "But we understand, don't we, Joe, that I'm only the Omineca's *temporary* gold commissioner and county court judge. One season will be more than enough."

When the colony's Legislative Council convened on January 5, 1871, he knew that this might be his last session as a member. Once BC was a province, all future representatives to the legislature would be elected and, as he had recently again assured Carry, he could never be a politician.

He began the preliminary preparations for his departure while Confederation was debated throughout Victoria. In the legislature, Governor Musgrave presented the terms negotiated by Trutch, Helmcken and Carrall: first, for calculating the cash-per-capita grant BC would receive, its total population was to be considered one hundred and twenty thousand. That was over double the actual number of all people living in the colony: the Indian population continued to decrease with the annual smallpox and measles epidemics, and many Chinese had departed to work on American railways.

The second term was the assumption by Canada of all BC's debts.

Third, a wagon road was to be blasted out of the Rockies and to be usable within three years, connecting BC with the Territories (as the future Alberta, Saskatchewan and Manitoba were called) and with Canada's five original provinces. Surveys for a transcontinental railway were to begin immediately, and agreements were legalized about the time frames for its completion. Last but not least, a representative government was to be phased in for British Columbia.

Finally, on January 18, 1871, Joseph Trutch moved, and Dr. John Helmcken seconded, that the terms be accepted. All the elected and appointed members assented.

Over dinner that evening, O'Reilly reported the details of that momentous happening to Carry. To his surprise, she was not as glad as he was that it was over. She questioned whether the benefits would be adequate. "Has this not all been done rather quickly?" Seemingly she, along with many others, had forgotten that Confederation had been ordered by Britain and was not a matter of choice.

"Even if Canada accepts all those terms, what will we do if they don't stick to them?" Carry worried that once they were part of Canada, colonial officials would no longer have any responsibility for British Columbians and their well-being.

"We can only trust, Carry. Joe is comfortable with the terms." O'Reilly had voted for the agreement without worrying, partly because Joe was so adept at looking after his own personal interests.

As soon as the BC newspapers announced that the legislature had passed the motion, O'Reilly began hearing from friends and settlers who hoped he could help them to purchase strategic acres of land, or be assigned leases, before surveying for the railway began. Some farmers wanted more land, fearing that if there were an influx of new settlers, they might not be able to expand. He was firm that all such requests had to be applied for through the usual procedures, but he did assist some of them.

When a newspaper reporter bluntly asked, "Commissioner Trutch, how will the relationship between BC's lands department and the Dominion officials responsible for Indian reserves be shaped?" Joe had declined to comment, saying that would be up to Canada's managers and it would be presumptuous of him to make any forecasts. He had recently directed O'Reilly and all the assistant land commissioners to revise as many reserves as they could. "Reducing them to ten acres per family this spring is your priority. Work hard, and accomplish as much as you can."

O'Reilly privately asked him later, "Why the rush? Do you think that Canada will be able to dictate to us about reserve size and how to manage BC's lands and waters?"

"Certainly not! But having a number of reserves with the ten acres per family will set a precedent." Joe then hinted to O'Reilly that there was a possibility he was going to be at the helm when BC became part of Canada.

CHAPTER THIRTEEN

Confederated . . . Or Seceding?

Joseph Trutch was appointed British Columbia's first lieutenant-governor. "Who else but our Joe? Mother is so pleased," Carry said to her husband proudly. In her opinion, Governor Musgrave and Prime Minister Macdonald had chosen well. O'Reilly did not reveal to her that he had heard that Joe was their third choice; Dr. Israel Powell had been asked, as had Henry Crease.

He was not sure that Joe would be generally accepted and was relieved when Chief Justice Matthew Begbie was as pleased as Carry. When he came to Point Ellice House for Sunday dinner, as he did whenever he was home in Victoria, Matthew said, "I suspect the final decision was made by the British Colonial Office and Lord Carnarvon. Joe Trutch is their best chance for shaping an efficient provincial government here."

O'Reilly passed him the baking powder biscuits. "He does understand the underlying issues between the mainland and the island."

Even those who were questioning his appointment agreed that Trutch's years as a private contractor, elected legislator and land and works commissioner had given him a broad overview of the future province. He also understood every clause in the statutes linking BC with Canada.

Carry rang for the rice pudding to be brought in. "More than anything, Joe will not let Canada bilk us." As she spooned Begbie's favourite dessert into crystal bowls, she said that Mrs. Musgrave was relieved to have her husband's replacement decided. Shortly after the governor learned that his leg injury would need long-term treatment, he had notified London that he was not able to stay on. Once his duties ended with Confederation, they would return to London.

Joe's promotion had an unexpected spinoff for his brother-in-law. In late February 1871, O'Reilly became the temporary head of the BC Land and Works Commission. Assisted by a team of acting land agents, mostly former BC officials and Royal Engineers who were now in the process of developing their own pre-emptions, he supervised the allocating of more Indian reserves. Joe wanted the boundaries revised for as many of the lower mainland and interior bands as possible before the Dominion Indian Affairs Department became involved. "Staking those lands for future settlers must be finalized, Peter, despite any Aboriginal protests about the ten acres per family," he told O'Reilly.

Ben Pearse, now BC surveyor general, was to be appointed BC's interim land and works minister when O'Reilly went north to be the gold commissioner and county court judge for the Omineca.

O'Reilly was relieved to pass on those duties. Before he left to board the HMS *Sparrowhawk*, he said to Carry, "Perhaps going north is easier than being the land commissioner."

He disembarked at tiny Port Simpson and promptly slipped in the thick mud covering main street. He hoped it was not a harbinger of the months ahead when he would again have to endure sleeping in a canvas shelter, being eaten by bugs and disturbed by bears, wolves, wolverines and even mice. As he was also doubtful whether a profitable gold rush was about to happen, having to come up and live that life for the summer was frustrating. The legislators and the public were hoping that the Omineca was as rich as the

Cariboo because it would help resolve BC's financial woes. Few people had any concept of how far away the Peace, Parsnip, Finlay and Omineca rivers were, or how expensive mining there would be. O'Reilly was travelling in from Port Simpson because he was searching for an alternative route to lessen the costs and risks of getting supplies in and gold out.

He and his four Nass paddlers left in a heavily loaded canoe at dawn, heading up against the dangerous currents of the Skeena River. They would then go up the Bulkley River to Babine and Stuart lakes to a rendezvous with William Fitzgerald at inactive Fort St. James. The Cariboo's chief constable, he would be O'Reilly's second-in-command and constable in the Omineca, and was bringing in a pack train from Quesnel.

Although O'Reilly stopped to designate eight small reserves as he and his paddlers worked their way east, it was the portages that delayed them. For thirteen days, they stumbled over the miles between the many lakes, climbing over fallen trees and wading across wetlands while they carried the

The family on the steps at Fairfield, *ca.* 1871. In front, left to right, Frank O'Reilly and Joseph Trutch, recently appointed lieutenant-governor. Above, left to right, Peter, Carry and Kathleen O'Reilly, Julia Trutch, Mrs. William Trutch.
IMAGE D-03510 COURTESY OF ROYAL BC MUSEUM, BC ARCHIVES

freight and canoe. O'Reilly's forty-three-year-old body ached as it never had before, though his loads did not compare to what each Indian carried.

Fitzgerald ran to the shore to greet them when they finally reached the almost-deserted fort. "I was getting a wee bit concerned, sir! You are six days late, Mr. O'Reilly."

"I was worried myself and wondering whether my crew were on the right route," O'Reilly admitted. He paid off the paddlers and set up his tent.

His assistant passed over a mailbag. "You read your mail and I'll go and cook us up that fine-looking trout you brought."

O'Reilly leaned against a fir tree, ignored the many government envelopes and found Carry's letters. He ripped open the two envelopes from his wife, hungry for her news. She reported that Pop's health seemed to be improving, though the doctor remained concerned about her back. Kitty and Frank were fine but quite a handful. "I have had no word from brother John, and although Zoe gets brief personal notes from him, he has not told her if he is making progress." John was surveying north of Quesnel, hoping to find a water route to connect that area to the Omineca.

O'Reilly reread his wife's letters. He then decided he would not feel as bereft if he wrote to her, even if it could not be forwarded for weeks, and found his paper and pen. He started telling her about his migraines, heavy cold and cough, but quickly realized that would worry her. Instead, he told her about the gardening tip that the *Sparrowhawk*'s steward had passed on:

Carry, put well-ripened horse manure in a large bucket, add considerable water, stir it thoroughly every day for at least a week and have the gardener dig a ditch around each flower, bush and tree. Pour the mix in each depression. Make sure he does not put too much . . .[1]

Fitzgerald called, "Ready, sir." While they ate beans, bannock and fish, they discussed their base camp and decided that, depending on where they found the most miners, they would build it either on Manson Creek or at Germansen Landing. Miners in the Omineca would be widely scattered so tracking and licensing them would be difficult. As help was over four hundred miles south and there was no communication, the two of them were responsible for controlling the whole area.

O'Reilly lit his pipe and drank some tea. "Well, I certainly discovered that coming in from the Pacific will never be a feasible supply route. That boggy ground between the lakes is hard travelling, Will. Except for a few Indians and all the wolves, grizzlies and black bears, it's empty country. Those wolves! At Babine Lake, their howling at night was overpowering. Mind you, they always make me nervous."

He related how, years ago in the East Kootenay, he had been squatting beside a stream one dawn when a grey shadow had fallen over him. He looked up and a wolf was right above him. "I tripped on my drawers as I stood up, hollering and waving my arms. It fled, but I still dread them."

Fitzgerald murmured sympathetically and said a bull moose had once terrified him. "Luckily, the beast chose not to knock me off the branch I was clinging to, but I now detour around moose whenever I can."

At sunrise, they headed their small pack train north on the Hudson's Bay Company's brigade trail, now overgrown, and found it was far too wet for transporting the tons of supplies miners would require. "Do you think John Trutch's surveying will result in a water route this year?" Fitzgerald asked.

"Maybe. If John can figure out how to reclaim that old Giscome Portage." The previous spring, businessmen from Quesnel had petitioned Governor Musgrave for funding to rebuild the former portage that led to the chain of northern waterways, and money had been allocated. They wanted to be able to supply the Omineca miners, but without a viable route, they could not risk sending flour, beans and whiskey north.

By mid-May, hundreds of prospectors had been licensed by O'Reilly and Fitzgerald, and each knew that a tax had to be paid on all gold acquired, be it dust or nuggets. Also, as the officials issued the necessary paperwork, they checked each man's supplies and experience. The poorly equipped or the neophytes were warned that heavy snow could fall in August.

"Some will listen but not all, and some will disappear up here without anyone knowing," Fitzgerald reflected when they shared their evening mug-up by the campfire. Once they had set up a permanent camp at Manson Landing, they also established a routine: one went off for a week, identifying where mining was under way as he roughly mapped that area of the vast Omineca, and when he returned, the other headed out. By mid-July, they had covered hundreds of square miles and had estimated the total number of miners at under a thousand.

That limited the amount of work O'Reilly had to do as county court judge. The season's worst incident was a bloody fight between two partners, and when O'Reilly learned of it, he located the beat-up pair and held court under a big cottonwood. He fined each man heavily for breaking the peace and ordered them to end the partnership. He then continued his journey to the distant Osilinka River. When he returned, on August 15, 1871, he discovered to his pleasure that John Trutch had just arrived at Manson Landing.

"The Giscome Portage is now open," his brother-in-law announced. Their big freight canoe had been loaded with tons of merchandise plus six paddlers, one trader and himself, yet it had taken them just four days to make the trip. They had come up the portage to Salmon River, Summit Lake, Crooked River, McLeod Lake, Parsnip Reach and, finally, down Manson Creek to the landing.

Trutch told O'Reilly that he had recently received a letter from Carry and all was well at Point Ellice House and with his own dear Zoe. He then passed over a satchel of letters, along with an apple pie and a bottle of wine which he had exchanged for two gold nuggets in Fort George. "To celebrate Joe and Confederation. Did you know it was delayed for three weeks? Quesnel residents are afraid that is a sign that Canada won't treat British Columbians justly."

"Well, since it was our only viable option, I will continue to be optimistic. I'm relieved Joe is part of the transition." O'Reilly wondered what he would do if Confederation did not work out as expected.

They raised their tin mugs and laughed aloud when they considered each other's scraggly beard and worn-out clothes. Neither appeared a suitable relative for BC's first lieutenant-governor, they agreed, before repeatedly toasting the Honourable Joseph Trutch, official representative of the British Crown.

O'Reilly later lit a precious candle in his tent and arranged Carry's three letters by date, then read them. He missed her in so many ways. She told him how, since Joe and Julia had become BC's senior dignitaries, she was dining out often. Everyone she'd visited with had been annoyed when Confederation was delayed from July 1 until July 20, 1871. However, once Queen Victoria had belatedly signed the imperial Order-in-Council, the celebrations were enthusiastic:

> Joe arranged for considerable funding and much is happening . . . picnics, races and dances. The Royal Navy will fire a 21-gun salute, which the children are most excited about as the roman candles will be exploded in the Gorge . . .[2]

In the next letter, she reported that Kitty, Pop and Frank and their new nanny had watched the festivities on the Gorge while she had attended the grand party at Cary Castle. Hosted by Governor and Mrs. Musgrave to both say goodbye and celebrate Joe's appointment, it had been an elegant evening. Carry had been seated beside BC's interim premier, John McCreight, a very quiet man, but as Matthew Begbie had been on her other side, she had enjoyed the dinner. She had danced often and received many compliments on her dress, which she'd had hand-sewn and studded with pearls. It was made from some soft peach silk she had brought from India all those years ago. O'Reilly chuckled when he read, "Yes, my dear, it was costly—but well worth it."

She reported there had also been a few noisy demonstrators near the governor's mansion; they still questioned the sanity of joining a country four thousand miles away. This time, each sign had had either "Equity?" or "Justice" scrawled on it. They had been gone by the time she and the other guests departed, to her relief.

O'Reilly had a restless sleep after reading Carry's letters and rose at four AM to find that John was already up, throwing evergreen boughs on the fire to make smoke. "Peter, these bugs are the worst I've ever endured. And their noise! Awful."

O'Reilly said unsympathetically that he usually had to start his days before the insects began their dawn feasting, and he passed John the clipping Carry had sent him from the *Colonist*:

Today is the last in the life of British Columbia as a distinct colony of the British Crown. Tomorrow by the Grace of God and Royal proclamation, this colony becomes a Province of the Confederation in the Confederated Empire of British North America. It is about to lay off the chrysalis shell of the Crown colonial existence and don the garb of a full-fledged self-governing people.[3]

In the following weeks, O'Reilly continued to wonder whether he could ever identify himself as a Canadian; saying he was a British Columbian rather than an Irishman had taken him years. On the other hand, now that BC was part of Canada and would supposedly be connected to the eastern provinces by rail, he hoped its ongoing financial problems would lessen.

Each time he thought of the costs and physical challenges involved with laying the track, he mulled its feasibility and decided that when, and if, it was built, he and Carry would take the family across.

On October 15, 1871, he closed mining in the Omineca district and left for Port Simpson in an Indian canoe while Fitzgerald took their horses back to Quesnel. O'Reilly had to return to the coast and meet the HMS *Zealous*; there had been a possible murder reported in the Nass area and he was considered to be the nearest official. When he received the order, he'd been furious.

William Duncan at the Metlakatla Mission had reported that the Nass and Tsimpsean tribes were almost at war and, as usual, he had demanded help before his mission's Indians became involved. Because of severe sleet and snowstorms, O'Reilly's return trip was even slower than his travel in, and much colder. When he and his five paddlers reached the Pacific, Captain Samuel Nelson of the *Zealous* welcomed them with relief; doubting that the gold commissioner was still alive, and nervous about the winter storms, he had just ordered that they would start for Esquimalt the next morning.

The exhausted O'Reilly enjoyed the on-board barber's services and buckets of hot soapy water, and then joined the captain for dinner. He sipped a hot toddy and declared, "It's amazing we survived. We hit whiteout blizzards and then we got terribly lost. When the canoe tipped and dumped our supplies into deep water, I didn't expect to see my family again."

Captain Nelson toasted him. "What an awful ordeal. Thank goodness you survived."

At Metlakatla, O'Reilly was rowed ashore in the ship's longboat and learned that Duncan had left for the winter. When he asked for information about the reportedly murdered man, Duncan's assistant, a congenial mission Indian said, "Well, sir, the dead man was long in the water. Maybe it was not murder, as Mr. Duncan believes. Maybe he had drowned."

"Maybe so," O'Reilly said tartly, and when he reboarded the *Zealous*, he requested that Captain Nelson head for Esquimalt.

He finally got home six weeks after he had left Manson Landing, and Carry hugged him desperately. Later she told him that she had almost accepted that she was a widow.

O'Reilly was now being paid by Canada as a county court judge, though he had actually been working as a gold commissioner, a provincial responsibility. When he visited with Lieutenant-Governor Trutch, he asked, "How's the transferring between provincial officials and the Dominion going? Am I supposed to be doing two sets of financial records? I haven't yet had any directives from Canada's justice department, but I am receiving my stipend."

Joe said that sorting it all out was more challenging than expected. "Like you, most BC officials fulfilled many roles, and dividing up what is now a BC or Dominion expense continues to be somewhat muddled." Most of the terms of Confederation were going well, though he, the premier and the legislative members were concerned about where BC's revenues would come from during the next few years, before railway construction started.

"I wish I could report that the Omineca's gold has great potential, but it's nothing much yet," O'Reilly said.

"Well, perhaps the bonanza will be found next season. Once the railway is under way, I predict that new investors and settlers will come in droves." Joe confided that Prime Minister Macdonald had written him a private note, confirming that the railway's funding was almost in place.

Later, O'Reilly asked Begbie for his perspective on how the transfers were going. Canada was responsible for providing justice, except for policing, and for managing shipping, defense, international affairs and BC Indian policies.

"Relatively well," the judge replied, "though slowly. As I've had little communication from my new superiors in Ottawa, I have almost no information about how to manage the new court system." Like himself, most people were waiting for the railway route to be announced and the necessary surveys and expropriations to begin; they needed a demonstration of Canada's good faith.

"We certainly do. Will those start as scheduled?" O'Reilly asked bluntly.

Begbie considered. "Who knows? According to our premier, he is continually 'waiting for mail from Ottawa,' while Joe's become surprisingly close-mouthed. Did you happen to read the editorial accusing him of being Macdonald's appointed dictator? Although it has some validity, I still prefer that Joe be allowed to run the show after this silly election." McCreight, who had been picked by Trutch as the interim premier, was expected to be elected, as were most of the members who had been part of the last legislative council.

The mechanics of electing BC's first fully representative government were convoluted. The vote was being staggered between October and December 1871, and there were many misunderstandings about who could vote. When BC had been a colony, only male landowners had the vote. Now, theoretically, all men could vote—but did that include Chinese or coloured men? Did men with residences in two districts vote twice? The only clear exclusions were Indians, part-Indians and women.

Victoria's general unrest did not at all dampen O'Reilly's delight at being with his family and enjoying Point Ellice House's comforts. Memories of the season's difficulties lessened, his vitality returned and he gained weight. When he commented that his family and household appeared to have functioned well without him, Carry hugged him and disagreed, pointing out how much Frank and Kathleen needed time with their father.

"As much as their antics delight you, Peter, you must take them in hand. And do include Pop."

O'Reilly said he would, wishing their frail youngest daughter had some of her siblings' energy. A sweet child, she was often in pain, despite the tiny, custom-made corset the doctors were now having her wear; they hoped it would support her back, give her lungs more room and enable her to walk more easily. The two-year-old liked to snuggle quietly in her father's big chair while he worked in his study, and he liked having her nearby.

Point Ellice House itself continued to please the O'Reillys. Its gardens were maturing and they enjoyed sitting beside their new wharf on the Gorge, watching the boat traffic. When O'Reilly learned that the three lots across the street were for sale for four hundred and fifty dollars, he immediately purchased them, despite Carry's admonition that the house needed repairs. "Peter, the stove and the cranky water system have to be fixed. Very soon!"

O'Reilly promptly had a new water system installed but announced, "We will have the old stove repaired, Carry, just one more time. I promised the children a pony."

Carry acquiesced. Her husband's abilities with, and love of, horses appeared to have been inherited by their offspring. Kathleen, who would not be five until New Year's Eve, was as comfortable around any animal as her father.

Christmas that year was crowded with invitations and public celebrations. While Joe and Julia relished their duties and Carry thrived on being entertained as the lieutenant-governor's sister, O'Reilly did not enjoy the socializing. After four outings in five nights, he said, "Carry, this gallivanting is more hectic than organizing the Omineca. Can't we stay home more?"

Carry replied that although he preferred dining with Begbie or the Pembertons or the Creases, discussing horses and cricket, she enjoyed the larger social gatherings. And since he was so infrequently available to escort her, she would appreciate his graciousness when he was.

"Of course, my dear." He fastened on his stiff formal tie again and resolved to consider these outings beneficial. The night before, he had visited with Amor de Cosmos who reported that many Victorians, particularly owners of businesses, were struggling to keep themselves afloat.

Many were doubtful about Confederation's viability while others forecast that the railway would be delayed indefinitely.

When all the Trutches came to a family dinner at Point Ellice House, O'Reilly asked, "Joe, is Confederation working out the way you and your fellow negotiators hoped?"

Joe said that it was, in most areas, and used his own family's benefits as an example. As a federal county court judge, O'Reilly was now receiving three thousand dollars per annum for at least five years, and John was being remunerated well to survey. Canada had also paid out all BC's colonial debts and enacted excellent new tariff and excise laws. Tolls on the Cariboo Road had been abolished, and improvements to public schools, mail delivery and telegraph systems were under way. He did not mention the railway as he knew his relatives were dubious about that term.

After Joe and Julia left, John reminded O'Reilly of how Joe had built the Alexandra Suspension Bridge despite all the naysayers. "I didn't think that was feasible, either."

Because many lower mainland residents and Vancouver Islanders had never been up to the interior, they had no concept of the physical challenges involved in constructing a railway; their issue was its route, and they wanted that decided right away. The islanders were adamant that its terminus had to be Victoria, but O'Reilly knew that was not likely. He also had growing doubts about the overall construction. How could the track be built across the prairies, the Rockies and BC in just ten years?

When the O'Reillys visited the Dewdneys in New Westminster, Ned admitted he was also wondering how that could be achieved and the extremely high costs managed. His employees were currently surveying the Homathko Valley from the head of Bute Inlet as a possible rail route but, since Joe had previously stated that the rock there was potentially unstable, Ned suspected that the survey was being done to satisfy Victoria's businessmen.

O'Reilly asked Dewdney's opinion about the terminus and he said that as it certainly could not be Victoria or Nanaimo, New Westminster would be ideal. Neither mentioned the property each still owned in Hope, but it would become valuable, if the Fraser route was chosen. When their conversation switched to the Omineca, O'Reilly repeated what he had reported officially; his projections for 1872 were for only eight hundred to one thousand miners.

"Are you going to have to run it again?"

O'Reilly sighed. "Yes." He would have headed north already except that Joe had decided he should accompany Hector Langevin, Canada's minister of public works, through the interior. Langevin was coming at Prime Minister Macdonald's request to survey southern BC, tally its residents and businesses, and assess BC's potential for development.

When Langevin arrived, he stated that only whites, Chinese and coloured, as black people were called, were to be counted in the census. He made no mention of Indians.

To O'Reilly's relief, Julia questioned this at a dinner party she and the lieutenant-governor hosted. "Do BC's Indians not need counting, sir?"

Langevin said, "That is a different department's responsibility, Mrs. Trutch. Those administrators will count that population when they are ready and I will not be doing so."

O'Reilly and Langevin departed from Victoria two days later, and in Yale they were greeted by another report about a dispute between settlers and Indians. O'Reilly realized that the boundaries he had set, or revised, for reserves were being ignored because no official had done any enforcement while he had been in the Omineca. Apparently most of his district's Indian bands were behaving as if they still had open rights to hunt, fish or harvest firewood. When he asked two local chiefs about people going outside their reserves, they were puzzled and replied that, of course, their lands would always be theirs. Neither had expected their people to use *only* the lands O'Reilly had had staked and surveyed. Why would they?

"Please tell the Canadian officials who are responsible for the Indians that I don't think trespassing in the Nicola and Shuswap will stop, Mr. Langevin." O'Reilly added that he suspected that would be true for most areas.

He said goodbye to the minister of public works, then spent his days on the stagecoach up to Quesnel considering what he could do about the numerous Indian protests in his own districts. Despite all his hard work, the Natives' refusal to stay on their reserves made him appear inept. He decided to be much firmer in the future.

A telegram from the lieutenant-governor was waiting for him in Quesnel, ordering him back to Victoria. When O'Reilly arrrived and reported in, Joe commanded, "Read these, Peter," and passed him a stack of letters and telegrams.

They were copies of the messages Joe had sent to Ottawa to inform officials that the Chilcotin Indians had chased off three of Dewdney's surveyors and were threatening to kill any white men who intruded on their lands. Trutch and Premier McCreight had decided a show of force was necessary. On July 6, 1872, Joe's letter to the newly appointed Governor General, Lord Dufferin, explained:

[Regarding] the Secretary of State for Canada directing that a Magistrate of the Dominion Gov't should confer with the Chilcotin Indians, I selected Judge O'Reilly for that purpose . . .

As the Mission could be most expediently carried out by way of the Bute Inlet route, I . . . request . . . the service of four of H.M.'s ships under his command to convey Mr. O'Reilly to the landing place on the Homathko River at the head of Bute Inlet . . .

I am confident that Mr. O'Reilly who has had large experience in settling similar misunderstandings during his past 13 years service . . . will not fail to adjust the complaints which this tribe may have to make . . . [4]

"Four ships?" O'Reilly asked, afraid that many people must be dead.

"No, the Royal Navy decided to supply only one ship, the HMS *Boxer*, and the assistance of its crew, if you need it."

"Has there been bloodshed?" O'Reilly was still puzzled about why Joe had requested four ships.

The lieutenant-governor shook his head. "Not yet, to my knowledge. But a settler up there has threatened the Chilcotins with bringing in the smallpox, the fool! The disease is more dreaded than soldiers." He had asked for four ships to make Ottawa understand the urgency. Nothing must delay the railway, and Dewdney's surveyors refused to continue on up to the Chilcotin plateau until the problems had been resolved.

When O'Reilly was dropped off by the *Boxer* at Bute Inlet, the surveyors awaited him and told him they were not going to resume their work without a guard. He said that was what he was, then he returned to the *Boxer* and released it, reporting that there had been no further conflict or threats. He and the surveyors headed up the rough track through the Homathko canyon to finish their task for the railway. To O'Reilly's delight, he spent the rest of July and early August in the Chilcotin district, riding through tall, sweet-smelling grass, catching trout or shooting grouse for his and the surveyors' meals.

He wrote Joe that the few Chilcotins they encountered appeared co-operative and they all knew that the problem-causing settler had left his pre-emption. O'Reilly had ordered him to do so, at least temporarily, and warned him, "Plan thoughtfully before you come back. Because of your own stupidity, you are now a marked man."[5] He had debated telling the settler that he was a dead man if he returned, but decided that anyone ignorant enough to threaten Indians with smallpox would not understand.

When the surveyors finished, having decided the Chilcotin region could not be recommended as a route for the railway, O'Reilly's interlude ended and he sent off a final report to Joe. He recommended that the Chilcotin plateau be classified as a risky area for settlers, so there was no reason to designate reserves at the time.

When O'Reilly finally arrived at Manson Landing in late August, Fitzgerald told him, "Most of the miners have already left. It has been a very poor season."

O'Reilly had been directed to assess the northern Indians but, dreading to be caught in winter storms again, he decided he could do so only while the weather allowed. He and his guide journeyed through the northern portion of the Omineca country, mostly by canoe, then explored the wilderness between there and the Skeena River. They travelled as quickly as they could, though the portages were again over numerous bogs, and they encountered few Indians until they came to the villages on the Skeena. One band's homes and supplies had been completely burned in a forest fire, and O'Reilly was delayed as he had to find food for them. Winter descended and on December 6, 1872, he recorded in his diary, "improvised snow shoes."[6]

He met the HMS *Sparrowhawk* at Port Simpson and returned to Esquimalt, anxious to be home with his family. At Point Ellice House, O'Reilly did not receive his usual warm welcome from Carry—she was expecting again.

Through her tears, she asked him, "How often are you here, Peter? Four children! How will I manage?"

O'Reilly held his wife but remained silent; he knew she understood that he could not ensure their financial well-being by staying home. When he went into Victoria the following day, he found that BC's political climate was almost as unsettled as his relationship with his wife. As he listened to officials and friends complain about the legislature's increasing dissension, his unease grew.

On December 23, 1872, McCreight's government fell. Lieutenant-Governor Trutch immediately invited Amor de Cosmos, who had a slim majority of support, to become premier. De Cosmos accepted and said that he planned to continue as both an elected member of the BC legislature and a member of the Dominion Parliament.

Almost half of the members of the legislature were enraged at de Comos's appointment, as were newspaper editors and concerned citizens. Many demanded, "Whose interests is de Cosmos going to put first—BC's or Canada's?"

The powerful George Walkem, owner of a large ranch in the lower Cariboo, was appointed commissioner of land and works, and his first official action was to disallow Edgar Dewdney's appointment as surveyor general. He insisted that Dewdney had to resign as MP for Yale before he could be on BC's executive, but Dewdney declined and told Premier de Cosmos that he preferred to continue representing the Yale district in the Dominion Parliament. He wanted to be there to help shape upcoming legislation about the railway in BC's favour; he and Jane moved to Ottawa.

In their first letters to the O'Reillys, Ned admitted that after just one meeting with Sir John A. Macdonald, he was converted. He'd agreed that the Atlantic-to-Pacific railway was feasible; however, he had not discussed his main concern with the prime minister. O'Reilly knew that was whether the track through the Rockies could survive winter avalanches.

Carry read Jane's enclosed note aloud. "I do like Lady Macdonald very much. I am not impressed with Ottawa and have never seen such a collection of downright ugly and awkward looking men."[7]

O'Reilly had repeatedly promised Carry he would be home with her for the birth of their fourth child, but when a court in Yale became necessary two weeks before her due date, he left briefly. Arthur John O'Reilly arrived on April 4, 1873; his father hurried back and presented Carry with a ruby-and-diamond ring. When the doctor reported that their second son, quickly nicknamed Jack, was healthy, his parents sighed with relief; Pop still needed assistance and comforting most nights.

During that same week, Ottawa, Toronto, Montreal and Victoria were catapulted into the Pacific Scandal. Prime Minister Macdonald was accused of accepting bribes, as an estimated three hundred and fifty thousand dollars had been donated for his and the Conservative Party's election expenses. The donors were a powerful consortium headed by Sir Hugh Allen of Montreal and David Macpherson of Toronto. In exchange, they wanted the charter rights to build the Canadian Pacific Railway.

Dewdney's letter to the O'Reillys confirmed that the Conservative government under Macdonald had received illegal contributions and predicted the prime minister would soon resign:

> Great disarray here. The charter is worth $30 million in government grants plus 50 million acres of land, to build the Canadian Pacific Railway."[8]

He wrote it was dreadful news because Macdonald's successor, the dour Alexander Mackenzie, was not a supporter of the CPR, nor of anything Macdonald had achieved:

> I find Canada's next prime minister to be a pedantic man with nothing to say.[9]

After Carry read Dewdney's letter, she said, "How sad! How can Confederation survive without the railway?"

"So much for BC's main demand," O'Reilly grumbled. "I was afraid of that."

"Don't let your Irishness make you gloomy, Peter! Britain will not let Canada renege."

"Carry, London will have to support Mackenzie even if he reverses Macdonald's decisions." Would BC's county court judges be at risk?

O'Reilly fretted. How could his family manage, if his appointment was cancelled?

After being sworn in as prime minister, Mackenzie immediately questioned the railway's feasibility. Premier de Cosmos, assisted by Joe, shaped a terse reply to Prime Minister Mackenzie: The railway was an irrevocable term of Confederation. Construction was expected to begin as agreed on July 1, 1873.

That promise was the core of BC's agreeing to join Canada, and it was all that was enabling the province to remain financially viable, though barely so.

July came, and no extension of the deadline had been requested nor had Mackenzie's government apologized for the delay. BC residents were infuriated and some began to investigate union with the United States again. Others wished forlornly that BC was still a colony, and seceding from Canada became a frequent topic of conversation.

Lieutenant-Governor Trutch's world had also gone awry. He was Macdonald's man and thus distrusted by Prime Minister Mackenzie. Shortly before the Pacific Scandal hit, Amor de Cosmos had forced Trutch, once he had read the throne speech, to withdraw from the legislature. He had ordered Joe not to attend any sessions, not even as a spectator, telling him that the premier had to be in charge of the BC government, not the lieutenant-governor.

Joe was devastated; he was almost powerless, as he admitted to the family after Jack's christening. "Except for ceremonial duties, de Cosmos and Walkem allow me nothing! Julia and I are considering touring Europe so I may request that my term be shortened."

"No, Joe! What about the railway?" Peter protested.

"It might proceed—if BC has a different lieutenant-governor."

British Columbians began seriously to discuss seceding if the railway was not started. On July 25, 1873, the BC legislature formally charged the Dominion with "non-completion of terms," in official notifications to

Prime Minister Mackenzie and his parliament, Canada's Governor General Lord Dufferin, and Lord Carnarvon, now colonial secretary for the British Empire. Mackenzie continued to waffle and refused to discuss the delay with any BC official; London watched and waited.

In February 1874, BC had another bitter election during which secession was loudly debated and Walkem became premier with a two-seat majority. He left to confer with officials in London and to call on Prime Minister MacKenzie in Ottawa on his return, hoping to get rail construction started by summer. Few British Columbians expected that he would be successful, and more packed up and left the troubled province.

Canada was also delaying taking over other Confederation responsibilities, particularly the management of BC's Indians. In O'Reilly's districts of Yale, Lillooet and Kamloops, disagreements between Indians and settlers escalated. The Dominion's new superintendent for BC Indian Affairs was Dr. Israel Powell, and he was in Victoria to explain why the Indian Act was still being revised. In addition, he wanted to confer with his old acquaintance, Peter O'Reilly, about a petition from fifty-six Indian chiefs in his district:

July 14, 1874
. . . We feel like men trampled on, and are commencing to believe that the aim of the white men is to exterminate us as soon as they can . . . [through] encroachments of the whites. Some of our best men have been deprived of the land they have broken and cultivated with long and hard labour, a white man enclosing it in his claim and no compensation given . . . white men had taken places where those cattle were grazing . . . [our people] obliged to cut rushes along the bank of the river to feed their cattle . . ."[10]

O'Reilly read it and said, "We have received similar complaints." He hesitated and decided not to point out to Powell that he believed he should be accountable only for the settlers, that a federal county court judge should not be making decisions about Indian lands issues, but he did not want to appear uncooperative.

"Until Canada has its regional Indian agents in place, it is confusing. Do you have any suggestions?" Powell asked.

"No," O'Reilly answered.

He and Dr. Powell had known each other since the Fraser gold rush. After that era, the doctor had practised medicine in Victoria and had looked after Pop and Carry when Dr. John Helmcken was away. When he became involved in the united colony's politics, he had been appointed its first education minister and later, as one of BC's three negotiators, he had helped define the terms of Confederation. O'Reilly believed that he was the man best qualified to shape the way Canada took over its responsibility to the Indians but remained unsure whether the task was beyond even Powell's abilities.

O'Reilly's headaches had returned as he again debated how to manage all his duties, which seemed to multiply each year. Adding to his depression was Joe's lack of hope. Still powerless as lieutenant-governor, he had realized that Mackenzie would not honour Canada's obligations to BC and confided to Peter that most British Columbians now favoured seceding from Canada. "Who could have predicted this sorry situation?"

CHAPTER FOURTEEN

Lord Dufferin Pacifies British Columbians

Britain intervened. Lord Dufferin was instructed to visit British Columbia in 1876 and try to pacify those pushing for secession. He had a reputation as an astute unofficial negotiator and in a recent speech had acknowledged that:

> [He] likened himself to the engineer of a vast and complicated machine who moves about with his oil can, keeping the wheels of government moving.[1]

Since the semi-royal visit was announced a year early, Victorians, including Carry O'Reilly, began preparing and planning outfits for the numerous social occasions. One morning as she and Peter were drinking tea on their porch and admiring their garden, she asked, "You and Lord Dufferin both grew up in Ireland. Did you ever meet him, Peter?"

O'Reilly chuckled. "I saw him once at a race, but it was my horse he met, not me."

"Well, next spring, he will meet you. Won't it be lovely to have pleasant gatherings? I am weary of listening to moanings about the railway and Canada's reneging on the terms as I dine." Julia and Joe had decided to delay their departure for Europe because of the Dufferins' visit. Even though Joe's term as lieutenant-governor would officially end just before their arrival, the Trutches had been asked to host the welcoming ball.

"I just hope I'm here next summer, Carry," Peter cautioned. They understood that he had no control over where he would be sent next as a county court judge-cum-gold commissioner.

He'd often been home at Point Ellice House through the winter as he'd been filling in as New Westminster's judge, but he was about to leave for the interior. He and Carry knew he would be away for at least two months, accompanying Dr. Israel Powell on a tour of reserves as O'Reilly was still responsible for the Yale, Lillooet and Kamloops districts. He and Powell hoped to resolve the usual springtime disputes between the Indians and settlers before they escalated; another dry year was forecast.

In mid-April, O'Reilly met Powell in New Westminster and they boarded the stage for Yale. They were the only travellers and analyzed the Indian–settler situation as they journeyed. Powell had learned that the Dufferins expected to visit many bands and host celebrations in various places, and predicted that might help lessen tensions. "I hope it will reassure the Fraser Indians. They're nervous about where the railway tracks will eventually go. All the chiefs could come to a welcoming ceremony for the Dufferins in Yale."

"As long as there's also one for settlers." O'Reilly again observed how Dr. Powell's and Joe Trutch's views differed. The doctor usually referred to the general needs of the Aboriginals ahead of those of the white people coming into the country whereas Joe's priority was the well-being of the settlers.

They moved on to discussing the Indian Act which, after having gone through many revised drafts, was scheduled to be ratified by Parliament soon.[2] Powell commented that the latest one was a consolidation of earlier statutes and new legislation, attempting to interpret the relationship between Indians and the Dominion, and he was concerned that it had been developed with inadequate consultation. "Ottawa's experts were not interested in my knowledge and experience," he confided.

O'Reilly asked if the revised act created clear rules and procedures. He disliked grey areas.

"No it is confusing. This Act gives Canada's officials the power to protect all Indians as wards of the state, rather like needy children. It even curtails where Indians are allowed to go." Powell commented the act did not recognize the way traditional Native systems were structured. "The bureaucrats have decided that Indian chiefs and councils have to learn to use the white man's election system." Officials enforcing and interpreting the Indian Act had been given the final authority over the sale of Indian lands and timber rights, and how each band could use its money. The act also enforced the ban on alcohol and defined who was an Indian.

O'Reilly considered the doctor's bluntness and realized that Powell reminded him of Brew, a dedicated man who was sure of his values. He expected BC Indians to receive justice, proper health care and education when they became the Dominion's responsibility. No wonder he's even more frustrated than I am about the delays, O'Reilly thought, wishing Powell sounded more hopeful about the new Indian Act.

As the six horses pulled the stage along the narrow, dusty, rutted canyon road, they discussed where a railway track could be built along this narrow strip of flat land above the Fraser. The line would mean deep cuts into reserve lands and blockage of some river access, and they puzzled over how much land might have to be expropriated.

"As I have repeatedly told many of my fellow Dominion officials, what works on the prairies will not work here at all," Powell said ruefully.

They left the stage, stayed at the Cornwalls and, as the weather had changed overnight, rode out in drizzling rain to visit the nearby Indian bands. While they were greeted as usual at a few villages, they encountered more distrust than either had previously experienced. In some villages, where the chief was away or not available, no one would even talk with them.

Last week, when they called on Chief Louis of the Kamloops Indian Band, they were served tea as they visited. He was a man they respected and who knew them well. He asked if they were aware of how the Indians' discontent was increasing; most Indians had little patience left. He then carefully questioned Powell about what was happening with the new Indian Act and the railway, and both officials again realized how well-informed Louis was. He also said that he and his people were uneasy over the ways in which the railroad might interfere with salmon fishing, and concerned about whether the location of the tracks would affect their usual fishing spots.

As they rode away from the Kamloops reserve, Dr. Powell said to O'Reilly, "I certainly hedged about Canada's various procrastinations, didn't I? And I suspect Louis is right about the salmon. Assuming the railway will eventually be built along the Thompson, it will have to be built on the south bank, even if that doesn't please the settlers."

O'Reilly did not admit that he was now one of those settlers. He had recently invested, with two other men, in a horse ranch west of Chase and they would be most displeased if the tracks cut off their river frontage. They expected the railway to go along the north bank.

"Louis is as astute as you and I are, isn't he?" Powell continued.

O'Reilly hid his surprise. Did Powell actually believe Louis was his equal? He himself certainly did not; even the idea seemed absurd, and he changed the subject. "Along both the Thompson and Fraser, the track and the railway land grants will cut into reserves and the Indian lands will have to be adjusted. Have you considered the potential for sabotage?"

Dr. Powell said that if the local Indians were hired for railway construction and maintenance, as he had been pushing for in Ottawa, then the railway would be a benefit to them. "We need to get that policy in the Railway Act." He suspected that since Sir John A. was flexing his political might again, Mackenzie would have to proceed with the Canadian Pacific Railway.

There was progress in Ottawa after Lord Carnarvon arrived. As the Queen's representative, he instructed the Canadian government to agree with the terms of Confederation, and when Prime Minister Mackenzie acquiesced, the construction of the CPR was again a certainty.

O'Reilly returned to Point Ellice House for a brief visit before heading up north again. Carry gathered the family together and after dinner, when the ladies retired and O'Reilly poured port for his brothers-in-law, they toasted each other and discussed the railway.

"What do you think about me buying an acreage that might be on the route?" John asked.

"No, you'd best not!" Joe ordered his brother. Since the Pacific Scandal, charges of conflicts of interest were common, and being related to BC's unpopular lieutenant-governor made John and O'Reilly particularly vulnerable.

O'Reilly understood that warning and, shortly afterwards, he sold his ranch shares to his partners. That had an unexpected benefit: When two lots adjoining Point Ellice House became available, he had the funds to purchase them, increasing his property to two acres. Carry was as pleased as he was, and before he left for Quesnel, they sketched ideas for where to put a barn. They needed more stalls because eight-year-old Kitty had grown almost too large for the pony she had inherited from Frank, and wanted a horse.

Ned and Jane Dewdney came for a short stay, announcing they had come to pamper the O'Reilly children, and they also reviewed the barn plans. Then Peter asked, "Ned, where should I put the cricket pitch?"

Dewdney chuckled. "Somewhere where you will not beat me as often as you do now. Have you heard about the new cricket-grass seed? Carpet smooth, they say. Remember how awful that mowed hayfield in Hope was? It was probably why I could outbat you then."

Over dinner, the foursome talked about Ottawa's latest events and confrontations. Dewdney reported that a number of the MPs and Macdonald had been pushing for an election. "But Mackenzie is adept at avoiding a forced vote. I dread talking with my Yale–Cariboo constituents next week and having to admit that I don't know when laying the rail track might start."

Jane changed the subject, asking O'Reilly if he had heard about anyone else seeing a long, fish-like monster in Okanagan Lake. Since her sister, Susan Allison, had observed it three years before, family and friends had been seeking other sightings. All O'Reilly knew was that the Indians there had a myth about a lake creature.

Shortly after the Dewdneys' departure, O'Reilly planned his own. To his chagrin, as he read the instructions that had recently been delivered, he learned he was to head up to the Peace River and the Cassiar as well as the Omineca; he had been temporarily appointed to be those regions' county court judge and acting gold commissioner. His party was to explore, enforce licensing and law and order, and evaluate how many prospectors and miners were up there, as mining was under way in the extensive Dease Lake region. He was also to investigate how many Natives lived in BC's extreme northeast and to draft maps up as far as the abandoned fur-trading Fort Nelson, a distance of about twelve hundred miles. They were to circle west to the Dease Lake and Laketon mining areas, and oversee the miners there on their return. How much gold was being found in the far north was unknown, and everyone was optimistic that it would be a bigger rush than the Cariboo, which had almost completely petered out.

O'Reilly debated questioning the feasibility of performing all those duties before winter but decided it was pointless. Instead, he wished again that Chief Constable Fitzgerald had not died and went to ask British Columbia Provincial Police Superintendent John Sullivan to choose an assistant for him; since he, his constable and their guide–interpreter would be on their own in that distant wilderness, he hoped for a man with Fitzgerald's skills. Although he did not yet know Sullivan well, Begbie did and predicted he would return the force to the high standards set for it by Chartres Brew.

When O'Reilly met with Sullivan, the superintendent admitted that many of the more experienced constables had resigned when the province had stopped covering their policing expenses, and his choice of whom to send with O'Reilly was limited. He decided on Constable Donald Redgrave. "He has a quiet nature and is very strong, sir, but he is relatively inexperienced as a constable. I do hope he works out."

Still disgruntled about being assigned such a huge task, O'Reilly had similar hopes of Redgrave. He missed being able to visit with Begbie, who would have immediately understood, but Matthew had left in the fall on an extended leave to look after pressing family matters in England, and Peter and Carry knew that he might not return.

O'Reilly's headaches, and his nightmares about being trapped under ice, returned as his departure neared, and he became impatient with the children and with Carry. Once he'd left and reached New Westminster, that haunted him. He wrote her, apologizing for being surly. He told her how grateful he was to have her as his wife and how thoughts of her and "our dear chicks," would be constantly with him.[3]

At Quesnel, O'Reilly met Constable Redgrave; he found the man overly diffident and tried to explain what their relationship would be. "When we are managing the north, I expect you to become my right hand, Mr. Redgrave. We will accomplish what we can and will have to travel many miles every day, sometimes separately. And before the snow stays on the ground, we will be heading south!"

Their first extended stop was at McDame, and O'Reilly found that region less busy than the previous year. He related to Redgrave that, on his trip to Quesnel, he'd encountered Henry McDame at the Lac La Hache roadhouse, and the old black man had talked about the big strike he'd made, over a decade before. "He's still pleased that the biggest camp in the Omineca was named after him."

"Yes, sir," Redgrave said, and O'Reilly understood that his constable was a taciturn man.

When they reached the Peace River and went farther east than O'Reilly had been previously, he found to his surprise that he was captivated by the grassy, park-like landscape. The rich plains, groves of trees and lakes differed radically from the Omineca's dark swamps and damp countryside. He rode through knee-high grasses, burnished to gold by the sunshine, and admired rows of towering poplars against the vivid blue sky. Others would find this area appealing, he knew. If its soil could grow grains, this country would eventually be settled. He watched a herd of deer bounce along in the near distance and wished he could develop a prime horse herd here.

When his party encountered Indians, his interpreter tried to find out who they were and where their main village was. O'Reilly realized the man did not understand much more than he did and recalled Begbie lecturing him years ago on how few interpreters could really speak as many Native languages as they claimed.

The first three men they met were from the Denethah tribe while the next group of five said they were Slave people. Farther west, they met a number of Kaska and then a whole family group of Tahltan, including women and children, on a buffalo hunt. They also met two Cree, travelling to the Pacific to get seal oil. Since O'Reilly's main duty as gold commissioner that season was to organize the Dease country, his party turned west and headed to the Cassiar. There, he learned that few large finds had been made and most of the Dease Lake miners had left. When the few remaining men told him they had mixed opinions about whether their season had been profitable and whether they would return next season, O'Reilly understood that the Dease was not yet a prolific gold-mining area. He was relieved.

When he returned to Point Ellice House on November 5, 1875, Carry welcomed him and told him that their younger daughter was becoming frailer every day. However, he was only there overnight because a telegram summoned him to settle a confrontation out at Chase, sixty miles east of Kamloops. A settler had ripped out Indian fish weirs, and the incident had grown into a potentially large conflict. The settler was supported by most of the other whites in his area and over a hundred angry Indians had gathered on the north side of the Thompson, right across the river from the village.

Reluctantly, O'Reilly left Carry and Pop, and in Chase, he sorted out the dispute in record time. He fined the settler who had destroyed the weirs a token amount and lectured him at length. That satisfied the Indians who were in attendance without offending the area's pre-emptors. During that fast trip, he also discovered that the Shuswap and Okanagan tribes had formed some sort of confederacy out of their dissatisfaction with white settlements on their lands, and the failure of the Crown to intervene.

After achieving a temporary peace, O'Reilly rushed back to Victoria, wanting to be with Pop, who appeared to have improved, enough that her parents were able to go and greet Begbie when his ship docked. Knighted by Queen Victoria, he was now Sir Matthew. Although O'Reilly was not sure whether they would now have the same relationship, he and Carry were on the wharf with the two bands and the sizable crowd. Begbie greeted the officials, then went directly to the O'Reillys, embraced Carry and shook Peter's hand warmly.

In February 1876, Premier Walkem lost a confidence vote, thirteen to eleven, and resigned. He was replaced by Andrew C. Elliott, a Dublin-educated lawyer. O'Reilly reported to Joe and John Trutch that he had always found Elliott, a fellow gold commissioner and county court judge, to be honest and capable.

"Confidentially," Joe said, "he is not going to have an easy time of it. I've heard the Bank of British Columbia is going to refuse to loan our government any more money. And, of course, there is that outstanding four-hundred-and-fifty-thousand-dollar loan that Walkem weaseled out of the Dominion. I am relieved my term is up in July." If Sir John A. Macdonald were re-elected, Joe Trutch was to become the Dominion agent for BC, responsible for supervising the agents obtaining the land to build the CPR. O'Reilly was relieved that his brother-in-law would again be connected with government: If his term as a county court judge was not renewed by Canada, Joe might find him something else.

Governor General Lord Dufferin and Lady Dufferin arrived in late July, 1876, and were welcomed by great archways on the main streets in each town. Although one arch in Victoria caused a stir as it stated "Separation," it was quickly changed to "Reparation" because the Governor General refused to pass under it.

Lord Dufferin met with numerous delegations concerned about the railway, how the decisions about what was Indian land were being handled and other contentious issues. He tried to reassure everyone. At Esquimalt's future dry dock, he drove in the initial piling, and in Victoria, he and Lady Dufferin were feted almost every evening. The Sir James Douglases, Trutches, O'Reillys, Dewdneys and Sir Matthew Begbie attended most of the grand dinners and dances, though they privately concurred that Joe and Julia's was the best. That extravaganza celebrated the Dufferins' arrival and that of BC's new lieutenant-governor, Albert N. Richards, and his wife—even though not all British Columbians believed that a lawyer from Ontario was the best choice.

At the Trutches' party, Carry and Peter danced for hours and were pleased when Lord Dufferin referred to O'Reilly as his "fellow Irishman."

He told Carry she had one of the sweetest voices he had ever heard. As they returned to Point Ellice House in the early dawn, Peter pulled Carry as close as her many petticoats allowed and whispered, "Mrs. O'Reilly, even the Governor General of Canada is charmed with you."

Most British Columbians were comforted by the vibrant representatives from Canada and began to believe that the Governor General would ensure that the terms of Confederation were honoured. Lord and Lady Dufferin travelled extensively and visited even more Indians and settlers than Dr. Powell and O'Reilly had hoped. Both felt that the Governor General had impressed the chiefs, as he had listened and asked relevant questions.

After the Dufferins' departure, the O'Reillys and Trutches decided that the visit had improved morale, on both the mainland and Vancouver Island, as they had breakfast at Point Ellice House. Joe and Julia were sailing that afternoon for San Francisco, then continuing on for an extended holiday in New York, England and Europe. Joe said, "I expect that by the time we return, British Columbia will be thriving."

∽ ∽ ∽

Seven-year-old Pop's health deteriorated again. Since O'Reilly had to fulfil his county court duties, he left for Yale, and Carry wrote him frequently:

Thursday, October 26, 1876
My dear beloved husband,

I have left writing to the last, hoping that I might be able to tell you that our darling is better . . . a difficulty to write with calmness. The principal symptom now is fever. She has severe fancies in her head and she cannot bear any light in the room. Dr. Helmcken fears inflammation of the brain . . .[4]

Her next letters related that their daughter was enduring awful pain and that the neighbours were looking after the other three children. Carry's mother had been helping to nurse Pop but became ill herself, and returned to Fairfield where John and Zoe, who were staying there, cared for her.

O'Reilly hastened home from Kamloops, arriving just days before Pop died on November 7, 1876. The following day, to everyone's horror and Carry's devastation, Mother Trutch's heart gave out. Their funerals were held jointly, and the O'Reillys' cherished daughter was laid to rest with her beloved grandmother.

Sick with grief, and with worry about his distraught wife, O'Reilly stayed with her for two weeks, then had to go to New Westminster. On December 15, their thirteenth anniversary, he wrote her:

My darling Carry,
. . . I have been very dreary. Our lost darling is constantly before me—I cannot realize that I should not be greeted on my return with her usual welcome and the sight of her dear face . . .[5]

After a dreadful Christmas season, O'Reilly left Carry looking gaunt and unwell, and in deep black mourning, when he returned to New Westminster in January 1877. Only three-year-old Jack was rosy and healthy. Frank, now eleven, was hesitantly preparing to join Joe and Julia next June, then to begin boarding school in September; he'd told his father he did not want to leave Victoria. Kitty, who had just turned nine, was to start attending Angela College two days a week, if her fits of weeping ceased.

O'Reilly felt as if he had no energy left and he suffered from headaches most nights. He tried to concentrate on the court cases he was hearing but it was difficult.

CHAPTER FIFTEEN

The Consequences of the 1876 Indian Act

Shortly after O'Reilly returned to New Westminster, he dined with Dr. Powell and Begbie, who were concerned about how depressed he was. After they had extended their sympathies over his and Carry's losses again, Powell, still the Superintendent of Indian Affairs for British Columbia, asked, "Do you believe the joint commission will work? Or do you find it as fraught with potential problems as I do?"

When O'Reilly looked puzzled, Sir Matthew explained that Ottawa had just announced that the Joint Indian Reserve Commission for BC, initially created the previous spring after the 1876 Indian Act had been passed, was to proceed. "The three commissioners are to begin sorting out the land and water problems between the settlers and Indians next month."

The members were A.C. Anderson, to represent Canada's interests, and Archibald McKinley, to look after BC's, while Gilbert Sproat was the joint appointee. Anderson had most recently been the federal fishery inspector for BC while McKinley had held several official positions in BC and was respected for his extensive knowledge of the Indians on both the mainland and the island. Sproat had been BC's first agent-general, responsible for promoting immigration.

The commission had been stalled for months, due to a dispute between the governments of Canada and BC. McKinley had been instructed by the BC government that as their representative, he was "to ensure no unnecessary large reserves were apportioned."[1] Canada's government had informed the BC legislators that that was not feasible and they replied that the Joint Indian Reserve Commission for BC could not proceed until it was. The federal ministers remained adamant that the formula for acreages assigned to Indian bands in one province was to be used to size the reserves in all provinces, including BC.

Finally, Canada's minister of justice had issued a proclamation excluding the Indian lands and reserves in the province of BC from the operation of the Indian Act.[2]

"I was sure the commission would be cancelled," Powell admitted. "And most surprised when I received notice from Ottawa that it would begin this spring. What a change of policy! Probably it will have long-term consequences."

"I agree," Begbie interjected. "Allowing BC's reservations to differ in size from those elsewhere in the Dominion is a fundamental revision."

O'Reilly was astounded. "Do you mean that BC does not have to conform to the "s" section of the Indian Act?"

"That's correct," Dr. Powell said. "However, the consequence is that establishing the acreages for BC's reserves becomes unclear. It's no longer shaped by Canadian law."

Begbie forecast that the exemption for BC would make it challenging for the commissioners. "Although each of them is well-qualified, agreeing what to assign will create ongoing disputes."

"It will be hard for the commissioners to function." O'Reilly wondered whether Joe's old ten acres per family would be used. "Maybe all the boundaries I set won't have to be revised."

Powell chuckled, said that he didn't know how the reserve acreages would be set and changed the subject. He asked if either Begbie or O'Reilly had encountered James Lenihan, the Dominion government's new census taker for BC Indians, who had not reported in as expected. The man had planned to begin his task somewhere in Burrard Inlet and was to record in detail how many people—adults, youth and children, male and female—lived on all the reserves. He was also to count the houses, barns, stables, cattle, oxen, horses, pigs, fowl, ploughs, harnesses, scythes and corn mills that each Indian family owned as well as to note each individual's occupation and his or her ability to speak English.

"English? Why? What about their own languages?" Begbie asked, his annoyance showing.

Powell bristled. "Sir Matthew, I did not set the census questions. In fact, I was not informed it was under way until Lenihan came with his instruction from Ottawa."

Begbie refilled the wine goblets. "I'm afraid the Indian situation is going to deteriorate. For instance, the Okanagan and Shuswap tribes are traditional enemies, yet I keep hearing about them meeting in large gatherings. Jointly, they would be able to drive off all us whites, at least temporarily."

They all thought that the Dominion's Indian Superintendent General, L.P. VanKoughnet, was ill-informed about British Columbia and had questioned whether one system could work for all of Canada's Aboriginals, as it did not factor in the differences between each area's climate and terrain.

തന്ത തന്ത തന്ത

The next morning, O'Reilly awoke with a pounding head but pleasant memories of a long evening. With Begbie admitting his unease, he was even more aware of the potential of future Native unrest in his district. Joe had given him a summary, made for BC's legislative members, of

Lord Dufferin's report to Lord Carnarvon about his concerns for British Columbia. O'Reilly sorted through his satchel until he found it:

> Dufferin has suggested that the province's 60,000 Indians must be considered a resource to be raised to a high level of civilization and become part of the wealth. He has also warned that a sense of injustice could provoke the Indian population to violence or into collision with our scattered settlers.[3]

Considering what the Natives would do was just one more worry for him but not nearly as acute as his concern about his wife.

When O'Reilly returned to Point Ellice House in mid-February, Carry was not eating and had a chest cold, but she was again coping with the children and the household. She was working endless hours in the garden and had had their two Chinese gardeners dig a heart-shaped flower bed on the path down to the wharf. "For Pop and Mother, Peter," she explained, tears welling.

He held her tightly. The following day, he took her to the best nursery in Victoria and they chose two dozen white and pale pink rose bushes.

Before O'Reilly returned to Yale, he was sent to Nanaimo to assist with settling a long conflict between strikers and the owners of the Wellington coal mine. James Dunsmuir and his partners, who were reported to be increasingly confrontational with the strikers, had accused the local sheriff of interference. However, by the time O'Reilly got there, the matter had been resolved so he found passage to New Westminster, then caught the stage to Yale to begin his delayed circuit.

He spent his fiftieth birthday, March 27, 1877, in the Lytton courtroom, then dined on a tough steak and undercooked beans. He received Carry's card and parcel the next day. Her note described the private tour she and Kitty had had through Begbie's almost-completed house, "with three tennis courts." She also wrote that John, Zoe, Kitty and Jack had gone to the wharf to see Frank off to England, but she had not been well enough. She sent him birthday greetings, but her note seemed overly cool.

During the next months, O'Reilly wrote in his diary about headaches, weather and finances, keeping track of every penny he spent or received. In Kamloops, feeling gloomy as usual, he settled into a white wicker chair on the verandah of the Grand Hotel to open Carry's latest letter. She reported proudly that Joe had been recognized by Queen Victoria and was now a Companion of the Order of St. Michael and St. George. O'Reilly wondered pensively whether he would ever receive comparable recognition for all his work, then realized that Carry sounded more like herself. He reread her note, perked up and went to reply, and to ask Carry to send his congratulations to Joe.

When Sir James Douglas died in Victoria, O'Reilly did not return for the massive public funeral on August 7, 1877, nor did Carry go; she was shaken up over a break-in at Point Ellice House. Upon receiving that news, O'Reilly wrote from Ashcroft:

August 8, 1877

My dearest Carry,

I am deeply grieved to hear of the fright & annoyance you have been occasioned by the rascals who broke into the house. The loss is bad enough, but nothing to the worry & shock you must have had. Is it not strange that troubles always come when I am away?[4]

O'Reilly learned that the Okanagan was on the verge of more confrontations and reported to Powell that a great council of Shuswap and Okanagan Indians was under way. He had heard that the BC Natives were being advised by their American relatives, some of whom were or had been engaged in armed battles with the United States military.

The three joint commissioners hurried up to Kamloops and O'Reilly met them in the large carriage he'd arranged for their travel down to the Okanagan. During the trip, he discovered to his surprise that McKinley and Sproat had not realized that most Natives in the Thompson and Okanagan regions were now engaged in farming and ranching. Anderson was as startled as O'Reilly at their ignorance, and impatiently told them it was the main reason for the disputes over grazing lands and water. After that discussion, the commissioners resolved to consider the conflict created by that factor as they designated the Indian reserves.

> Between June and December 1877, the Commissioners assigned reserves for seven Shuswap Bands and four Okanagan Bands. Also assigned were two commonages, i.e., grazing lands to be used jointly by Indians and Whites in the area of Okanagan Lake . . .[5]

To Sproat's chagrin, as he was the commissioner keenest on commonages, O'Reilly disagreed with the concept, forecasting that having joint lands with common use might create more problems. "For instance, I suspect everyone will disagree about who owns which calf and how the creek water is being used."

The commissioners said those were good points but as they had already assigned some commonages, they were obliged to continue doing so, for the time being. They would certainly assign fewer, they assured him.

Later, O'Reilly heard from John Allison that after he had met with the commissioners, he'd begun moving his large family back to Princeton. Much of his own backup supply of water had been apportioned out to a reserve and he'd decided to leave. "Peter, I expect nothing but trouble in the Okanagan over land and water. Why stay?"

After completing his autumn court circuit, O'Reilly returned to Point Ellice House, prepared to be sympathetic about the health problems

Carry had been describing to him in her letters. To his relief, he found she had recovered her balance and sense of humour. The house was beautifully decorated for Christmas, smelling of polish, cedar and ginger. Puss informed her father she had baked his favourite spice cake without help and little Jack greeted his father with a handshake, then held up his pudgy arms and demanded to be picked up.

Later that evening, Carry told him that she had rejoined her choir and had decided to be involved with fundraising for a nursing home for destitute mothers. She'd also been following what the newspapers were reporting about the commission and asked his opinions, particularly about the three commissioners' disagreements, and whether the fact that the commission had been recently cancelled might affect him. "Do you think that Sproat being appointed as the sole Indian Commissioner is a good solution?"

O'Reilly replied that he was leery of having only one commissioner. "According to Dr. Powell, the joint commission hasn't worked because none of their decisions have yet been gazetted by either government. That's the only way all their judgments could have become legal and enforceable legislation. Must have been frustrating for them. As well, they had some serious disagreements and Anderson has been ill."

In his own area, he was still swamped with disagreements between settlers and Indians over land, water and timber rights. Although the BC lands department expected the recently appointed government agents to begin resolving local matters, those men had neither the time nor the expertise. "For instance," O'Reilly told Carry, "Will Teague in Yale and Johnny Ussher in Kamloops are excellent men, but they are the provincial constables as well as the government agents and each of them has a vast territory. They can't do more than they're already doing. Perhaps Sproat will be able to sort out what needs to be done—I find him pleasant enough, if only he could be a little less passionate about his beliefs. The chiefs like him, although Powell is still hesitant about him."

"Yes, it's complex," said Carry, "but so is raising children. I just heard that Frank isn't doing well in school." Joe had recently written that he'd hired a personal tutor for their son and that he would be staying with them over Christmas. They were going to the Musgraves for dinner, Carry laughed. They would also be with a Musgrave on Christmas Day, as Zoe and John had invited them to dine at Fairfield and she'd accepted.

He reached for her hand, knowing that the first Christmas away from their eldest child was hard for her, especially after losing Pop and her mother just before the previous year's holidays. Wanting to cheer her, he told her some good news. Their property outside Hope had sold for a good price, half to be paid in January 1878 and the balance a year later. "Carry, we will now be able to afford to paint and renovate a little."

"Perhaps even buy a new stove?" she asked, smiling at him.

The new year continued to bring positive changes for the O'Reillys. Point Ellice House received two coats of paint in the spring and a pipe was laid to bring the newly available city water into the kitchen. As Carry's year of mourning had ended, they started to entertain close friends and plan outings with their children. Kathleen, as she now wanted to be called, was blossoming at school and Jack continued to be an easy child.

O'Reilly left for his spring circuit feeling renewed and hopeful, as many British Columbians were. Although there was still no contract to build the railway, considerable surveying was going on, which was reassuring. The population of BC had stopped declining and the number of new pre-emptions was increasing. The lengthy worldwide depression had staggered to an end and most people expected that their province would become economically stable, despite the ongoing discord in its legislature.

In Ottawa, as the date of a critical election grew nearer, Macdonald's supporters continually confronted Mackenzie's government, some MPs filibustering for hours. Members were roaring songs, blowing toy trumpets and throwing blue books as Parliament fought day and night over the railway.[6]

In mid-June, O'Reilly returned home after eight weeks away and found the Dewdneys there, happily playing croquet with Kathleen and Jack. Carry was at a choir practice and had asked them to meet her downtown for a late dinner, Ned explained. He and Jane had left Ottawa early because he'd had quite enough of the silly nonsense going on there. He'd decided that campaigning in his Yale district would be more beneficial.

Jane laughed as she helped Jack smack a ball. "Actually, Ned's homesick for his ranch and its isolation. He wants to be with his cows and horses."

"Well, yes, and to ensure I'm elected for a third term. Do you think I'll encounter much opposition, Peter?"

They met Carry at the Driard Hotel and discussed the coming federal election over dinner. They all wanted Macdonald to be prime minister again, now that the Pacific Scandal was old news. Ned worried that it might be a close race but Jane had a different opinion. "Despite the amount of alcohol Macdonald drinks, people like the old character, much better than Mackenzie. He's so straitlaced, he can barely bend over. Ned, the voters will elect Sir John—and you, too."

They did. Macdonald swept back as prime minister and Dewdney was returned as MP for the Yale district. British Columbians were jubilant, sure that now it would be just a matter of months before railway construction would start.

Sir Matthew disagreed when he encountered O'Reilly at Lytton. "The investors haven't yet funded our railway and that might still take years."

"Gads, Matthew, they've been debating the railway for almost a decade now! Why not get it started?"

"Investors are very cautious. Macdonald has to re-establish credibility with them, both his and Canada's." Begbie switched to discussing the Reserve Commission and observed that Sproat had not gained co-operation from either government in his first year, although he was gaining approval from the Indians because of the generous size of reserves he was recommending.

"Neither government has gazetted anything yet. Will his recommendations be accepted?"

"Probably not, Peter. The reason BC politicians fought the 1876 Indian Act was to limit the size of acreages allotted to reserves," the judge reminded O'Reilly. "Canada excluded BC from its formula and Sproat can only set new boundaries or increase reserve size if the province agrees."

∞ ∞ ∞

Joe and Julia returned for a short stay that September, having come across from New York with the Musgraves in a private coach attached to a fast train. The family were delighted to be together for the first time in three years and congratulated Joe on being knighted by Queen Victoria. Julia nodded regally. "For an American like me, it's interesting to see how enthusiastically people in England now seek our company."

Joe was finally about to be appointed the Dominion agent for BC. He reported that almost enough investment was in place to start the construction of the CPR. Once it was, rails would be laid in many locations across Canada as quickly as possible, and he would be overseeing the BC section. He and Julia would return to live in Victoria the following spring.

Later that week, Joe arrived at Point Ellice House unexpectedly. He hugged Carry and Kathleen, and said he had come for a visit with Peter. Carry had just told Jack that he could have a swim, if his father would supervise, so the brothers-in-law and the five-year-old went down to the wharf.

"You've developed quite an estate," Joe commented, as he settled his round frame into the sturdiest padded chair.

O'Reilly responded proudly, "Yes, it's coming along. These latest renovations have certainly made the house more livable." He was pleased to have been able to build a new kitchen for Carry, finally, even though the large new stove they had ordered had still not been delivered.

Jack dove expertly and shouted, "Did you see that? I didn't flop!"

His father and his uncle clapped, then Joe sighed and explained that part of the reason he'd called was to discuss Frank. His progress at school continued to be weak, but a recent possibility had opened up. One of Joe's engineer friends did construction in South America and had offered to take Frank on as his apprentice, once he was seventeen. Joe knew Carry would be dubious, but considering Frank's marks and inattentiveness, finding him suitable employment was going to be difficult.

O'Reilly thought it might be Frank's best chance and suggested that his courses should be revised to accommodate that.

They watched Jack dive again. "I wonder what career will suit this boy? If I had my preference, it would be law. This family needs a lawyer, Peter."

O'Reilly thanked Joe again for supervising his older son's education in England. "Frank is shy whereas Jack is a completely different child—he loves to talk, and to argue. So perhaps he *will* become a lawyer. He might even end up being a county court judge." O'Reilly was aware that his own contract was nearing its close.

Joe asked what he expected to do once his years as a judge ended.

"I'm looking at different options," O'Reilly lied. Actually, he was regretting that he had done the expensive renovations to Point Ellice House instead of squirrelling funds away. Although he and the other county court judges being released would get a pension, the amount had not been decided.

A flight of ducks skimmed into the shoreline nearby, interrupting Joe's response. When they stopped quacking, he said that he did not expect Sproat to last very long as the Indian Reserve Lands Commissioner. In his quest to assign reserves and commonages, he was offending powerful people; even Prime Minister Macdonald was receiving complaints. That position might become available, Joe speculated, as would one connected to finding and transferring property to the CPR. "The Railway Lands Act legislation is almost drafted, making sure the investors will be secured, and it will be passed, along with the Railway Act."

"Any employment around building the railway would only last for a few years, Joe," O'Reilly noted. He hoped his next position would take him into his retirement.

His brother-in-law asked whether he would consider running as an MP or MLA, then laughed when Peter shuddered visibly. O'Reilly chuckled with Joe and said that it certainly was not a possibility for him. He could not sway people to a point of view; he liked things to be black or white, structured, not always changing. He had also realized that he found listening at length to the opinions of men who were not his friends quite tedious.

Joe watched Jack swim, as well as the distant rugby game going on in the park across the Gorge, pleased at the idyllic setting O'Reilly had managed to create for his cherished sister and their family. "Peter, if you end up being the Indian commissioner, it would mean travelling to isolated regions again. Are you prepared for that?"

After pondering for a few minutes, O'Reilly decided he was. In expeditions as the Indian commissioner, he would have staff to make his camp comfortable and prepare him decently cooked food. And it would be his surveyor who would do most of the riding around the countryside; he would only go when he chose.

Being the commissioner did appeal to him. "Here's a strange thing, Joe. I just had a letter from Dewdney. He's agreed to become Macdonald's Indian commissioner of the Northwest Territories." Ned had said there were even more problems with the Natives on the prairies than in BC, what with American Indians moving into Canadian territory. "Won't it be peculiar if I become the BC lands commissioner and Ned's doing the same thing on the other side of the Rockies?"

Shortly after that conversation, Government agent and constable Johnny Ussher was killed, trying to retrieve a stolen horse from a local teenager and three McLean brothers, sons of a respected Indian woman and a former Hudson's Bay factor. O'Reilly went quickly up to Kamloops, saddened to lose such a fine man. He had to oversee Ussher's land registry duties and appoint a temporary constable until a new agent could be selected.

Parliament finally ratified the long-awaited Railway Act in 1880 and BC's economy boomed as immigrants and confidence returned. Even before the act was officially notarized by London, signed construction contracts were awarded and an American railroad builder, Andrew Onderdonk, moved his crews up to Yale and prepared to lay track. His family settled into their new house, right beside Joe and Julia's cottage.

Also that year, as Joe Trutch and Sir Matthew had forecast, Commissioner Sproat resigned, or was nudged into doing so. He was succeeded by Peter O'Reilly, much to the displeasure of BC Indian Superintendent Powell. He was not happy with the appointment because it had been initiated by Joe Trutch, and when Trutch had been the BC land and works minister, his policies had been enacted by O'Reilly.

Dr. Powell charged that the decision made by Prime Minister Macdonald's Privy Council had ignored due process and he questioned its validity. He respected how diligent O'Reilly was and knew he had an excellent reputation for accomplishing set tasks. However, he was concerned that after so many years as a county court judge, he might not be able to adapt to and undertake the complex negotiations required, and he repeatedly questioned whether Mr. O'Reilly was the best choice.

When the appointment was confirmed, Dr. Powell acquiesced, and instead of leaving as he had been considering, he took a promotion and became Inspector of BC Indian Agents. Six new Indian agencies were being created in BC: Cowichan, West Coast, Kwawkewlth, Fraser River, Kamloops and Okanagan. Powell also continued to be the BC Indian superintendent. Responsibilities of that position had been increased to a national level in the new federal Department of Indian Affairs, as under the Indian Act of 1880, which amended the Indian Act of 1876, provincial superintendents were to assist in setting future Indian policy. The revised act also created Indian agencies and redefined the administration of Canada's Indians; perhaps the most powerful new clause prohibited Indians from assembling.

In addition, it changed who would ratify the reserves that O'Reilly was to map out. His recommendations would be legally confirmed by BC Land and Works Commissioner T.G. Vernon, in conjunction with Superintendent Powell. If they could not reach agreement, then the prime minister, acting as the secretary of state, would decide. However, Macdonald had predicted in a letter to O'Reilly that he might have to adjust some of Sproat's recommendations, "guided by the terms of Union . . . and claims of white settlers."[7]

As O'Reilly completed his court cases within the Yale–Kamloops district before his retirement as a judge, construction of the CPR was moving along quickly in the Fraser Canyon. Carry had become good friends with Delia Onderdonk during the winter in Victoria, and the contractor's wife insisted the O'Reilly family come for a visit to her home in Yale. O'Reilly methodically recorded in his diary:

Sunday, September 26, 1880
Arrived at Hope at 2 PM—We all paid Mrs. Dewdney and her Mother a visit . . . Arrived at Yale at 7 & went to stay at Onderdonks, Carry, Puss, Jack & self.[8]

O'Reilly and his fellow county court judges were officially pensioned off on January 15, 1881, and the next day, he was sworn in as BC Indian Reserve Lands Commissioner. Early in February, he and Joe Trutch sailed for San Francisco, then boarded a cross-country train and endured a cold and miserable trip to Ottawa, where O'Reilly was to report to Prime Minister Macdonald. As his diary recorded over the next weeks, receiving his new instructions was an interesting combination of social events and long-awaited meetings:

Friday, March 4, 1881
A most unpleasant day, snow with a high wind . . . After dinner went on the floor of the house to hear discussions on estimates, high words between Ogden & Brunet(?)

Sunday, March 6, 1881
Fine bright warm day-thawing rapidly. Went to St. John's [church] with Mrs. Dewdney. Took a walk . . . Dinner with Carrall at the Queens-J. McDonald, M. of Justice & Dewdney were also of the party.

Monday, March 7, 1881
Fine bright clear day-Rec'd letter fr. VanKoughnet to say Sir John would see us at 11 ½—Went to his office at ll:15 with Dewdney . . . . [to find] Sir John does not want to see us until he had seen J.W.T. [Joe Trutch] . . .

Wednesday, March 9, 1881
Had an interview with Sir John, Joe Trutch, Dewdney & VanKoughnet where BC & Indian matters were discussed. Sir John promised to try to get Walkem to agree to deciding on reserves . . . He wanted to grant an allowance for Camp from which I was to make up my salary. I objected, he promised to reconsider . . . [how to cover my expenses]

Friday, March 11, 1881

Remained in house all forenoon. After lunch had my photo taken . . . Rec'd a message fr. Sir John to say that my salary as I.R.C [Indian Reserve Commissioner] should be $3500 . . .[9]

Since Joe Trutch had to continue to London, O'Reilly returned home on his own and enjoyed the trip along the same route much more than the one seven weeks earlier. His diary of April 3, 1881, described train-window views: "Flowers & fruit trees in full blossom, a perfect spring day."[10] When he finally disembarked in Victoria, he was greeted by his waiting family and escorted to Point Ellice House.

∞   ∞   ∞

Later, when he and Carry were alone, he told her that the trip had given him time to analyze his duties as the Indian Reserve Lands Commissioner. He was looking forward to shaping the way BC lands would be used in the long term and, in some ways, it was as if his life had come full circle. The mandate of the Irish Revenue Police had been to ensure that the revenue from Ireland's lands, whether from manufacturing poteen or raising sheep, benefitted the whole country.

"My talks with Sir John and the officials in Ottawa were often about how BC's lands and water have to benefit all of us. I believe I can accommodate the rights of the settlers with those of the Indians, challenging though it will be."

CHAPTER SIXTEEN

Indian Reserve Lands Commissioner

Carry was relieved that her husband's long years of uncertainty were over. When his career as a county court judge had neared its end, Peter had seemed unsettled, but since he'd been appointed the BC Indian Reserve Lands Commissioner, his confidence and good nature had returned. She was also pleased that he was receiving suitable remuneration as the commissioner and a pension as a former county court judge. When Carry thanked Joe for his assistance, he assured her that this position would take Peter to his retirement, assuming all went well.

Later, Sarah Crease said she understood her friend's relief at having O'Reilly's new position decided. Before Henry had been appointed a chief justice, the waiting had been hard on them. "Peter is a good choice. Although the Indian land issues are complex, he knows how to sort them out." She had met many Natives when she had travelled with Henry on his circuit in the summer. "One Indian woman who spoke reasonable English told me that her people had had no idea so many white men would come. Mind you, how could they? It's rather like if they started mining coal across the Gorge. We wouldn't be able to do anything about it, but it would certainly change our world."

Carry recalled a friend of her mother's, from Nanaimo, who had been horrified when Dunsmuir established a coal mine where she'd picked red currants.

"Perhaps you will eventually travel with Peter," Sarah continued. She enjoyed seeing the scenery and meeting different people, even though she and Henry often stayed in dilapidated places.

Carry laughed and said she found preparing to take Puss and Jack to England was as much as she could manage. They were leaving on March 29, 1882 for San Francisco, whence they would go by rail to New York and sail to Portsmouth. O'Reilly hoped to join them for the following winter, after he finished his second circuit of assigning reserves. "I expect to be away for two years. Exciting as that is, I will miss you and my other friends in Victoria, and my gardens."

While the women chatted, O'Reilly was working in his home office, completing the paperwork from the previous season. After Sarah left, he told Carry that he'd completed his reports for how he'd set up or revised reserves in the Cariboo, Thompson and in most of the Fraser districts.

In the reports, he acknowledged that former Commissioner Sproat had done a lot of work there, dividing land into four categories: reserves with permanent boundaries; reserves with indefinite boundaries assigned during colonial times by assistant BC land commissioners or Royal Engineers; commonages which were joint grazing lands to be shared with another tribe or with nearby settlers; and temporary reserves, which were those which Sproat had found basically unsuitable. They either lacked adequate water or the land was not useful for agriculture or grazing, but it had been assigned because of being "all that was currently available."[1]

O'Reilly usually confirmed the boundaries that Sproat had designated for permanent reserves, but he found the other categories difficult to work around, particularly in the Thompson and Fraser canyons. The railway right-of-way often interfered with lands assigned to Indians. As well, sections of the Cariboo Road had collapsed and needed replacing, and other portions needed to be moved to make room for the track. That was unsettling for everyone but frequently devastating for the native residents who could be cut off by a slide caused by the construction, or have their reserve's boundaries moved again.

As O'Reilly pointed out to Joe Trutch, who was often in Yale and met with him regularly, those Indians had been affected by white men's activities repeatedly over the past two decades. The gold rush and the building of the wagon road had often intruded into their lands and their fishing areas.

Joe agreed but said the construction had to take precedence over those concerns, whether it was a hindrance to Indians or settlers. "The railway will create permanent change to this land—think how a train passing through a landscape dominates it. And think of the numbers of people and quantities of supplies it can deliver in one fell swoop. Quite a different effect from a stagecoach or pack train."

O'Reilly thought about Joe's statement often that winter while he tried to set boundaries for adequate reserves and accommodate the pre-emptors and the railway. His task was quite overwhelming as he understood more about what being the Dominion's BC Indian Reserve Lands commisioner involved. Answering the questions from all the Canadian and British Columbian offi-cials using his reports often became onerous for him.

Before he had completed re-examining and revising Sproat's work in the canyon areas, he was sent up to the lower Skeena, where a large fish cannery had recently been built. The cannery's fishermen were taking large quantities of salmon from river mouths and other traditional Native fish-ing areas, sometimes even demanding the Indians not catch salmon there at all. The BC commissioner of land and works, Robert Beaven, had ordered O'Reilly to go up immediately, calm the angry Natives and prevent them from destroying the cannery. Dr. Powell had directed that he was also to define reserves to protect the Native fishing areas, without offending the owner of the cannery.

In late November 1881, O'Reilly returned to Victoria and reported to Beaven. "I have established set areas for Indian fishing but neither side intends to abide by them. I also marked boundaries for two reserves but it means nothing because the Indians didn't even understand why I was doing that." He predicted that everyone would continue to use the land, water, timber and fish exactly as they had previously.

Beaven agreed that the point of establishing reserves was bewildering for some Indians. However, now there were lines on maps defining who could fish where and he asked, "Who will supervise that?"

O'Reilly thought the Dominion perhaps had an appointment pending.

O'Reilly's study as it is preserved at Point Ellice House. When O'Reilly was away, Carry frequently used the room, taking her tea by the fireplace or working on her household records and writing letters at his desk.

IMAGE COURTESY OF LYNNE STONIER-NEWMAN

Later, he wrote to Powell. "Who will be overseeing the foreshore use in the Skeena? I cannot be in the Okanagan and there at the same time—and more canneries are about to be opened."

Powell replied that he had asked the BC Police superintendent to look after it but been told that anything to do with fisheries was a Dominion responsibility. And other than the two constables at Port Essington, charged with keeping the peace, no manpower was available.

O'Reilly was relieved that their relationship, strained by Dr. Powell's objections to his appointment, seemed to have improved. They met frequently, and Powell had recently passed over a copy of a letter addressed to O'Reilly but initially mailed to Ottawa. It had then been returned with a terse note from Indian Superintendent General Vankoughnet to find out what the complaint was, and try to resolve it.

Port Simpson, Oct. 5, 1881

Indian Reserve Commissioner Peter O'Reilly,

What we do not like about the Government is their saying this: 'We will give you this much land.' How can they give it when it is our own? We cannot understand it. They have never bought it from us or our forefathers. They have never fought and conquered our people and taken the land in that way, and yet they say now that they will give us so much land . . . our own land! . . .[2]

The Chief and People of Port Simpson

They assumed the letter had been written by a white man—"Probably a missionary," Powell said—and thought that there was nothing to be done about it because he had to set the boundaries.

O'Reilly often received similar letters when he and his survey team appeared in Indian villages. In some, he was asked how he could give land to the Indians when it was already theirs. The chiefs and elders cognizant of O'Reilly's power were beginning to become angry when he showed up, as it frequently meant more changes to their lands. On occasion, he was told he and his men were not welcome; most of the time he persisted, but ordered his team to move on, if it seemed dangerous.

"Makes me aware of how vulnerable we are, Dr. Powell, particularly when I order the markers to be placed. Even though a British man-of-war or a search team will be sent if we disappear, I prefer not to require that." O'Reilly always tried to assign the lands and water a band had traditionally used, but he often had to revise that to accommodate settlement.

"Establishing legal boundaries will enable us to sort out disputes, and that protects the Indians as well as settlers," Powell said, and complimented O'Reilly on his meticulous maps of the reserves he had assigned during the previous season; he had recently forwarded them to Superintendent General VanKoughnet and to Prime Minister Macdonald. For the coming season, O'Reilly was to survey and assign reserves first in Barkley Sound and on the Queen Charlotte Islands, and then continue the work he had started in the Nass and Skeena region.

Shortly before he was scheduled to leave for Barkley Sound, O'Reilly received a note from Carry. Their Atlantic crossing had been terrifying.

May 15, 1882

My own beloved husband,

No words can tell you our thankfulness for recovering from the danger we were in . . . the shaft on the *Catalonia* broke with fearful noise and the ship trembled as if torn to pieces . . . it became apparent she had no sailing capacity. The *Sarmatiac* arrived . . .

We had to climb down the ship's side on a rope ladder and as she is 5000 tons, you may think how high she is out of the water . . . Atlantic wonderfully calm but it was a trial of courage to go in a crowded small open boat . . . easier to get on board, a stairway was let down & the

Sarmatiac is only 3000 tons . . . towed our disabled ship 240 miles, out of danger of the Icebergs as we were in their corridor . . .[3]

Sir Matthew Begbie came to Point Ellice House shortly after O'Reilly had read the disturbing letter and was equally upset. He insisted Peter return home with him, judging that he should not be rattling around in his empty house, worrying about what might have happened. O'Reilly saddled up, and after a refreshing canter, the two of them settled in Sir Matthew's den, each sipping a restorative dram of brandy. Then O'Reilly noticed he was ensconced in a new and well-padded chair and complimented his friend on its comfort.

Begbie laughed aloud, knowing that Peter was not really interested in furnishings except to agree with Carry about her choices. "All right, Peter, you've done your duty. Now we'll eat."

They proceeded to the dining room, which would seat twenty-four, and O'Reilly smelled the starch from the white tablecloth. "It's an impressive table, Matthew, and it suits your new home. Now, have I told you that I will be joining Carry for almost six months next winter? My leave of absence starts in the fall, as soon as I wrap up my reports."

The chief justice said that, quite apart from being reunited with his family, it would do him good to leave BC; it would give him a fresh perspective. He then asked if the O'Reillys would be touring at all.

"Probably not, unless Carry wants to go somewhere. Since my parents are gone, I don't have to go to Ireland this trip, though I'd like to see my family there."

"I hope you do. My year away was settling for me, and I suspect that your leave will do the same for you. It's good to see the reality over there instead of reviewing old memories. Though you do appear to be less anxious. How do you like being the lands commissioner as compared to a county court judge?"

O'Reilly considered at length. "I'm glad to have the position and I think I do prefer it, although I don't like everything about it. Other than my surveyor and my interpreter, who also does the cooking, I sometimes only see Natives for weeks on end." He commented that it was easier to organize his schedule now; it was certainly more controllable than when he'd been a county court judge. Although he still had to be away from home for months at a time, his new position suited him.

"You must see many unique artifacts and be beginning to understand how one tribe differs from another. Does that interest you?" Begbie asked.

O'Reilly was startled. He did see many differences between tribes and how they built or what they created. "But Matthew, I find it all so primitive that I don't actually notice much. Mind you, Carry complains that if something doesn't have four legs, I barely see it." What he did absorb and remember in minute detail was the land: the shorelines, hills and mountain ranges, what trees and plants grew where and often the birds.

"Carry's right, you know. A horse or a dog does get your full attention," Begbie agreed as he rang for another bottle of wine.

O'Reilly told his friend that he had received a long letter from Ned Dewdney. He was now out on the prairie, liking its big skies and bright stars, but still missing BC. "Macdonald has appointed Ned the commissioner of Indian Affairs in Manitoba and changed his title to lieutenant-governor for the Northwest Territories. He wrote that despite the fancy titles, he only has 'railway workers and Indians to govern'." Ned and Jane had had a good winter in Ottawa and had often visited with Sir John and Lady Macdonald.

"Did he say anything about what's happening with the American Indians who have moved into Canada?"

"Yes, they are causing problems, mainly because of their desperate shortage of food." Dewdney had picked a central site for his headquarters and had quickly renamed it Regina—previously it had been known as Pile of Bones.

They chuckled, then Begbie said, "It puts the objections you encounter from BC chiefs and elders into a more favourable light, does it not? At least most of our Indians aren't hungry."

O'Reilly wondered aloud if Ned's Indians were as influenced by missionaries as some BC Natives were. Personally, he found most men of the cloth helpful, and liked many of them, but not all. "I also meet some who are overly opinionated, too dedicated to converting Indians. And I find the competition between missionaries for Christian adherents repugnant."

Begbie thought differently and said that despite the few bad apples, almost all of the missionaries were well-meaning men and their contribution was invaluable. He believed the Natives could not continue living as they had earlier. With the increasing influx of outsiders, it was best they learned what they needed to survive, and churches were opening schools.

Although O'Reilly questioned the value of some schools, he suggested a game of chess instead of replying, knowing that Begbie liked to argue much more than he did.

∞   ∞   ∞

By mid-June, O'Reilly and his surveyor and interpreter had set up a camp in Barkley Sound and were proceeding with mapping out reserves; they did not encounter much opposition. When they left for the Queen Charlotte Islands three weeks later, O'Reilly intended to have that region completed by mid-October, as he was to sail for England on November 2, 1882.

They completed their surveys and the marking of boundaries in the Queen Charlottes faster than expected because when O'Reilly went to meet the chief of the first village, he had not been formally acknowledged or greeted at all. Although the tension caused by being unwelcome lessened a little in the other villages, he was very aware that he and his men were on an island and they could only leave by ship. They worked quickly and finished up in record time. He wrote to Carry that he was glad to depart as he found those Indians' log houses quite overwhelming and the people overly proud.

As they travelled up and down through Queen Charlotte and Hecate straits, O'Reilly saw how busy the Pacific coast was becoming. Ships, fishing boats and barges plied its waters, transporting salmon from canneries and logs from isolated sawmills. The white population was increasing yearly as more settlers arrived to build homesteads and start to farm. Businessmen came and opened up stores or saloons while a few investigated the feasibility of another cannery.

The commissioner was repeatedly told about the number of bootleggers around Port Simpson and Port Essington. A BCPP constable confirmed that and said that he suspected more Indians than before were buying liquor. That was probably true, O'Reilly thought, perhaps because their traditional methods of gathering for various celebrations had recently been disallowed. Although under the earlier Indian Acts and in the latest one, Natives could not legally be supplied with alcohol, the revised 1880 act made holding potlatches illegal.[4]

O'Reilly personally disagreed with that new regulation; he believed potlatches were more beneficial than harmful. Since they had been outlawed, he concurred with his current interpreter and cook's opinion. "Now the money the Indians spent on potlatching will probably go to bootleggers."

That season, as O'Reilly travelled, he worked hard to complete his reports and make maps of the reserves. Whereas he had usually made rough drafts that he finalized during the winter months, he needed to have everything finished before he could leave for England: one copy went to BC's new chief commissioner of land and works, T.G. Vernon, and three were forwarded to BC Indian Superintendent Dr. Powell and officials in Ottawa. When O'Reilly returned to Point Ellice House in late

October, he had two secretaries making the copies as he finished up the originals.

O'Reilly had a set formula and all his reports began with:

I have the honor to enclose herewith for your information, and approval, sketches, and descriptions of the lands reserved by me for the . . .[5]

He would then add the specific details:

. . . use of the Ohiet, Opetchis Aht, Teshar, Toquart, Ucluclet, Uchucklesit, and Pachen Indians, situated at, or near to Barkley Sound on the West coast of Vancouver Island . . .[6]

When he continued up to the Queen Charlotte Islands, he wrote in the names of those tribes:

. . . for the use of the "Massett" and "Skidegate" tribes of Indians.[7]

Information about the reserves assigned in any area included detailed reporting on who had owned what previously, and the current users, as well as descriptions of its land features, water and timber. As in Governor Douglas's era, O'Reilly often used the markers available.

Massett a Reserve of Seven hundred, and Seventy (770) Acres, situated at the mouth of Illasset Inlet, Queen Charlotte Islands. Commencing at a Spruce marked "Indian Reserve", on the North bank of Massett Inlet, and running East ten (10) chains, then North to the Sea Coast . . .[8]

When Begbie learned O'Reilly was back, he sent a messenger, inviting his friend to tennis and dinner. O'Reilly went, hoping for a game of croquet rather than tennis, and anticipating hearing the judge's summary of what had happened during the summer.

"Did you know we had a smallpox outbreak in Yale?" Begbie asked as they had an ale after playing tennis.

O'Reilly said he did not. "How bad was it?"

"I'm not sure. Onderdonk immediately shipped out any of his workers who were exposed, to control its spread." The contractor was also losing many workers in construction accidents, mostly Chinese. As with the smallpox, the number of deaths was hushed up.

"That's awkward. Now, one of the things I want to know is whether Gilbert Sproat is still the government agent for the Kootenays?" O'Reilly asked.

"Yes, he is. How is the work of redoing his reserves?"

"Mixed. Sproat certainly was popular with the Natives and I'm not nearly as liked, but I believe I'm achieving more. Compared to his reserves, I think that mine are reserving adequate land for the Natives but still leaving enough available for future development." O'Reilly wondered if he seemed immodest.

Begbie reassured him how necessary it was to balance land use between the Natives and the newcomers, then asked, "Are your reserves being confirmed by both Canada and BC officials?"

O'Reilly replied that that was still being processed, which took time. But he'd decided it didn't matter to him, once his own report about a reserve was accepted.

After a pleasant afternoon and evening, he thanked Begbie and said, "See you next October. I am off to London—and Carry."

CHAPTER SEVENTEEN

Peter O'Reilly Visits England and Ireland

On O'Reilly's trip from New York to Portsmouth, the weather was good and the passage fast, not at all like his family's harrowing journey. The only other time he had crossed the Atlantic was when he'd emigrated to British Columbia. He recalled his relief when Governor Douglas hired him; suddenly, he also remembered his uncertainty, his dreadful homesickness—and taxing the captain's pork. What a nervous and arrogant young man he'd been. He reflected on it and decided it was like trying to compare the comfortable feather bed on this ship he had now to the narrow, hard, upper bunk he'd been assigned in 1859.

He considered how isolated he'd felt and it made him think of Frank, down in South America, and Jack. He expected his sons to grow up strong and capable, yet he knew that being trained to be an engineer was not his eldest's choice. He had wanted to be a hunting and fishing guide on Vancouver Island. For the first time, O'Reilly understood why his father had been such a firm man, and regretfully accepted that he'd become somewhat like him. On the other hand, being a guide certainly would not have enabled Frank to enjoy the quality of life he expected.

Carry met him at Portsmouth, looking healthier than she had for years, and said that the sabbatical from daily mothering was agreeing with her. Jack was in a private boarding school while Kathleen was at Lady Murray's Finishing School in London. After their perilous crossing, they had settled into their rooms in London and had a good visit with Frank, shortly before he had left for Argentina.

"Did he seem reluctant to go?" O'Reilly asked.

"No more than usual. You know that Frank dislikes change. Now, Peter, I have a request. Before you and I get tied up in schedules after Christmas, I would like us to go and tour France."

Kathleen, Frank and Jack in London, *ca.* 1883. Frank, age seventeen, is about to begin his career as an apprentice engineer. Kathleen is fifteen and Jack is ten.
IMAGE C-03940 COURTESY OF ROYAL BC MUSEUM, BC ARCHIVES

O'Reilly agreed it was a fine idea.

They began preparing for their Christmas holiday in Glasgow, and he went with her as she shopped, searching for the right gifts. Carry's cousin, Agnes, and her husband, Gordon McArthur, had invited the O'Reilly family to their large townhouse, which had over thirty rooms; it much impressed Kathleen and Jack. The festivities were constant and O'Reilly was glad when their stay ended as he found Gordon pleasant but boring. He was an accountant, not interested in anything outside financial matters. As O'Reilly knew how much Carry savoured the elaborate teas, dinner parties and balls, he tried to be social but it was wearying.

What he did take pleasure in was being with his children. They rode together most days, although Peter again realized that his younger son was not nearly as skilled with or interested in horses as his sister. Kathleen, whose fifteenth birthday had just been celebrated in Glasgow, was a natural with horses. She was also blossoming into a woman and O'Reilly watched the gentleman callers greet his daughter. He asked Carry one evening, "Do you and Puss talk about how some men are unsuitable and how cautious she has to be?"

"I have been doing that for years," Carry laughed.

When the children returned to school, the O'Reillys left for France. They had a lovely month, full of long walks, leisurely meals, interesting excursions and, in Paris, extravagant shows. Everywhere they went, Carry shopped. Since it was their first extended holiday together in the seventeen years since Frank had been born, O'Reilly told her to buy whatever she wanted and, most of the time, he managed not to cringe when she did. After all, they had funds in the bank.

They returned in mid-February because Carry had arranged for them to stay with an old friend of her mother's in London. O'Reilly decided that, instead of accompanying his wife, he would go to Ireland to see his family.

He enjoyed most of it. Being with each of his six sisters, who reminded him of Mamsey, and with their families was the highlight of the visit for him, although he had a difficult time sorting out his numerous nieces and nephews and their children. His eldest brother, Frank, who was just five years older than himself, looked worn out and sounded as depressed as their father had been. He and his family lived in Ballybeg House which was in need of serious repair. O'Reilly realized that almost all his relatives were still struggling to make a decent living and was thankful that he'd left. Ireland was not nearly as green or as appealing as he'd remembered, yet its horses were even more impressive, and O'Reilly spent as much time visiting stables as he did with his family.

On his return, he and Carry moved to a house they had been loaned outside London. He again wearied of her social schedule and tried to hide his displeasure when she went on at length about whether they were being considered provincial. She was sensitive to any perceived slight. Overly so, he felt.

O'Reilly began to go to horse meets where he found people as interested in the breeding and characteristics of horses as he was. He was invited to their homes and stables, and there, time passed quickly for him. After the children's school terms ended, the family enjoyed two pleasant months together, touring the countryside around York and the Lake District, then staying at a seaside cottage near Dover.

In early October, after helping to resettle Kathleen and Jack in their respective schools, and Carry in a small suite in London, O'Reilly sailed from Portsmouth. As Begbie had forecast, he was looking forward to returning to BC, to resuming his duties and to being back at Point Ellice House; it was his home.

He had been instructed to stop in Ottawa to discuss various issues about BC Indians. Once he arrived there, he had a busy schedule as he recorded in his diary:

October 25, 1883

Called at Ind. Office. Saw Sinclair, VanKoughnet absent.

October 26, 1883

A glorious day. Called on Sir John at his new residence & was referred by him to McPherson, minister of the interior.

November 1, 1883

A fine bracing day. Spent a couple of hours in Indian office-Dawson lunched with us . . .[1]

After many meetings and much discussion about where O'Reilly was to assign reserves in the coming season, it was decided he would return to the Okanagan and Kootenays during 1884. When that became known, many people, including politicians, stressed how accommodating he would have to be. He had to safeguard the needs of the established settlers, Sir John A. privately cautioned him. When Macdonald said, "Land and water rights for Indian reservations have to balance the needs of current and future settlers,"[2] it could have been Joe Trutch speaking.

When O'Reilly met jointly with the prime minister and Indian Superintendent General VanKoughnet, they expressed their satisfaction with what he had achieved to date but pointed out that complaints were increasing. A number of letters from powerful BC residents had been received, charging that the reserves he was allotting were overly generous. A greater number, written on behalf of chiefs and elders of some BC Indian bands, complained about the small size and poor quality of their reserves and the lack of adequate water and timber rights.

"I function within your instructions," O'Reilly told them.

VanKoughnet moved on to his next item: how to teach the Native children in BC. Another act regarding education for Indians had recently been passed in Parliament and he was being contacted by representatives of the Methodists, Anglicans and Catholics, requesting that their churches be subsidized to create boarding houses and schools. "In your opinion, does that work? How do you think education can best be achieved?"

O'Reilly replied that he'd been told most Natives made good employees and some Indians had already requested that he arrange for them to be taught "white men skills." He recommended educating the older children first, by establishing industrial training schools, one on Vancouver Island and another on the mainland. "Then hire travelling teachers, preferably not missionaries, to go to the bands in the more populated areas to teach the children, and any adults interested, a little English."

VanKoughnet said that was not how it was done in other parts of Canada. He believed that the advantage of using churches was that some such schools were already built in BC and the costs would probably be lower if churches oversaw teaching all the children. "After all, Mr. O'Reilly, it is estimated that in BC, there are over one thousand Native bands."[3]

O'Reilly was learning why Dr. Powell was often frustrated with Ottawa; he did not believe that church-directed education made sense for the BC Natives. Although that system might work in other provinces, what they wanted and needed to learn was how to make money, like the Chinese and white men. Ranchers, farmers and logging operators were searching for employees who would not move on every year. Also, when Indians could find work near their homes, it helped to create local stability, and that required them to learn the skills to do those jobs.

                                             ∞ ∞ ∞

After a month of conferring in Ottawa, O'Reilly boarded a train to San Francisco, then a ship to Victoria. On his arrival home, he wrote Carry about how lonely Point Ellice House was without her but how glad he was to be there. He reported that the gardens were flourishing and the house had been kept in excellent shape.

He settled in and caught up on all his reports and correspondence, finding it peaceful to be home with only Lee, the newest Chinese house boy, who looked after his needs and did the cooking. However, the evenings were long for him, and he gratefully accepted Joe and Julia's invitation to spend Christmas Day at Fairfield. He was even more pleased when he learned that there would only be the Trutches, Sir Matthew and himself for dinner.

John and Zoe Trutch and their two-year-old daughter, Charlotte, came down from Yale to stay with him for a brief holiday before the Christmas season, Zoe explaining that they no longer stayed at Fairfield because they felt their daughter disturbed Julia. John described how much they liked living in Yale. Even though it was jammed with the rough construction crews, he found the surveying fascinating and enjoyed watching the trestles being built. "Onderdonk's crews are laying track so fast that he believes a train will run right across the country within two years."

Later, when he and O'Reilly went to look at the expanded barn and the latest horse, John said, "Did you know that the dilly-dallying has ended about which route to use to cross the Rockies? The Rogers Pass was finally chosen." He was pleased because, despite that pass's engineering challenges, it was the most direct route to Calgary and the east.

⁂

At Christmas, when O'Reilly and Begbie joined Joe in his den for the traditional hot toddies, he proposed they make their first toast to Onderdonk. The builder had recently informed him that the track between Port Moody and Savona would be completed by the end of January 1884. After more toasts, Joe and Sir Matthew began arguing about the land grants for future railways in the Okanagan and Kootenays. Dinner interrupted the discussion, much to O'Reilly's relief.

As they were sharing a carriage, Begbie returned to fuming on their way home. "Does your brother-in-law not realize he is helping to create feudal land barons by these railway grants? Not only will they finesse the Indians out of their lands, even established settlers are at risk. And just how many railways might this province actually need?"

Although he'd just received another letter of complaint, forwarded from the Indian department in Ottawa, and knew that more of his own decisions were unpopular, O'Reilly did not tell Begbie that. Instead, full of good food and feeling relaxed, he said, "Matthew, you know that I often do not agree with Joe's opinions or his tactics."

∞ ∞ ∞

O'Reilly was just about to leave for the Kootenays when, on February 26, 1884, he received a telegram from Superintendent Powell, asking him to come to Chilliwack immediately. A fifteen-year-old lad, Louie Sam, from the Sto:lo tribe, had been lynched after being accused of killing an American shopkeeper.

A mob of about a hundred vigilantes from nearby Nooksack, Washington, had raced to Chilliwack, knocked out the provincial constable and taken Louie Sam from the cell he'd been put in for his protection. They hanged him, just five hundred feet north of the Canada–United States border. Hundreds of Sto:lo had hurried to the area, and some wanted to begin killing Americans immediately.

The Sto:lo elders who disagreed with this action managed to prevail, backed up by the BC Provincial Police constables and numerous government officials, including Dr. Powell and O'Reilly. On their arrival, they learned that the accusation had been made by the man who was probably the murderer.[4] After lengthy discussions, Louie Sam's relatives and band members decided to leave it to Canada to punish the guilty.[5]

Powell told O'Reilly to continue to the Kootenays and he left to meet

Andy Brown, his surveyor, in Hope. They headed out to Wild Horse Creek with a pack train of six animals and four men, knowing that they would not be back until November. O'Reilly sent Joe Trutch a message to please meet Carry when she returned in late April. Kathleen and Jack were remaining in England for at least another year, to continue their schooling.

꩜ ꩜ ꩜

O'Reilly learned on his arrival that the East Kootenay region was also having confrontations with Indians. Chief Isadore of the Kootenae tribe was threatening to remove any settlers encroaching on their lands. Gilbert Sproat, now the government agent for the territory between Wild Horse Creek and Farwell, explained that he had not taken any action because BC's new premier, William Smithe, had ordered all agents not to attempt to resolve any of the Dominion's problems.

O'Reilly knew that Smithe, who had been the provincial treasurer and secretary before being elected premier, had campaigned on his strong belief that the Dominion must assume its constitutional responsibilities. That included all the administration of Indians, including costs.

Sproat told O'Reilly that was why he had not been authorized to do anything about the settlers' difficulties with Chief Isadore. As well, he had only one constable assigned to patrol the whole East Kootenay, and when it appeared that man's safety might be at risk, he'd told him to leave. He also warned, "Do not expect these Indians to accept just a pittance of land." Both were aware that many members of the large Kootenae tribe moved back and forth across the border and knew that the American government was granting miles of land for reserves there. "And, Mr. O'Reilly, you had best begin assigning reserves before all the good land is taken up." Sproat was obviously mindful of the generous settlements being made by Joe Trutch to investors who were claiming they intended to build railways in the future.

During March, O'Reilly assigned a number of reserves, though marking the boundaries on each one was difficult. The Kootenae bands were demanding acreages larger than he could authorize, and when their elders did not agree with his decisions, they refused to co-operate further and ordered his team to leave. After one confrontation, the commissioner suspected that he and his men were in increasing danger and decided to return to the Okanagan.

When they reached that area, he discovered it was not peaceful either, and there were again potential risks. The Okanagan Indians and settlers were at odds, threatening violence to each other over water, timber rights and joint pasturelands. After O'Reilly learned of some non-English-speaking immigrants who were reportedly creating secret societies to support each other, he felt that they were more dangerous than any Indians. If one of those settlers did not like the location of a reserve boundary, he ignored it, then threatened any Native who protested, knowing he would be well backed up if it came to actual fighting.

O'Reilly tried to find out more about those informal groups but without success. He told his men that no one was to work alone or take any risks as they continued to reassess and change the boundaries on the reserves assigned by Sproat in 1879 but not ratified by Canada. When the season ended, he and his surveyor felt it had been a tough year.

When he finally returned to Point Ellice House, exhausted and looking forward to a peaceful winter with Carry, a letter from Premier Smithe awaited him:

Since you have assumed the work of laying out reserves, I am bound to say that it is much fairer and more accurate . . . but in the Kootenay, you overestimated the requirements of the Indians and under-estimated those of the whites . . .[6]

O'Reilly replied on December 4, 1884:

I had the utmost difficulty in persuading the Kootenaes to agree to the boundaries fixed on by me, and they looked upon them as meagre in the extreme, compared to the millions of acres set apart by the United States Government for American Indians, a few miles south . . . I think it important . . . Indians living on the frontier should have no reasonable ground of complaint, and in this view I feel sure you will concur.[7]

He was unsure whether the premier would agree but hoped that Prime Minister Macdonald and Superintendents Powell and VanKoughnet would; he had of course copied his reply to them. They were well aware that although BC had had the clauses about their lands exempted from the Indian Act in 1876, the province and Ottawa were about to be united by the Canadian Pacific Railway. He hoped that the Dominion and, more particularly, the Department of Indian Management, would finally administer their responsibilities to BC's Indians more efficiently. As well, he knew the rail connection would allow Canada to transfer militia from other areas quickly, if required.

When he mentioned that to Carry, she pointed out that their own personal world was also changing. With all their children away, she had briefly considered travelling with him as he worked but had soon realized that she was not Sarah Crease. Although her friend was willing to accept primitive conditions to go with Henry occasionally when he was holding his courts, Carry had decided she needed her comforts. She could meet him in New Westminster or spend a week or so at the Cornwalls or in Kamloops, but more than that would not suit her.

O'Reilly did not tell his wife that having to share his tent would not have been comfortable for him either. He also did not volunteer that his task was becoming more perilous in the field. It would only worry her to know that few tribes were staying within their reserve's boundaries and that the number of confrontations between Indians and settlers was increasing.

Both sides regularly reported to government officials and journalists that O'Reilly's decisions displeased them, and more formal complaints were being made to Ottawa about the size and limitations of BC reserves. To date, the Nootka, Kwatiutl, Comox, Secwepemc, Okanagan, Kootenae, Sto:lo, Nlaka'pamux, Lillooet, Chilcotin, Salish, Gitxsan, Nisga'a, Tsimshian and others had challenged the limitations being imposed on their people.

O'Reilly believed that it was only a few Indians who counselled violence when settlers or canneries or mines encroached on their livelihood but was aware that could change overnight. When VanKoughnet queried the situation, he said that, at the current time, most Indians remained patient, probably because the number of infringements on their lands was still relatively insignificant. He did not point out that whenever previous pasturelands were fenced off or almost all the available water taken or the salmon harvest restricted by fishery regulations, most Native people showed their anger.

He was always nervous about saying something that might make Ottawa officials overreact, although on occasion, he found some native positions justified. One such situation had occurred with the Songhees, whose reserves were within Victoria. A year ago, some of their land was desired by white residents and the chiefs adamantly refused to consider being moved to a new reserve. O'Reilly had reviewed the situation as requested, conferred with Superintendent Powell and written to Sir Alexander Campbell, Canada's minister of justice on their behalf:

I see no present necessity for removing, from their dearly prized present reservation, the Victoria Indians. [Songhees] The men work on the wharves and otherwise, and the females do as washerwomen, seamstresses, laundresses, earn much and spend it all in the City—The money might otherwise go to chinamen who would spend but a fraction of it in the province . . . I can think of no defensible, humanitarian plea for now disturbing the Songhees . . .[8]

O'Reilly thought the issue was closed and he was disturbed when it arose again in early 1885; a group of Victoria's residents again decided that the Songhees had to move. He contacted Ottawa and was annoyed to be told that the matter was being studied and a decision would be made in due course.

O'Reilly was also told that more mission schools were to be funded, despite Campbell's recommendations after a recent tour of BC. He had been sent to assess whether the established mission schools were fulfilling the Natives' education needs, and his conclusions had been similar to O'Reilly's. Campbell had decided that it was best to fund industrial schools, to concentrate on teaching the Indian children skills rather than religious training and British ethics.[9]

O'Reilly wondered whether Campbell's advice was ignored because Ottawa officials were overwhelmed with work. The prairies had exploded into open warfare, which probably meant that the issues of managing BC Indians were receiving little consideration. Or perhaps the decision about educating BC Indians was a demonstration of the power held by the churches that owned the existing missionary schools. He was aware that the related government grants added significantly to church coffers and that each student brought into a residential school was immediately counted as a Christian, increasing the count for that denomination. He poked around through unofficial channels but was unable to find out why Campbell's recommendations had not been heeded.

֍   ֍   ֍

On April 18, 1885, O'Reilly and Carry were in a dreadful accident as they drove into Victoria to meet friends for dinner. The spirited gelding was startled by a newspaper page blowing in the wind; it then became tangled in the harness and panicked. Their light carriage overturned and the horse dragged it for quite a distance, trapping O'Reilly inside. Carry was thrown out and was badly shaken up, her shoulder and back very bruised, but her husband was severely injured. The doctors found that he had significant internal damage and that his right leg, which had been broken in three places, could not be completely repaired.

Transferred immediately to his own bedroom, O'Reilly spent the first month in a blur of pain and medication with full-time nurses; then his long recuperation began. He had to stay flat in bed for weeks, and when he was finally allowed to start sitting up, he realized that no matter how much he willed himself to move, his body did not respond. He began to accept that he would probably never fully recover.

When Sir Matthew returned from an extended trip to the interior, O'Reilly admitted he was not an ideal patient. "Even Carry is becoming quite terse with me." He explained that her favourite maid had recently quit after he had been too abrupt with her, and Carry had since demanded that he not talk directly to any of the servants. He was allowed to ask only her for anything he needed. She'd also pointed out that, although she was assisted by the orderly who came in for part of each day, she was still suffering considerable pain herself. He had apologized profusely, but the reality was, he was a burden.

"It is hard. It takes a long time for a body to heal but you will," Begbie said.

"Maybe. I hate this, Matthew. I don't know whether I will ever be able to ride a horse again."

Begbie bluntly told him he was lucky to be alive and that he had best be more patient and much more considerate, particularly with Carry and the servants. He asked what books O'Reilly was reading to pass the time, and when he confessed he hadn't started one because he was also getting headaches, Sir Matthew lectured him. "Well, start! There is no point letting your brain go to mush, just because your body is badly injured." Then he changed the subject. "What do you hear from Ned Dewdney?"

"Just condolences so far. What do you expect will happen out there? Ned must be right in the centre of the conflict with Louis Riel and his Métis. I don't know much about it because Carry has decided I'm better off if I don't read the newspapers yet. They depress me." O'Reilly had been told by another visitor that the military had been sent in to end the fighting on the prairies.

"Riel will either be killed in the fighting or hanged," Begbie predicted.

In fact, Riel was hanged on November 16, 1885, just nine days after dignitaries, investors and builders had gathered at Craigellachie, BC, to celebrate the last spike being driven into the CPR main line. By that time O'Reilly was reading every newspaper available. Edgar Dewdney, lieutenant-governor of the Northwest Territories, had signed Riel's death warrant, directed to do so by Sir John A. Macdonald, and O'Reilly recalled that when he'd been the colonial sheriff, Ned had hoped he would never have to do such a thing.

By then, O'Reilly was moving around but with great difficulty, confined to an invalid chair and requiring help to be transferred in and out of it. In September, he had started doing a few of his official duties as he was worried about how long Ottawa would give him to recuperate on full salary before they replaced him as commissioner.

He had also gone to Nanaimo when settlers ignored reserve boundaries there. Frank, now nineteen, had come home on leave in late September and agreed to take his father and his chair up the island. After O'Reilly had settled the dispute, he felt better about himself than he had since April. He then decided that he would like to resume all his work, if his son would join the commission staff, technically as a surveyor but mainly as his father's assistant. Frank did so, and they made three more short trips, but even with that additional help, O'Reilly found travelling painful and his leg became ulcerated again.

When Frank was asked to return to Buenos Aires by the engineer supervising his training, he left, first having a private talk with each of his parents. He told his father that he was glad to have spent time with him and was sure that his leg would heal. Then he lectured his cherished mother about her well-being and pointed out that even though his father had lost a lot of weight, he was still too heavy for her to lift. They must hire more help.

When Carry told Peter what Frank had said, they found William, a strong giant of a man who was charmed with Carry and took charge of Peter's needs. He joined their household staff and stayed on for almost two years.

After the holiday season, O'Reilly began to instruct his surveyor, Andy Brown, on where and how to have the commission team do the fieldwork; his doctor had demanded he remain at Point Ellice House until the latest ulcer healed. He sent his men to areas of Vancouver Island and the lower mainland where the Indian bands would accept the final surveying of boundaries. Then, when all the maps and measurements were returned to him, he produced his usual precise reports, although his physical descriptions were shorter.

He also persisted with a rigorous exercise schedule and endured many manipulations of his leg, trying to regain more use of it. Eighteen months after the carriage overturned, O'Reilly started to walk again with the aid of two canes, celebrating each slow, short trip with Carry. Shortly after that, he bought himself a low cart and a pony so he was able to travel about again.

When he arrived home after his first outing, to a nearby horse breeder, Carry said, "My prayers have been answered."

The injury to O'Reilly's leg changed his life. Although his walking improved, he almost always needed a cane, and he never knew when another ulcer would erupt. He would then have to keep that leg raised to lessen the possibility of its becoming gangrenous. He and Carry went to San Francisco to have his overall health reviewed, and the results of those medical tests reassured them. His internal injuries had healed and, other than his leg, he was in excellent condition for a man of fifty-nine.

O'Reilly rejoined the commission in the summer of 1886 and, with William assisting, he managed well. Since he could no longer tramp over fields and through forests to decide on the reserve boundaries himself, he directed his survey team from his tent. He stopped calling on chiefs and elders before beginning the surveys; instead, and without any explanations for his lack of mobility, he ordered that they come to him. That offended many of them, as he learned during an evening with Sir Matthew in New Westminster. The judge had been at an Indian village whose chief reported that O'Reilly had been there recently and that he was an unfriendly and arrogant man.

"Why do you not explain how hard it is for you to walk?"

"I've decided not to do that. I'll just keep on doing the best I can," O'Reilly replied good-naturedly.

"You do seem less prickly than you used to be, at least to me," Begbie said.

O'Reilly considered that comment as he sipped a small glass of wine. He did not confide that he seldom had a headache anymore. He had told Carry, who said that perhaps it was because he was not drinking brandy or port since he'd become cautious about his balance.

In January, she'd also told Peter that she was tired of all the long months on her own, and she was lonely without any of her children or family in Victoria. John, Zoe and Charlotte were still in Yale while Joe and Julia were again in England. "We need to resume our social life," she declared, and he said she was right. The O'Reillys began accepting invitations, having small dinner parties at Point Ellice House and meeting friends in town.

Neither of them could ride after the accident so O'Reilly sold two of his horses, keeping only the mare, which Kathleen had claimed as her own, and his pony. He bought a reliable old horse to pull Carry's new cariole, which was the latest style and even had a folding canvas top. They spent much time planning how to expand Point Ellice's landscaping, where to add on to the house and how to redecorate it.

They entertained often, and some of the guests who decided to visit surprised them. This was the case when Sir John A. and Lady Macdonald sent a messenger to see if it was convenient for them to come for tea. Lady Macdonald and Carry toured the gardens while the men visited, and she asked for a clipping from one of Carry's cream-coloured roses.[10]

Most people continued to refer to O'Reilly as "Judge," and it became usual for newspapers to report on the social activities of Judge and Mrs. O'Reilly. He corrected them occasionally but then decided it didn't matter. What was important to him was that he and Carry were again healthy, and cheerful with each other, most of the time.

After the Point Ellice Bridge was built, the O'Reilly family could watch its traffic from their wharf on the Gorge.
IMAGE C-00463 COURTESY OF ROYAL BC MUSEUM, BC ARCHIVES

CHAPTER EIGHTEEN

The Last Years

By the 1887 season, O'Reilly's leg had healed enough that he and his men were able to go to northeast Vancouver Island, the Kootenays, the Okanagan and, finally, the Fraser district. With the increasing number of lake steamers and the railway, he found travelling easier, especially as he stayed at roadhouses when they were available, rather than in his large tent. The survey team assessing what land to assign to each Indian reserve was supervised by his assistant, Ashton Green, who, O'Reilly had decided, was as adept as himself. So, once he agreed with Green's recommendations of the new boundaries, he worked on the related reports and maps while the surveyor oversaw the placing of the pegs.

A provincial commission looking into settler–Indian relations had recently been announced and, since O'Reilly would be a primary witness, he was reviewing all his reports. A powerful delegation of northwest Indians had requested the commission be set up because of the serious confrontations and ongoing threats in the Skeena and Nass regions. They charged that their lands were being illegally taken over by white men and that Canada was ignoring it, and they wanted Premier Smithe to formally examine whether all the land transactions under dispute were legal.

When Smithe suddenly died, his replacement, Alexander Davie, expanded the terms of the commission and added more questions. He wanted to know details of the land, water and timber grants as well as information about the Natives' general well-being and what was being done to educate them. He asked bluntly, "Why are Indians not being hired when many business managers and the owners of canneries and mills claim that they are unable to find employees?" Davie was against bringing more contract Chinese labourers to British Columbia and was demanding to know more about the supposed labour shortage.

The provincial commission started hearings in the spring of 1887 when it sat briefly in Port Simpson; then it moved to Victoria and continued to drag on for months. O'Reilly's letters and reports to Ottawa, of which copies were always sent to the BC land and works commissioner, were often read aloud and formed the basis of discussions. He was frequently called to the witness stand to explain and interpret, which was quite nerve-wracking for him; he clearly understood how his replies might upset his Dominion employers. Indian spokesmen and journalists often excerpted his words and reported the issue incorrectly, as though O'Reilly had publicly stated that faith had not been kept with the Natives.

"Well, the only thing that really matters is how Ottawa reacts and whether they keep on paying me. We'll just have to wait and see. Let's go to bed," O'Reilly said, after one such misinterpretation.

Carry had expected him to be enraged; she laughed and said that he certainly was not the man she'd married. That one would have stayed up all night, worrying.

Over the next years, formal protests by BC Indian bands became common and resulted in numerous hearings and commissions by the Canadian and British Columbian authorities. O'Reilly usually had to attend these and to explain what he had intended in his decisions. It was a challenge for him because many of the acreages, and water and timber rights, being questioned had been assigned by him in the early 1880s and since then, some reserves had been revised for railway right-aways or other reasons. He found the hearings tedious, but he also believed they helped make Natives more comfortable with the radical changes that had happened in their lives—and if the Dominion wanted to pay him for that rather than setting reserve boundaries, so be it.

☙ ☙ ☙

After bloody conflicts between the Kootenae Indians and some settlers, the Dominion decided that the Kootenaes needed a lesson. The North West Mounted Police force had men available, since the railway was completed and the prairie rebellion was over, and about a hundred of them were transferred to the East Kootenay for one year. They established Fort Steele and built solid barracks, barns and offices. That clearly demonstrated Canada's power to the few settlers and the elusive Kootenae bands, and so did the troops parading and patrolling throughout the countryside. They engaged in no encounters and their only enemy was mountain fever (now called typhoid).

In November 1887, O'Reilly again left for England as he had been granted a leave of absence. He was meeting Carry and Kathleen, and they would then stay with Julia and Joe Trutch in their leased mansion in London. Carry had gone earlier, excited that Kathleen had finished her schooling, and wanting to help prepare her wardrobe before she was to make her debut as an eligible young woman. Jack was still in school, planning to become a lawyer, as his Uncle Joe continued to encourage him.

The O'Reilly family had a relaxing Christmas with the Trutches before the main event of the season. Joe and Julia gave a gala party for Kathleen's twentieth birthday on December 31, 1887, and her closest friends from her school years, and their brothers, attended, as did many of her extended family in England and Scotland. Kathleen wore a layered, white tulle dress that she and Carry had taken weeks to choose; her father had not been told its cost. The gifts were extravagant and included her Grandmother Trutch's precious piano from her mother and a harp from her Aunt Julia. She also received a surprise trip from Carry and Peter; the three of them were to depart for Spain in March.

They enjoyed that spring visit, particularly the spectacular cathedrals and the flamenco dancers. However, all three found the food did not suit them, and O'Reilly learned that Kathleen had a tendency to question many of her parents' comments or suggestions. He was glad to return to England and told Joe, "Travelling with two women is a lot different from being with just one."

In May, he and Carry left for Switzerland as, at Zoe Musgrave Trutch's instigation, O'Reilly was going to be assessed at the Zurich clinic by the doctors who had helped to ease her brother's leg pains. During his stay at the impressive clinic, he gained some additional leg flexion, but he was vexed by the doctors' and nurses' concern about the two small, weeping ulcers on his leg. O'Reilly explained they were quite usual, but the doctors recommended he stay for another few weeks and take experimental

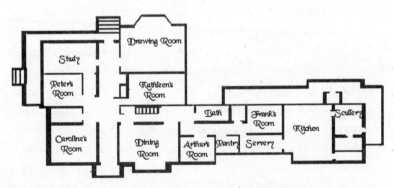

Floor plan of Point Ellice House after its expansion in 1888–89.
IMAGE COURTESY OF POINT ELLICE HOUSE

medication that might eliminate the possibility of gangrene. Because many medications made O'Reilly ill, he declined. He was discharged and he and Carry carried on to France for a holiday.

As they travelled, Carry shopped for materials to complete the redecorating of Point Ellice House from her sketches and measurements of their renovated house. They had enlarged the dining room and kitchen, and the parlour and den were to be redone on her return.

O'Reilly accompanied her while she looked for the carpets, mirrors, wallpaper, drapery materials and china required, but she no longer asked him whether she should buy something. Since he had few helpful opinions, and had allotted her the budget she'd requested, their arrangement was that she would make the purchases without further consultation. When he dared to question the cost of a large mirror, she was enraged, and he apologized in a letter:

> I must again impress on you that I have never intended to object to your getting anything you want or like . . . what I had intended to say was that there is a great necessity for keeping a correct entry of what you spend & to get what you want as cheaply as you can.[1]

When O'Reilly's leave was almost over, he wondered how his wife and daughter would manage in the little suite they had recently leased. The Trutches were also returning to Victoria, but Carry had decided to stay for another six months, partly to be close to Jack, as he had difficult exams coming up, and partly to chaperone their daughter. Kathleen's antics were wearing on her nerves, she admitted to Peter and asked for his suggestions just before he left to catch his ship.

He wrote her from the Cunard Royal Steamship *Etruria* on June 24, 1888:

My dearest wife:

The first & best will be to take care of yourself & not worry about trifles. The next is to teach dear Puss to go to bed in proper time, get up early and do something useful every day & to be punctual; this would tend much to her happiness . . .

Good bye, my dearest Carry

Always your aff. loving husband

P. O'Reilly[2]

He was in Ottawa in time for meetings with Sir John A. Macdonald, Dr. Powell, Indian Superintendent VanKoughnet and Ned Dewdney, who had recently been named Canada's minister of the interior. This appointment meant that Dewdney would also become the new Superintendent General of Indian Affairs since VanKoughnet was to retire shortly.

O'Reilly was pleased, although somewhat chagrined that his longtime friend was to become his most senior superior officer. His discomfort increased when he tried to discuss the differences between the tribes in BC from those on the prairies and Ned became huffy. After that, despite the necessity of his salary for his family's well-being, he decided he would not moderate his opinions to appease Ned, and they became quite formal with each other.

In the spring of 1890, the Methodist Church questioned whether Commissioner O'Reilly had a bias against missionaries and churches educating Indians. He had to travel to Ottawa to answer those charges and was on the witness stand for days, feeling that he was being put in an impossible position. He considered resigning as the BC Indian Reserve Lands Commissioner but realized the only way he could do that would be to sell Point Ellice House, and he was not prepared to do so. He became pragmatic as the years passed and even more taciturn.

Increasing numbers of studies into how to better manage the needs of the Indians were under way, funded by both BC and the Dominion.

The Methodist Church underwrote an extensive investigation in which Joe Trutch, now Sir Joseph, was cited as being mainly responsible for the problems of the BC Indians, and O'Reilly was named as the man who had imposed most of the policies his brother-in-law had initiated. Carry and Kathleen were upset by the publicity that followed, but O'Reilly was not. "I have always done my job to the best of my ability and as I was directed. What more can a man do?"

After his return from testifying in Ottawa, O'Reilly met with Sir Matthew and John Trutch for an evening and volunteered that he'd found the official climate in the capital quite changed. Sir John A.'s various underlings were positioning themselves to support his successor, and the conversation turned to what would happen when Macdonald retired or died.

O'Reilly said he'd have to tread carefully himself since the Indian complainants from BC normally named and blamed him, and many of the bureaucrats in the Indian Affairs department in Ottawa agreed. They did not understand that assigning reserves did not make Peter O'Reilly responsible for all facets of the Natives' well-being and education. Also, there would be changes in the management of BC Indians; Dr. Powell had confided that he was resigning soon, frustrated with Ottawa's ongoing delays in authorizing the programs and improvements he was trying to establish. "Powell said he is getting too old for all that nonsense."

John Trutch commented dryly, "Yes, aren't we all? Joe's last letter from Ottawa said that he and Julia are glad he retired, and I'm considering doing that soon myself."

O'Reilly said that he hoped to continue working for a number of years, though he did not point out that it was mainly for his stipend.

"You will be, because both governments have ratified those decisions of yours. If they change commissioners now, it will look as if your decisions were wrong, and there will be more challenges to the reserves," Sir Matthew said.

"I hope my superiors agree." After being questioned by Dewdney, O'Reilly had again been reviewing the records of the reserves he had shaped and had decided that there were only a few he would have handled differently. He now understood, although he hadn't at first, how critical it was to give the Indians adequate timber rights as well as water and land. Some bands did not own enough trees to cut for their winter heating and cooking. He knew that, in a few years and because of his decisions, the Dominion was going to have to buy firewood for some bands, probably at first in the lower Okanagan.

John said he'd been told that the province was finally meeting its annual estimates of how many immigrants were arriving. "I expect that now there will be more problems. The newcomers will pre-empt and immediately direct the local Indians not to trespass through their property."

O'Reilly considered that opinion in the following months, recognizing John was right about what was happening. When he was ordered to resurvey some original reserve boundaries to allow for more new pre-emptions or railways, the complaints increased. The reserve lands were again reduced or switched from one area to another, at either the Dominion's or the province's discretion, and often the new property did not have the same benefits.

When Dr. Powell left to become the first chancellor of the University of British Columbia, his assistant, A.W. Vowell, who had been O'Reilly's constable in the Wild Horse Creek gold rush, replaced him as the Indian superintendent for BC.

When he became O'Reilly's immediate superior, Vowell assured him that there would be few changes and said, tongue-in-cheek, "We'll just keep plodding along, attempting to accommodate the Natives within all the confusion." Every year, Canada's and BC's officials hotly debated who was responsible for what, and it became a challenge for officials to pick which orders to follow.

"Interpreting directions has become a little muddy, hasn't it?" O'Reilly remarked.

Vowell thought the same thing and volunteered that he had three main concerns. First, more smallpox epidemics were occurring in BC and, second, he was uncertain about the value of the churches' education: young Indians did not seem to be qualified for most jobs. "However, my greatest worry is the new fishing regulations. What if the Indians are not allowed to take enough salmon for the winter?"

O'Reilly noted that those were valid issues without giving any opinions, and again realized how weary he was becoming. He felt envious of Powell's decision to start a new career, but he did not want to risk making any such change himself.

He left on an extended survey trip with his team but was often distracted by thoughts of Kathleen, his dear girl, as he tried to help her decide what was best for her. A Royal Navy lieutenant-commander, Henry Stanhope, heir to the Earl of Chesterfield and a long-time friend of the family, had proposed to Kathleen and she and her father had debated the possible marriage at length before his departure. Reams of correspondence flew between O'Reilly, Kathleen and Henry as they dithered over what she wanted.

Henry was ideal in many ways, and Kathleen was very fond of him, but she was hesitant about moving to England. "Will I be happy living on his estate in England when he inherits it?" she wrote repeatedly to her father. In a multitude of letters to Stanhope over months, O'Reilly questioned his future intentions in minute detail.

Kathleen changed her mind regularly, but eventually, after much turmoil and drama, she decided that living at Point Ellice House with her "darling parents" was preferable to marrying a naval officer, even a future earl. She declined.

∽ ∽ ∽

After Sir John A. Macdonald's death, John J. Abbott became prime minister for two years, then it was J.S.D. Thompson for just over a year before he was replaced by Mackenzie Bowell. Similarly, in British Columbia, changes were frequent after Alexander Davie died. In just over six years, the premiership went from John Robson to Theodore Davie to John Turner (the O'Reillys' neighbour). Through all these political transitions and the increased delays in decision making, O'Reilly continued on as the BC Indian Reserve Lands Commissioner.

In November 9, 1892, Ned Dewdney was appointed lieutenant-governor of BC. Carry was pleased to have the Dewdneys living in Victoria; Peter had not told her that the relationship might not be as close as it had been.

On the tennis lawn at Point Ellice House. Kathleen O'Reilly is in the centre, with her brothers in front of her. Peter and Carry O'Reilly are behind her on the bench, with Henry Stanhope.

It was not until Sir Matthew Begbie died, on June 11, 1894, that the coolness between O'Reilly and Dewdney was healed. Dewdney's staff arranged the formal funeral, but the lieutenant-governor acknowledged that, as O'Reilly was Begbie's executor and closest friend, his suggestions were to be followed. He had to be the chief mourner, as Begbie's brother could not reach Victoria in time, and Ned thanked him for walking behind Sir Matthew's coffin, acknowledging how challenging it must have been because of his leg.

After that, the Dewdneys began to visit at Point Ellice House again; formalities were forgotten and the friendship resumed, as comfortable as it had been in earlier years. Ned and Peter now sat in lawn chairs rather than competing at croquet while Carry and Jane drank tea and often discussed Kathleen, mulling over who might be a suitable beau for her.

Carry enjoyed being meticulously dressed and, as she matured, people
began telling her that she reminded them of her mother.
IMAGE A-08347 COURTESY OF ROYAL BC MUSEUM, BC ARCHIVES

When the Point Ellice Bridge collapsed on August 16, 1896, O'Reilly was away, but Carry and the Dewdneys worked together to help. Tents were set up on the O'Reilly lawns to feed the people searching for survivors. Carry emptied her larder, got food from all the neighbours and organized the cooks using her kitchen. A few weeks later, she was recognized at Government House, formally thanked for her aid by Ned. The Dewdneys returned to Ottawa for Ned to preside at the celebrations marking Queen Victoria's diamond jubilee in June 1897, and the O'Reillys missed them.

The next year, Jane Dewdney returned for a visit and told Carry that after Ned's pending retirement, they planned to tour Europe for a year and would then buy a home in Victoria. "I'm looking forward to living close to you." The women spent much of their visit considering Kathleen. They were unsure whether the young woman had made the right decision turning down Henry Stanhope, particularly as she now seemed to be implying to her mother that she regretted it.

"Do you think she was still pining for Lieutenant Robert Scott, that young naval officer, when Henry was courting her?" Jane asked.

Carry suspected that was a strong possibility but she had never asked. She was glad that Kathleen was currently in Ireland, about to go to a grand ball and be formally presented to the Lord Lieutenant of Ireland. "Peter pretends to fuss about the expenses of her dress and flowers but he is pleased." She confided to Jane that she was hoping her daughter might meet someone there as she would be turning thirty-one in December; she wondered why none of her children had found mates. Her sons were now living nearby, though Frank travelled almost as much as his father did, and seemed to have few friends. Jack was busy courting a variety of girls and did not admit to being charmed by any one in particular.

Jane reminded Carry that at least she had children to be concerned about whereas she and Ned had not been so blessed. Then she laughed and asked whether Carry realized how lucky they had each been in her choice of husband. "We still like our men, all these years later. How many of our friends can say that?"

They were sitting in the little gazebo beside the wharf on the Gorge, looking up at Point Ellice House. "Yes, Peter and I are having a good life together, Jane, and so are you," Carry replied. "Isn't it incredible that it's over forty years since we danced all night at your wedding?"

In 1898, shortly after he turned seventy-one, O'Reilly received his notice of retirement. Superintendent Vowell was directed to take over his duties temporarily.

During O'Reilly's retirement ceremony, it was recognized that he had travelled to every corner of BC and had made twenty-six major trips to assign the majority of the province's Indian reserves. When he replied to the speeches, O'Reilly told his listeners about some of those journeys: how he'd felt being under a canoe in freezing water, how spectacular it had been to awaken to the sun coming up over the Rockies, how proud he had been when one chief, who had liked his band's land boundaries, named his first son Peter. In conclusion, he said, "I have been privileged to help us develop from a colony to a stable and powerful province. Like most of you, I'm an immigrant, but British Columbia became my home. I am grateful for that."

In late 1899, when Carry learned that Joe was seriously ill, she insisted she and Peter had to go to England. Julia had died four years before and he had no family with him. "We have to go. Joe cannot die alone!"

He could not refuse her, even though she was very frail herself, and he was relieved when Kathleen decided she would accompany her aging parents. The train trip to Halifax was cold and uncomfortable, and the Atlantic's winter storms battered and delayed their ship. Carry had been coughing and unwell when they boarded, and she became increasingly ill during the voyage. Kathleen and Peter were constantly at her bedside, often softly singing her favourite hymns and sponging her burning body. The ship's surgeon advised she had to have more liquid and they tried to feed her a little water or broth, but she could not swallow because she was choking on phlegm. When the ship docked at Portsmouth, Carry was transferred to a private hospital but it was too late. She died a few hours later.

O'Reilly confided to his diary and, later, used the same words to write to their closest friends:

My darling is gone. The brave, unselfish heart was worn out.[3]

Caroline Trutch O'Reilly was buried in Cheriton, Kent, England, in the pouring rain. O'Reilly and Kathleen then returned to Somerset with Sir Joe Trutch, who had been carried to his sister's graveside in a litter.

O'Reilly's grief overwhelmed him and he soon decided he had to return to Point Ellice House. He asked Kathleen to remain in England for a few months, both to give Joe the care her mother wanted him to have, and because he needed time alone; Frank and Jack could look after him.

By the time he reached home, gaunt and ill, he was able to walk only by using two canes and only for very short distances. He sat by the fire in the den for weeks, and what slowly revived him were the gardens he and Carry had cherished. He reminisced with her as though she were at his side when the early roses and honeysuckle began blooming in the soft colours she had loved. He told his sons that he was not at all lonely because he was having silent conversations with Carry, wherever he happened to be. "I need time to think about all my memories. Let me be alone."

Frank and Jack, still bachelors, worried about him, then slowly became their father's closest friends, along with his former surveyor, Ashton Green, who called on him every Wednesday afternoon.

Jack had recently joined the law firm of Drake Jackson while Frank was a well-established surveyor and engineer. By June, O'Reilly's health had improved somewhat and each son tried to interest him in outings, regularly inviting him for dinner or offering to take him to his club.

"Not yet. I cannot. I still need to stay home for a time, but I do appreciate it when you drop by and we can have dinner together here."

When Kathleen returned in midsummer, she took over the management of Point Ellice House and the two remaining servants. That October, O'Reilly began to question why she was still wearing black dresses. "Puss, times have changed."

She told him tartly, "Father, I like being traditional."

It was a full year after Carry's death when Kathleen began inviting close friends and extended family members for dinners and teas. She also managed to persuade her father to accompany her to St. Saviour's Church most Sundays, and that became O'Reilly's weekly outing. Except for going to the occasional meeting about his modest investments, he remained at home, perhaps because he was increasingly crippled. His leg was deteriorating painfully.

When Kathleen entertained guests at an elaborate dinner, a tennis or croquet tournament or a picnic for which everyone had to arrive by boat and be dressed in white, he warmly welcomed each person, but did not stay for long. After chatting with various individuals, usually about either their families or horses, O'Reilly retired to his den and closed the door. He told Kathleen it pleased him that most of her friends were the children or grandchildren of his and Carry's friends—the Turners, the Helmckens, the Pembertons and the extensive Douglas families.

His own visitors were few and he did not encourage many callers to stay for long. Some, like Arthur Vowell, still Canada's superintendent for BC Indian Affairs and the temporary Indian Reserve Lands Commissioner, were expected have lunch. Their discussions sometimes depressed O'Reilly as he found little had changed, but they also allowed him to find out what was happening and to recall all the various places he'd travelled.

One day in the fall of 1902, Vowell related all the latest complaints and disputes and asked, "Have you heard that British Columbia now has one hundred and fifty thousand non-Native residents? Amazing, isn't it, since we had fewer than fifty thousand ten years ago."

O'Reilly mulled that. "Joe was right. If you limit the Indians to reserves, settlers will eventually come and our province will flourish."

In the third year after Carry's death, O'Reilly grew concerned about Kathleen; she was in her mid-thirties and he still hoped she would find a husband. She seemed unsettled and when he asked why she seldom played her harp, she replied, "I miss Mother too much when I do." He encouraged

Peter O'Reilly on the lawn at Point Ellice House, *ca.* 1900.
IMAGE COURTESY OF POINT ELLICE HOUSE

her to return to England and, after Joe died, she did, mainly to wind up her uncle's affairs and to bring the Trutch treasures she had inherited back to Point Ellice House. When she returned a year later, she told her father that she had contacted the still-unmarried Henry Stanhope, who was now the Earl of Chesterfield. Henry had been civil but he had not wished to become reacquainted.

After that sad news, O'Reilly took his afternoon tea out to Carry's table, still in its usual place by the heart-shaped rose garden above the Gorge. As he frequently told his children, when he sat there, he believed Carry was nearby, waiting for him on the other side of the veil. He continued to share his thoughts and questions with her and, that day, he puzzled over whether their family tree might become a short-lived branch. Then he decided that did not matter as he and Carry had shared such interesting and fulfilling years.

When Vowell next showed up, he asked, "Have you any idea of how many miles you travelled in BC, Peter, as gold commissioner, county court judge and Indian land commissioner?"

"No, Arthur. I haven't even wondered. It is an interesting question though, and I'll try to make a rough estimate." In the following months, he calculated that he'd travelled over fifty-eight thousand miles in BC and wondered how many of those miles had been on horseback. He didn't bother figuring out the total for the trips to and from England, Ireland and Europe and those by train, back and forth to New York or Ottawa.

Another man who dropped in for visits was Superintendent Fred Hussey of the BC Provincial Police. He first came to discuss the northern Indian peoples, but, when O'Reilly showed him the meticulous horse lineage charts he was developing for stallions imported into BC, Hussey was fascinated. He decided he liked O'Reilly, whereas he had previously found him to be somewhat officious. He began searching out and bringing additional information about stallions, then staying to have a cup of tea with the chipper old man. He learned more about BC's early years and particularly enjoyed O'Reilly's stories about Chartres Brew and Sir Matthew Begbie.

O'Reilly wrote in his diary for August 20, 1905:

Seedy all through the night, heartburn.

The next day he scribbled:

Repairs to the kitchen going well. Kathleen also seedy.[4]

He made no further entries.

∾ ∾ ∾

Peter O'Reilly died at home on September 3, 1905. After a funeral at St. Saviour's Church, where his pallbearers were J. Musgrave, Lindley Crease, R.H. Pooley and B.H. Tyrwhitt-Drake, he was buried in the Ross Bay Cemetery, beside his little daughter and his mother-in-law.

When newspapers reported his passing, the various editors reminisced about his achievements. They all recognized that Judge O'Reilly was one of the BC pioneers who had shaped the province, through its gold rushes, railway years and land conflicts. Yet little was said about his extensive influence on the lives of BC Indians. The *Daily Colonist* wrote at length about O'Reilly's earlier careers, adventures and explorations, but the long article, published on September 6, 1905, gave scant coverage of his duties as BC Indian Reserve Lands Commissioner. Those eighteen years were covered in one sentence:

He became Indian reserve commissioner, an appointment he received from Sir John A. Macdonald, his duties bearing upon the Indian lands.[5]

EPILOGUE

Peter O'Reilly had three grandchildren, born years after his death. Frank married Jessie Blankiston in 1913 and they had two sons, Peter and Tom. As the marriage was brief, those boys were raised in England. Frank was a major during the First World War, and when he returned to Victoria, he lived on his own, though he often took holidays with his siblings. A keen gardener, he helped Kathleen expand the gardens at Point Ellice House and had its extensive greenhouses built.

Jack became a partner in Drake Jackson and Helmcken. He enjoyed shooting, riding, yachting, croquet, tennis, theatre and parties, often sharing those activities with his brother. He became an active member of the Conservative Party, where he met and then married Mary B. Windham. Their only child, John, was born in 1920. John eventually inherited Point Ellice House, and he and his wife, Inez Elson Whiffen, lived there after his Aunt Kathleen died in 1945.

Kathleen never married. She became one of Victoria's grand old ladies, carefully maintaining her social standards as she entertained and accepted invitations. Well known for her musical talents, her support of the arts and theatre, and as a respected gardener, she also became a water colourist.

Peter O'Reilly's legacy as the man employed by Canada to assign most of British Columbia's contentious Indian reserves remains to this day.

Many of his decisions continue to be disputed by BC's Native communities. Although a few of the acreages he assigned have been increased to a more viable size, most bands are still waiting for Canada and BC to agree upon and authorize the final revisions. It has been one hundred and ten years since Peter O'Reilly retired as the federally appointed BC Indian Reserve Lands Commissioner.

To preserve Point Ellice House and its treasure of Victorian artifacts and heritage gardens, the British Columbia government purchased it in 1974. It now operates as a BC Heritage Trust site, open to the public, and is also nationally designated as one of western Canada's finest collections of Victoriana in its original setting. The gardens, on two acres along the Gorge, have been restored, and the heart-shaped rose garden blooms every spring. Although the property is now surrounded by industry, it remains a pristine example of life in BC's early years.

ENDNOTES

Author's note: I gathered the resources used in this book over a twenty-year period. The materials relating directly to Peter O'Reilly were located between 2006 and 2009 while much of the BC history used was found between 1985 and 2006, during the writing of my previous books, *The Lawman: Adventures Of A Frontier Diplomat* (TouchWood Editions 2006) and *Policing A Pioneer Province: The BC Provincial Police 1858–1950* (Harbour 1991). Some of my references therefore use earlier identification systems and the access numbering has since changed. As well, some collections have been moved from one archive to another and there is increasing material posted to web sites. The Point Ellice House Archives have been reorganized and research documents are no longer available on site; most of the materials referred to here as PEH are now available on microfilm in the British Columbia Archives (BCA). Peter O'Reilly's diary entries are referred to as Diary.

CHAPTER ONE: O'Reilly's First Months as a Colonial
1   Colonial Papers, GR 1372 B, BCA
2   Diary, June 17, 1859, MS 2894, Box 5, BCA

CHAPTER TWO: Gold Commissioner and Stipendiary Magistrate
1   The history of Peter O'Reilly's family was gathered from his obituary in the *Daily Colonist*, September 6, 1905, from his diaries and from earlier works by PEH researchers.

CHAPTER THREE: Challenges and Rewards
1   Margaret Ormsby, "Some Irish Figures in Colonial Days," *BC Historical Review*, January–April, 1950 pp. 72, 73, University of Victoria
2   Ibid.
3   Ibid.
4   Diary, January 27, 1862, File—Peter, Miscellaneous, PEH
5   Diary, January 28, 1861, File—Peter, Miscellaneous, PEH

CHAPTER FOUR: O'Reilly Meets Caroline Trutch
1   Diary, May 5, 1862–May 12, 1862, File—Peter, Miscellaneous, PEH
2   Ibid.
3   Diary, June 20, 1862, File—Peter, Miscellaneous, PEH
4   Diary, August 13, 1862, MS 2894, Box 6, BCA

CHAPTER FIVE: Marriage and Two Governors
1   Robin Skelton, *They Call It The Cariboo*, Sono Nis Press, p. 146, excerpt from the *Daily Colonist*, August 17, 1863
2   Letter from Peter O'Reilly to Joseph Trutch, July 21, 1863, Reel A-01947, BCA
3   Miscellaneous files, PEH
4   Diary, November 30, 1863, MS 2894, Box 7, BCA

[5] *Daily Colonist*, December 16, 1863, and details from N. de Bertrand Lugrin & John Hosie (eds), *The Pioneer Women of Vancouver Island, 1843–1866*, The Women's Canadian Club of Victoria, 1928, Victoria and Regional Public Library

[6] Diary 1863, a draft written under Notes and ripped out, File—Peter, Miscellaneous, PEH

[7] Diary, April 8, 1864, MS 2894, Box 7, BCA

CHAPTER SIX: May Day Celebrations and the Chilcotin War

[1] Margaret Ormsby, "Frederick Seymour, The Forgotten Governor," *BC Studies*, Summer 1974, Thompson Rivers University

[2] Diary, April 22, 1864, MS 2894, Box 7, BCA

[3] Margaret Ormsby, Ibid.

[4] Mel Rothenburger, *The Chilcotin War*, excerpt, p. 23, from Report of a Journey of Survey from Victoria to Fort Alexander via Bentinck Arm, New Westminister, 1863

[5] May Day, 1864 report to Governor Seymour, Colonial Papers GR 1372 B1318, BCA

[6] O'Reilly to Governor Seymour, Colonial Papers, GR 1372 B1321, BCA

CHAPTER SEVEN: The Forced Amalgamation of the Colonies

[1] Rear-Admiral J. Denman to Governor A. E. Kennedy, November 18, 1864, AG 429 Box 1, BCA

[2] Ibid.

[3] Kennedy to Vancouver Island Executive Council, 1865, Journals of the Colonies, Legislative Library of BC

[4] O'Reilly to Chartres Brew, Colonial Papers, GR 1372 Brew files, BCA

[5] O'Reilly to Carry O'Reilly, July 5, 1865, File—Carry, PEH

[6] Rear-Admiral J. Denman to Lord Carnarvon, Kennedy file, 1864, AG 429 Box 1, BCA

[7] Seymour to Attorney General Henry Crease, February 11, 1866, Third United British Columbia Legislature, Journals of the Colonies, Legislative Library of BC

CHAPTER EIGHT: Point Ellice House Becomes Home

[1] N. de Bertrand Lugrin & John Hosie, Ibid.

[2] O'Reilly to Chartres Brew, July 19,1867, BCPP GR 55, Box 1, BCA

[3] Carry O'Reilly to Peter O'Reilly, September 2, 1867, File—Carry's Letters, PEH

[4] Ibid.

[5] Ibid.

[6] *Colonist*, December 4, 1867, Thompson Rivers University

[7] Diary 1867, O'Reilly wrote on a Notes page, File—Miscellaneous, PEH

[8] Diary, December 12, 1867, File—House, PEH

CHAPTER NINE: Indian Protests and the Genesis of Confederation

[1] Second session of the United British Columbia Legislative Council, March 21, 1868, is also referred to as the fifth session of BC's Legislative Council because some officials decided the pre-union British Columbia colonial sessions, dating from 1864,

were the formal starting point. Both have been used in various archival holdings. Journals of the Colonies, Legislative Library of BC

2   Second (Fifth) session of the United British Columbia Legislative Council, March 21, 1868, de Cosmos motion, March 26, 1868, re taking a census. Journals of the Colonies, Legislative Library of BC

CHAPTER TEN: Assistant Land Commissioner and County Court Judge

1   Carry O'Reilly to Peter O'Reilly, August 18, 1868, File—Garden, PEH
2   *BC Gazette*, October 5, 1866, Notice from Commissioner of Land and Works Joseph Trutch re Kamloops and Shuswap, Legislative Library of BC
3   O'Reilly note to Joseph Trutch, undated, with 1868 materials, Trutch Collection, Special Collections, Irving K. Barber Learning Centre, UBC
4   Terms of Confederation summarized at Yale gathering September 12–17, 1868, Akrigg, G.P.V. & Helen B., *British Columbia Chronicle 1847–1871*. Vancouver, Discovery Press, 1977
5   Resolution of Terms forwarded to Legislative Assembly, Executive Session of the United British Columbia Legislative Council, 1868, Colonial Sessional Records, Legislative Library of BC

CHAPTER ELEVEN: Musgrave Becomes Governor

1   *Daily Colonist*, May 26, 1869, Thompson Rivers University
2   Carry O'Reilly to Peter O'Reilly, June 28, 1869, File—Miscellaneous, PEH
3   Akrigg, G.P.V. & Helen B., Ibid.
4   *British Colonist*, August 24, 1869, Thompson Rivers University
5   Carry O'Reilly to Peter O'Reilly, August 30, 1869, File—Peter, Correspondence, PEH
6   Akrigg, G.P.V. & Helen B., Ibid.
7   The Granville Dispatch, *Daily Colonist*, October 21, 1869, Thompson Rivers University

CHAPTER TWELVE: Reluctantly Canadian

1   Chartres Brew's tombstone in Barkerville Cemetery, Lynne Stonier-Newman, *Policing A Pioneer Province: BC Provincial Police 1858–1950*, Harbour Publishing, 1991
2   Letter to Julia Trutch from Joseph Trutch, June 6, 1870, Trutch Collection, Special Collections, Irving K. Barber Learning Centre, UBC
3   Letter to John Trutch from Carry O'Reilly, October 25, 1870, Trutch Collection, Special Collections, Irving K. Barber Learning Centre, UBC
4   *Daily Colonist*, December 9, 1870, Thompson Rivers University

CHAPTER THIRTEEN: Confederated . . . Or Seceding?

1   Peter O'Reilly to Carry O'Reilly, June 16, 1871, File—Garden, PEH
2   Carry O'Reilly to Peter O'Reilly, July 11, 1871, File—Peter's letters, PEH
3   *Daily Colonist*, July 20, 1871, Thompson Rivers University
4   Joseph Trutch to Governor General Lord Dufferin, copy to the Honourable

Secretary of State for Canada, Lieutenant-Governor papers, GR 443, File 30, BCA

5   Undated note to Lieutenant-Governor Trutch from Peter O'Reilly, GR 443, File 31, BCA
6   Diary, December 6, 1872, MS-2894 Reel 01907, BCA
7   Edgar and Jane Dewdney to Peter and Carry O'Reilly, March 21, 1872, File—Carry's letters, PEH
8   Edgar Dewdney to Peter O'Reilly, April 6, 1873, File—Peter's letters, PEH
9   Ibid.
10   Unmarked file, loose copy, GR 868, Box 2, BCA

CHAPTER FOURTEEN: Lord Dufferin Pacifies British Columbians

1   Manitoba Historical Society:
    http://www.mhs.mb.ca/docs/pageant/11/lorddufferin.shtml
2   Drafts of proposed Indian Act of 1876, De Brou, W. & Waiser, Bill *Documenting Canada: A History of Modern Canada in Documents*. Saskatoon, Fifth House Publishers, 1992
3   O'Reilly to Carry O'Reilly, July 15, 1875, File—Carry's letters, PEH
4   Carry O'Reilly to Peter O'Reilly, October 26, 1876, File—Peter's letters, PEH
5   O'Reilly to Carry O'Reilly, December 15, 1876, File—Carry's letters, PEH

CHAPTER FIFTEEN: The Consequences of the 1876 Indian Act

1   Indian and Northern Affairs, "A Reference Guide to the Establishment of Indian Reserves in British Columbia, 1849–1911," from Proclamation dated December 15, 1876, published in the *Canada Gazette*, December 30, 1876, BCA
2   Indian and Northern Affairs, Ibid., quoting letter October 25, 1876, GR 494, Box 1, BCA
3   Sessional Records, 1880, Railway Papers, Legislative Library of BC
4   O'Reilly to Carry O'Reilly, August 8, 1877, MS-2894, Box 1, BCA
5   Indian and Northern Affairs, Ibid., Second Condensed Report by the Joint Commissioners Appointed by the Governments of Canada and British Columbia, December 1, 1877, BCA
6   Gordon Donaldson, *Fifteen Men: Canada's Prime Ministers from Macdonald to Trudeau*, Doubleday, 1969
7   Letter from Prime Minister John Macdonald to Peter O'Reilly, August 9, 1880, RG 10, Reel C-10125, BCA
8   Diary, September 26, 1880, MS-2894, Reel 01909, BCA
9   Diary, March 4,6,7,9,11, 1881, MS-2894, Reel 01909 Box 2, BCA
10   Diary, April 13, 1881, MS-2894, Reel 01909 Box 2, BCA

CHAPTER SIXTEEN: Indian Reserve Lands Commissioner

1   Joint Reserve Lands Commission, File, 1881 notes—P. O'Reilly, GR 2982, Box 3, BCA
2   Letter to Commissioner Peter O'Reilly from the Chiefs and People of Port Simpson, October 5, 1881, McKenna-McBride Commission, GR 2982, BCA

3   Carry O'Reilly to Peter O'Reilly, May 15, 1882, File—family letters, PEH

4   Indian and Northern Affairs, Ibid., revisions in 1880 Indian Act, BCA

5   Excerpts from Commissioner Peter O'Reilly's letters, October 26, 28, 1882, Joint Reserve Commission, GR 2982, Box 3, BCA

6   Ibid.

7   Ibid.

8   Ibid.

CHAPTER SEVENTEEN: Peter O'Reilly Visits England and Ireland

1   Diary, October 25, 26, November 1, 1883, MS-2894, Reel 01909, BCA

2   Diary 1883, notes, MS-2894, Reel 01909, BCA

3   Ibid.

4   Keith Thor Carlson, "The Lynching of Louie Sam," *BC Studies*, no. 109, Spring 1996, Thompson Rivers University

5   Ibid.

6   Copies of O'Reilly letters to and from Premier Smithe, Land and Works Department files, GR 2037, 1887, file 18, December, 1884, BCA

7   Ibid.

8   Diary, copies of correspondence to Sir Alexander Campbell, minister of justice, August 21, 1883, MS-2894, Reel 01909, Box 19, BCA

9   Diary, letter from Sir Alexander Campbell, minister of justice, to the superintendent general of Indian Affairs, September 18, 1884, MS-2894, Reel 01909, Box 19, BCA

10   Caroline Trutch O'Reilly, File—C/personal, PEH

CHAPTER EIGHTEEN: The Last Years

1   Peter O'Reilly to Carry O'Reilly, May 21, 1888, File—C/personal, PEH

2   Peter O'Reilly to Carry O'Reilly, June 24, 1888, File—C/personal, PEH

3   Diary, December 24, 1899, MS-2894, Reel A-01911, BCA

4   Diary, August 20, 21, 1905, Reel A-01912, BCA

5   *Daily Colonist*, September 6, 1905

SOURCES

BOOKS, SELECTED

Akrigg, G.P.V. & Helen B. *1001 British Columbia Place Names*. Vancouver, Discovery Press, 1973

———. *British Columbia Chronicle 1847–1871*. Vancouver, Discovery Press, 1977

Balf, Mary. *Kamloops, A History of the District up to 1914*. Kamloops Museum, Clow Printing, 1969

BC Department of Information and Education. *British Columbia Recreational Atlas*, 1975

Barman, Jean. *The West Beyond The West: A History of British Columbia* (Revised). Toronto, University of Toronto Press, 1996

Cail, Robert. *Land, Man and the Law*. Vancouver, University of British Columbia Press, 1974

Donaldson, Gordon. *Fifteen Men: Canada's Prime Ministers from Macdonald to Trudeau*. Toronto, Doubleday Canada, 1969

Duffus, Maureen and The Esquimalt Silver Threads Writers. *Beyond The Blue Bridge— Stories from Esquimalt*. Fleming Printers, 1990

Dunn, Joyce. *A Town Called Chase*. Theytus, 1986

Corporation of the Village of Ashcroft and Helen Forster. *Bittersweet Oasis*. 2002

Creighton, Donald (estate). *The Young Politician and The Old Chieftain*. Toronto, University of Toronto Press, 1998

De Brou, W. & Waiser, Bill. *Documenting Canada: A History of Modern Canada in Documents*. Saskatoon, Fifth House Publishers, 1992

Fisher, Robin. *Contact and Conflict: Indo-European Relations in British Columbia, 1774–1890*. Vancouver, University of British Columbia Press, 1992

Foster, Pat. *Historic Ashcroft—For the Strong Eye Only*. Kamloops, Plateau Press, 1999

Francis, Daniel. *The Imaginary Indian: The Image of the Indian in Canadian Culture*. Vancouver, Arsenal Pulp Press, 1992

Goodchild, Fred H. *British Columbia: Its History, People & Industry*. London, UK, Allen & Unwin, 1951

Gosnell, R.E. *A History of British Columbia*. Vancouver, British Columbia Historical Association, 1928

Gough, Barry M. *Gunboat Frontier: British Maritime Authority and Northwest Coast Indians, 1846–90*. Vancouver, University of British Columbia Press, 1984

Granatstein, J.L. & Hillmer, Norman. *Prime Ministers: Ranking Canada's Leaders*. Toronto, Harper Collins, 1999

Harris, R. Cole. *The Resettlement of British Columbia: Essays on Colonialism and Geographical Change*. Vancouver, University of British Columbia Press, 1997

———. *Making Native Space: Colonialism, Resistance, and Reserves in British Columbia*. Vancouver, University of British Columbia Press, 2002

Graham, Clara. *The Dewdney Trail: Hope to Fort Steele*. Heritage House, Surrey, 1987

Hill, Beth. *Sappers: The Royal Engineers in British Columbia*. Ganges, Horsdal & Schubart, 1987

Hutchinson, Bruce. *The Fraser.* Toronto, Clarke Irwin, 1950

Jackman, S.W. *Portraits of the Premiers.* Sidney, BC, Gray's Publishing, 1969

Johnson, Patricia M. *Canada's Pacific Province: Curriculum Resource Book.* Toronto, McClelland and Stewart, 1966

——and the City of Nanaimo. *Nanaimo, A Short History.* Tradex & Western Heritage, 1974

Jupp, Ursula. *Cadboro: A Ship, A Bay, A Sea Monster.* Victoria, Morriss Printing, 1988

Keshen, Jeffrey and Morton, Suzanne. *Documents in Post-Confederation Canadian History.* Toronto, Addison-Wesley, 1998

Laforet, Andrea and York, Annie. *Spuẓẓum: Fraser Canyon Histories, 1808–1939.* Vancouver, University of British Columbia Press, 1998

Langevin, H.L. *British Columbia: Report of the Hon. H.L.Langevin, C.B., Minister of Public Works.* Ottawa, 1872

McKechnie, Dr. Robert E. *Strong Medicine.* Vancouver, J.J.Douglas, 1972

Muckle, Robert J. *The First Nations of British Columbia: An Anthropological Survey.* Vancouver, University of British Columbia Press, 1998

Myers, Jay. *Canadian Facts & Dates.* Markham, Fitzhenry & Whiteside, 1986

Neering, Rosemary. *A traveller's guide to historic British Columbia.* Whitecap Books, 2002

Ormsby, Margaret A. *British Columbia: A History.* Toronto, Macmillan Company of Canada, 1958

Phenix, Patricia. *Private Demons: the tragic personal life of John A.* Toronto, McClelland and Stewart, 2006

Ramsay, Bruce. *Ghost Towns of British Columbia.* Vancouver, Mitchell Press, 1963

Robin, Martin. *The Rush for the Spoils.* Toronto, McClelland and Stewart, 1972

Rothenburger, Mel. *The Chilcotin War.* Kamloops, Ryan, McLean, Alaric, 1976

Roy, Patricia E. and Thompson, John Herd. *British Columbia: Land of Promises.* Don Mills, Oxford University Press, 2005

Skelton, Robin. *"They Call It The Cariboo."* Victoria, Sono Nis Press, 1980

Stonier-Newman, Lynne. *Policing A Pioneer Province: BC Provincial Police, 1858–1950.* Madeira Park, Harbour Publishing, 1991

——. *The Lawman: Adventures Of A Frontier Diplomat.* Victoria, TouchWood Editions, 2006

Swindle, Lewis J. *The Fraser River gold rush of 1858.* Victoria, Trafford, 2001

Switlo, Janice. *Gustafsen Lake Under Siege.* Peachland, TIAC Communications Ltd., 1997

Tennant, Paul. *Aboriginal Peoples and Politics: The Indian Land Question in British Columbia, 1849–1989.* Vancouver, University of British Columbia Press, 1990

The Women's Canadian Club of Victoria. *The Pioneer Women of Vancouver Island, 1843–1866.* Edited by N. de Bertrand Lugrin & John Hosie. Victoria, Victoria Press, 1928

Titley, E. Brian. *The Frontier World of Edgar Dewdney.* Vancouver, University of British Columbia Press, 1999

Union of British Columbia Indian Chiefs. *Stolen Lands, Broken Promises: Researching the Indian Land Question in British Columbia* (Second Edition). Vancouver, Union of British Columbia Indian Chiefs, 2005

Wade, Mark S. *The Cariboo Road*. Victoria, The Haunted Bookshop, 1979

Williams, David R. *". . . The Man For A New Country": Sir Matthew Baillie Begbie*. Sidney, BC, Gray's Publishing, 1977

JOURNALS AND MAGAZINES, SELECTED

Begbie, Matthew B. "Journey into the Interior of British Columbia." *Journal of Royal Geographical Society*, 1861

Brealey, Kenneth. "Travels From Point Ellice: Peter O'Reilly and the Indian Reserve System in British Columbia." *BC Studies*, No. 115/116, Autumn/Winter, 1997/1998

British Columbia Provincial Police Magazines. *The Shoulder Strap: Editions 1 to 16*. Victoria, 1932–1944

Harris, Cole. "How Did Colonialism Dispossess? Comments from an Edge of Empire." *Annals*, Association of American Geographers, 2004

Mattison, David and Savard, Daniel. "The North-west Pacific Coast Photographic Voyages 1866–81." *History of Photography*, Vol. 16, No. 3, Autumn 1992

Ormsby, Margaret A. "Frederick Seymour, The Forgotten Governor." *BC Studies*, No. 22, Summer, 1974

———. "Some Irish Figures in Colonial Days." *BC Historical Quarterly*, 14, 1950

The Beaver, wide selection of issues

Union of BC Indian Chiefs Resources Centre, Letter from the Methodist Missionary (Br [107] Brian Deer) and wide selection of documents

NEWSPAPERS

Barkerville Sentinel

British Columbian

British Colonist

Colonist

Victoria Daily Colonist

GOVERNMENT AND ARCHIVAL MATERIALS

British Columbia

British Columbia Archives

Attorney General records, 1872–1876

Colonial Papers, GR 1372 B-1297 re Ball, Begbie, Brew, Moody, Nind, O'Reilly

Colonial Office fonds AAAA0524, AAAA0528, AAAA0525

Gold Commissioners and County Court Judges

Land and Works Commissioner

Water rights and licensing

Land and Water Commissioner records, 1871–1876

Lieutenant-Governor records: Trutch, GR443, Vol. 24

Selected materials from
   Begbie collection
   Crease collection
   O'Reilly collection
   Trutch collection
Vital Statistics: births, deaths, marriages
British Columbia Heritage Trust
   Point Ellice House and Yale archives
      Selected correspondence
      O'Reilly, Carry and Peter, personal diaries
      Point Ellice household diaries and records
Legislative Library of BC Archives
   Attorney General reports
   BC Journals, re Parliaments of Canada, 1st–4th Session, 1871–1875 Sessional
Papers, Appendix
   Sessional Records of British Columbia
   Journals of the Colonial Legislatures of the Colonies of Vancouver Island and
British Columbia, 1851–1871, edited by James E. Henderickson
   Public Accounts, list and salaries
   Sessional acts, bills, ordinances: legislative assemblies, 1871–1876

Canada
Indian and Northern Affairs, Ottawa
A Reference Guide to the Establishment of Indian Reserves in British Columbia,
1849–1911
The Black Books
Parks Canada
   Various maps and descriptions of historical development

Glenbow Museum and Archives
   Dewdney records as related to O'Reilly
Kamloops Indian Band Archives
Journal of the Legislative Council of British Columbia, 1866–1871
Kamloops Museum and Archives
   Early history, colony to province
Nanaimo Museum and Archives
   Early history, colony to province
Thompson Rivers University Library
   Main source for research books and maps
University of British Columbia
   Special Collections Library and Archives
   Trutch papers (O'Reilly papers included)

X'wi7xwa Library and Archives assistance with sources
Vancouver Public Library
    Special Collections: Pacific Northwest Collection
Victoria Public Library
    Special Collections and early Vancouver Island history
Yale Historical Society
Trutch information and early Fraser River history

WEB ADDRESSES AND SITES, SELECTED
http://aabc.bc.ca/aabc/bcaul.html
www.barkerville.com/
www.bccls.bc.ca/cms/index.cfm?Group_ID=67530
www.bcheritage.ca/peh/gossip/famcon.htm
www.bcheritage.ca/peh/sitemap.html
www.canadianencyclopedia.ca/index.cfm?PgNm=TCE&Params=A1ARTA0003045S
UBLinks
www.canadiana.org/ECO/PageView?id=60c1b7f2a94eaf48&display=15637+0008
www.collectionscanada.ca/confederation/023001-2185-e.html
www.collectionscanada.ca/indianaffairs/index-e.html
www.crowsnest-highway.ca
www.e-ijd.org/printarticle.asp?issn=0019-5154;year=2004;volume=49;issue=3;spage=1
30;epage=131;aulast=Rathi;type=0
www.geog.uvic.ca/dept/wcag/sedgwick.pdf
www.kencom.ca/genealogy.htm
www.ktunaxa.org/who/index.html
www.lcs.gov.bc.ca/privacyaccess/Summ_IA_Order/ToC.htm#1995
www.leg.bc.ca/CMT/37thParl/session-2/aaf/hansard/a11102a.htm#586
www.library.ubc.ca/archives/bchistory/
www.quesnelmuseum.ca/Grtrail/canyon.html
www.ring.uvic.ca/00sept22/ethnohistory.html
www.royalbcmuseum.bc.ca/BC_Research_Guide/BC_First_Nations.aspx
www.ubcic.bc.ca/files/Pictures/McKennaMcBride/pages/A-01707.jpg
www.ubcic.bc.ca/Resources/ourhomesare/testimonies.htm
www.virtualmuseum.ca/pm.php
www.xaytem.ca/links.php

INDEX

ACKNOWLEDGMENTS

Many people have generously helped me with this book, and without that assistance, writing about forty years of British Columbia history would not have been possible. Topping the list are all the archivists, librarians and library assistants who not only found what I needed, they astutely helped to fine-tune my questions. And if they did not have the answers, they had the name, contact number or email of the person who might.

My thanks to the staff at the British Columbia Legislative Library, the British Columbia Archives and Royal BC Museum, the Thompson Rivers University Library, the Secwepemc Museum and Kamloops Band Cultural Resource Centre, Indian and Northern Affairs Canada, the National Library and Archives, the Ashcroft Museum and Archives, the Kamloops Museum and Archives, the Nanaimo Centennial Museum and Archives, the New Westminster Museum and Archives, the Greater Vancouver and District Public Library, the Greater Victoria Public Library, the University of British Columbia Special Collections Library and Archives, the X'wi7xwa Library and Archives and the Yale Historical Society.

I am most appreciative for the use of the archives at Point Ellice House, and to the managers, staff and volunteers who helped enlighten me about the flavour of O'Reilly's era, its challenges and pleasures.

Many thanks to Garth Stonier, Trudy Montgomery and Rachel McMillen for reading and commenting on the manuscript, to Brian Newman for his assistance with the research, to Carol Creasy and Garth Chorney for sharing their computer expertise and to Helen Knight, Sandra Williamson, Bev English and Lee Patjas for their ongoing encouragement. My thanks to TouchWood Editions publishers, Pat Touchie and Ruth Linka, and a special thank you to Marlyn Horsdal for her perceptive editing. Any remaining errors are mine as she could only work with my research and the interpretations I made in this book.

Peter O'Reilly was gold commissioner, country court judge and, in the years from 1880 to 1898, Canada's BC Indian Reserve Lands Commissioner. The history of that era is extensively recorded, sometimes in two or three different interpretations; in writing his story, I have used the one that seemed most credible to me.

O'Reilly's years of service to BC and to Canada shaped him from the reluctant immigrant who left Ireland because he had few other options to one of BC's influential officials. As BC went from colony to province, from fewer than ten thousand non-Natives in 1871 to over two hundred thousand when O'Reilly died in 1905, he regularly conferred with Sir John A. Macdonald, Sir James Douglas, Frederick Seymour, Anthony Musgrave and other notables. He probably found his relationship with brother-in-law Joseph Trutch, BC's first lieutenant-governor, a mixed blessing although without Trutch's influence, perhaps his own career would have been limited. Sir Matthew Baillie Begbie and Edgar Dewdney were his close friends.

O'Reilly also probably knew more Indian chiefs and elders in BC than most other men. Certainly, many of his decisions and his written reports about BC's Indian reserve lands, water and timber rights continue to be challenged and debated one hundred and ten years later.

He was a loving father and dearly cherished his wife, Caroline Trutch O'Reilly. When he wasn't away on long trips, performing his seasonal responsibilities around the province, he helped Carry to develop what has become a heritage house and gardens, Point Ellice House, on the Gorge in Victoria, BC.

Notes: Occasionally the spelling and capitalization used in this book has been changed from the archival sources to the style readers currently expect and read easily. The actual words and the grammar have not been changed. In that era, May Day and the Queen's Birthday were used interchangeably in correspondence and newspapers, possibly because many editors had an American heritage. Another confusing issue is the use of pounds and dollars. It appears both were used for a considerable number of years. Similarly, some geographic locations are known by a variety of names and I have used the one which has survived or appeared to be best known back then.

—Lynne Stonier-Newman, December 2009

Lynne Stonier-Newman is a freelance writer, communications consultant and British Columbia historian. Her publications include *The Lawman: Adventures of a Frontier Diplomat*; *Policing A Pioneer Province: BC Provincial Police 1858–1950*; an audiobook called *The Whys of Women*, a modern history about Canadian women; an illustrated poetry chapbook, *Canadian-Eh?*; and various articles, short stories and poetry. Born and educated in British Columbia, Stonier-Newman lives north of Kamloops, BC at Little Heffley Lake.